The Art Williams
PHENOMENON

By Bill Orender with Dona Bunch

Foreword by Mike Burroughs

Cover Design by Danny Woodard

The Art Williams Phenomenon by Bill Orender and Dona Bunch

Published by Orender's Champions Publishing: Frisco, TX

Foreword by Mike Burroughs

Cover by Danny Woodard

ISBN: 9798841241294

Printed in United States of America

First Printing, 2022

CONTENTS

Acknowledgements

To do anything well takes a team. I would like to say thank you to my team who worked with great enthusiasm, creativity and selflessness to help make this book possible.

Dona Bunch
Mike Burroughs
Chess Britt
Caroline Myers
Danny Woodard
Patrick Orender

Foreword

Since I grew up dreaming about writing for *Sports Illustrated,* the idea of making the giant leap from the newspaper business to corporate communications seemed daunting. That is until I learned the founder of the company was a former high school football coach.

It didn't take me long to realize that Art Williams ran his company like a football team, or that there wasn't anything remotely "corporate" about my new career.

It was the perfect fit for both of us, so we developed a special bond that would lead to a lifetime friendship.

Art changed my life, just like he had for millions of other people.

I became part of Art's Inner Circle, and I had a seat at the table for A.L. Williams' historic seven-year run as the No. 1 company in the life insurance industry. Art declared that we were the National Champions, even before the official numbers had been posted because he just knew in his gut that we had won.

"The enemy," as Art called them, didn't even realize they were in a game, much less playing for a championship. Actually, it was more like a revolution. And it was personal. Art summed it up with one sentence: "I never forgave them for what they did to my Momma."

The traditional financial services industry would never be the same after this old high school football coach from South Georgia got done turning it upside down.

More than 1,000 life insurance companies went out of business, and the rest of them were ultimately forced to stop selling traditional cash value life insurance, which Art called "the biggest rip-off ever perpetrated on the American consumer." The industry had been exposed.

Decades later, Art told me during an interview for a film on the history of the company, "We destroyed the largest, most powerful, most evil industry the world has ever known."

It became the epic punch line for the A.L. Williams chapter of the film, *A Company of Destiny*.

To this day, Art still tells stories about "how many times I laid my head on a pillow thinking we were going to be out of business the next day." Every time he tells one of those war stories, he says, "that's just one. I could tell you a thousand." He even told his team hundreds of times, "The odds are about like this of us surviving. (Holding his thumb and forefinger so close together, you couldn't even slide a piece of paper through there.) I'm not talking about beating Prudential… I'm not talking about being No. 1… I'm talking about surviving." Every time it appeared that A.L. Williams was not going to make it, something magical happened to keep it going, leading Art to start calling it "A Company of Destiny."

Art has always said, "God had his hand on our company." It also had a team of leaders with the strength and the courage to lay it all on the line to do whatever it took to win.

There was a relentless inevitability about A.L. Williams. That came from Art, the fearless leader whose gigantic vision, sheer toughness and unyielding positive attitude made the difference. Art could light up a room like Muhammad Ali, hit home runs like Babe Ruth, deliver in the clutch like Michael Jordan and stare down the competition and outcoach them like Vince Lombardi.

The number one question people still ask me today is, "What was it like to work with Art Williams?"

It was the honor and the privilege of a lifetime.

There is nobody like him. A true original. A national treasure.

Art motivated people to take their game to the next level, no matter what that level was. His teammates would run through brick walls for him, and they often did. He was a "do it first" leader, he always left it all on the field, and he demanded the same from everybody else. You always had to raise your game to meet his expectations. In the process, Art made everybody around him better.

Yet, no matter how tough he could be, and he was, Art's style of inspirational leadership always left people feeling better than he found them. His No. 1 mantra in A.L. Williams was always, "I want to be somebody." He kept that at the forefront through speeches, awards and t-shirts, and he instilled the belief in every single person in the company that they could, indeed, "be somebody." Art simply knew how to treat people the right way, motivate them and make them feel special, like no one you've ever met.

A few years ago, we were together at he and Angela's extraordinary hotel in Highlands, NC, Old Edwards Inn, and he kept introducing me to friends and hotel executives. Every single time, he would say, "This is my friend, Mike. We traveled the world together." Another time, we were having lunch at his golf club in Palm Beach, Trump National, and he kept telling everyone, "This is my friend, Mike. We were in business together."

It's simply not in Art's vocabulary to say, "Mike worked for me." He never viewed it that way. We went to war together against the traditional life insurance industry. We were in the foxhole together. We were in the locker room together. We were TEAMMATES. Art Williams didn't just write the book on *Pushing Up People*. He lives it.

Art taught me a long time ago that all it takes is a pen and a sheet of paper to recognize people in a very special way. I still have every letter Art has ever written me, and I have now sent my own hand-written letters to everybody from Hall of Fame athletes to owners of sports franchises to business leaders to invaluable teammates. It's a personal and far more effective form of communication than any email or text you could ever write – and nobody else does it.

If Art told you something, you could take it to the bank. He was the genuine article. "I don't blow smoke up nobody's butt," he said. I've seen him tear up pages from book signings because he couldn't bring himself to write something if he didn't mean it.

Those of us who were fortunate to be associated with Art have learned so many of his winning principles that apply to both business and life, "timeless truths" as he calls them.

Many of us have found, over time, that the most important one is "never quit." No matter what. "A winner," Art said, "will be motivated forever."

Positive attitude, positive action. "The single most important thing is a positive attitude," Art always said.

He is most famous, of course, for "Just Do It," which he was saying on stage long before Nike turned it into a massive international advertising campaign. "Winners do it… and do it… and do it… until the job gets done," Art repeatedly told us.

But for Art, these were always far more than advertising slogans. It was a way of life. He summarized it in his book *The A.L. Williams Way*, first published in 1985, and later edited and re-released in 2013. *The A.L. Williams Way* is now presented to every new Regional Vice President when they attend MIT (Millionaires in Training). The book is also available to every representative in the company, and many of its top leaders still teach its principles.

Through his books, videos, YouTube channel and occasional talks to small groups of company reps, Art Williams continues to coach and mentor a new generation of company leaders who were not even born when he left the company he founded 45 years ago. This new wave of dynamic leaders shares the same fire, enthusiasm and passion for the business held by the Original 85 and other company pioneers because of Art's influence, which will live on forever.

Today, Art's company is publicly traded on the New York Stock Exchange, a Fortune 1000 company and a respected industry leader that continues to shatter every record in the book by doing what's right for the consumer 100% of the time. The future has never been brighter, and Art could not be prouder of the company and the team.

This incredible new book by Bill Orender tells the inside story of Art Williams like it has never been told before, through the eyes of one of the biggest, most important leaders in the history of the company. Bill didn't just hear about what happened from Art and the other company leaders. Bill was there, in the trenches, and he was one of the men most instrumental in helping make it all happen. He was the first RVP to lead the expansion movement as the company went nationwide. A true company giant and a legend in his own right.

This is no ordinary success story, and there was no one better to help Bill write it than Dona Bunch, one of the original company executives who built and led the marketing and communications machine to support A.L. Williams' rise to No. 1. She also helped Art write the *New York Times best seller All You Can Do Is All You Can Do,* and his other books that played a key role in the success of the company: *Common Sense, Pushing Up People* and *The A.L. Williams Way.*

Art Williams changed the life insurance industry. But the fame and fortune that came from becoming one of the greatest success stories in the history of American business never changed Art Williams, the man. He's still the same person he was when I first met him almost 40 years ago.

Bill decided to write this book because he knew this story needed to be told and told the right way. I am so grateful that he did. The legend of Art Williams is captured here in great detail, and with unwavering respect, unabashed admiration, and the utmost appreciation. Reading this book is like spending time with a friend, and you won't want to put it down.

Mike Burroughs

Introduction

Art is known as the "man who changed the life insurance industry," but he was so much more than just that. He truly created a phenomenon that has lasted for 45 years.

A phenomenon is described as an exceptional, uncommon person, thing, or occurrence. Art caused a sensation in creating the first "general agency" to hire part-timers, but especially one that took a radical position from the cash value insurance industry's one hundred-plus-year dominance in America's financial realm.

Art's business systems, teachings, philosophies, style, books, and business coaching methods started a ripple effect throughout our country and has the power to continue.

Having witnessed the phenomenon firsthand, I've tried to relate to this generation, and future generations, the impact Art made on individuals, their families, their finances, their marriages and their becoming life agent influencers for their communities and North America. Art was a coach for all seasons by building relationships that seemed nonexistent in corporate America.

The purpose of this book is to extol what Art personally meant to so many. It will outline the history of how Art got started, the struggles that he fought, the men and women he influenced, and the purpose he placed in our hearts that transformed us and that of an entire industry.

To eulogize is "to speak or write in high praise of" a person regarding the life they lived. I originally intended this as a eulogy for Art. I began by wondering what I would say if asked to deliver his eulogy. Then I thought that it would be best if the book was delivered to his family after he was gone to give them a sense of how he affected us and made our lives better. I thought he would be too embarrassed to have others recognize him for the central role he played in how our lives have turned out. After interviewing numerous people, the conclusion became that he needed to hear what we had to say as well as the future generations that will benefit from the abundance of value that flowed from Art's life. The only word I found to properly capture it is "phenomenon." Whether phenomenon or phenomena is used, Art's life and legacy caused an extraordinary seismic shift in countless lives.

The Art Williams phenomenon is not based only on opinion. It can be measured financially. The record shows that his personal constitution and his beliefs created the business system that has transformed the financial landscape of our country since 1984:

- A NYSE company with $6.09B in market capitalization with 92.49% of the stock held by institutions
- $28.1 billion in total death claims paid
- 130,000 licensed agents
- Top 60 General Agents paid a combined $2.3 billion in compensation since 1984
- $903 billion in total life insurance in force
- $97.3 billion in investment assets under management

The crusade was Art's star to follow. Art identified that star he was meant to follow, and he followed that point of light his entire life. *(Goodwin, 2013)* His belief in the righteousness of the cause was beyond casual. No normal belief would do. "As it is the fierceness of the heat that melts the iron ore and makes it possible to weld it or mold it into shape, as it is the intensity of the electrical force that dissolves the diamond, the hardest known substance, so it is true that the law of belief attracts prosperity to those who think it is possible." *(Gladwell, 2021)* Art was the monolith that the titans of the insurance industry thought was a pebble and then found themselves crushed by the weight of Art's conviction. He was the rock they ended up breaking themselves against.

Art was one of the greatest business disruptors in the history of American business. When Art got into the insurance business, he looked at the way things were always done, saw a better way and made it happen. Art had an exaggerated view of what ALW could become. His bigger-than-life ambition built a legacy that's visible throughout North America. It can be said that much of ALW's success was due to the force of his personality. He did things no one believed was possible. Art saw each of us as partners, not agents. He only saw "team," not him as the star. His obsession with beating "Pru" was the rallying cry that defined our success. Beating "Pru" was a metaphor for righting the industry's wrongs. He didn't invent "buy term and invest the difference," but he perfected the system to bring it to the world.

Art's phenomenon was also seen in the effect he had on people. It was significant. The core meaning of significant is "sign or means to matter." Art's life mattered to us. Art's signature *was written on our hearts.* A deep impression that rippled through our marriages, our families, our relationships, our finances, and our faiths.

Words from the musical, *Wicked,* summarize the Art Williams phenomenon.

> "I've heard it said that people come into our lives for a reason,
> Bringing something we must learn, and we are led, by those who help us most to grow, if we let them
> And we help them in return.
> I don't know if I believe that's true, but I know I'm who I am today because I knew you." (*Schwartz and Holzman, For Good, 2003)*

The Art Williams Phenomenon is an ode to what one man with a vision can accomplish and the millions of lives that vision has transformed.

Bill Orender

Chapter 1:

FIRST STEPS TO GREATNESS

A PTA meeting and a family reunion seem unlikely situations to spark a business dynasty. But they did. Art's father had passed away at just 48, and his mother struggled to raise Art's two young brothers with the $10,000 of life insurance his parents owned. At a family reunion, Art ran into his cousin Ted Harrison, who was working as a CPA. As they talked, Ted explained term insurance to Art. Ted told him that it was possible to buy a significant amount of term insurance for a fraction of the cost of whole life insurance. Yet term was rarely sold because the commissions were much lower. As Ted explained the concept, something clicked in Art's brain.

It was hard to believe what Ted said was true, so Art went to the library and read everything he could find about life insurance — *Consumer Reports, Changing Times,* all the financial publications. What he discovered about whole life insurance infuriated him. "I realized that people like me and my parents were being ripped off, "Art said. "I was mad at what they did to my mother and father. I was mad that a former player's father sold me a $10,000 whole life policy when he could have sold me $150,000 of term. It started to create a crusade in me, and that crusade made me a driven person."

Looking back, Ted Harrison recalled the conversation, which hardly seemed historic at the time. "We were at Art's mother's house in Cairo, Art and his family, me and my family, his mother, and some other relatives," Ted said in a 1990 interview. "Art was coaching football at the time. We got to talking about term insurance, and I told him it might be something he would be interested in looking at.

"Art was surprised," Ted continued, "but at that time, it seemed most people I talked to didn't know there was such a thing as term insurance. I would have been surprised if Art had known anything about it. I don't think of it as something I got started because the concept had been around a long time. I'd like to take credit for it, but Art is the one who took it and saw something, researched, studied, and figured out how to make it work." (*Birth of a Legend, 1990*)

Art was shaken by his discovery at that meeting, but he was a football coach, not an accountant. How would he spread the truth to other people? Art never intended to quit coaching, but, like most teachers in his South Georgia school, he took part-time jobs whenever he could to make extra income. He'd refereed games, sold Christmas trees, even tried his hand at selling "Exer-Genies" — a portable workout system with ropes and handles that was used by the Apollo space program. None of these paid much, but every little bit counted. He loved coaching, but its income was far below what he wanted for his family. That's where the PTA meeting came in. As a winning football coach in South Georgia, Art admits that he only attended a handful of PTA meetings in his entire school history. But one meeting was prophetic. It's where Art met Forrest Smith, a man who worked for ITT Financial Services, and he presented Art with an opportunity that would be life-changing.

An Opportunity Appears

Smith told Art he believed in a concept called "buy term and invest the difference." Not only could you buy cheaper term insurance, but you could also use the difference between the price of term and whole life to start an investment program separate from your insurance policy. Art had found someone who understood his anger and frustration. Maybe this was a way he could act on his new knowledge during breaks from coaching. Unfortunately, insurance companies didn't hire part-timers.

But fate intervened. The ITT manager was so impressed with Art's passion about term, that he called the sales director at ITT and Art became the first part-time insurance sales agent in history.

Art had found the vehicle he needed to share the truth about insurance with everyone he knew. Yet selling term insurance was different from his other jobs. Art had to get both a securities license and life license just to go part-time. The pay scale was different too. "We only got paid on an 'as-earned' basis, so I only got 1/12 of what I sold each month," Art recalled, "Angela was furious because she thought I was going to get a lot of money upfront." Still, he made $42,000 during the first two and a half years (the equivalent of roughly $300,000 today). "That was the first time I'd ever made any real money." Art needed to make extra money, but it was the passion, not the money, that made this job unique. "I was never money-motivated early on. l wanted to be a coach forever. I thought I would never leave coaching. But ITT gave me a chance. I'd never sold anything like this before, but I ended up being very confident because what we were doing was right. I felt this was something I was called to do. Then I saw that I could make and save money, too. Angie and I saved all of my part-time income!"

The crusade was the second thing in his life that ignited a passion in Art. "When I started, in my first few years it was the only thing other than football that I could get excited about and work at. I wanted to know all about "buy term and invest the difference" from the beginning because if I was going to sell and recruit my friends, I needed to be right."

No one was more surprised than Art about the turn his life had taken. He had the best of both worlds, coaching and his insurance crusade, and was excited about the progress he was making. Just then the insurance industry reared its head. His success at replacing whole life with term insurance had gotten the attention of local whole life agents who had complained to the school where Art coached. The superintendent of schools gave Art an ultimatum. He could either quit selling insurance or quit coaching. Art couldn't believe it. What was wrong with selling term insurance? About that time, Art got a letter from the Georgia Insurance Department demanding that he attend a meeting regarding his conduct. The local industry reps were determined to stop Art from selling term. He met with Richard Kane, an investigator for the department who asked Art if he was replacing whole life insurance with term. According to Kane, that was called "twisting," and it could cause Art to lose his insurance license. Art admitted he was replacing whole life, but said he was doing it legally. He went on to explain "buy term and invest the difference" to the regulator. The result? Art could keep selling. Several years later, Richard Kane came to work with A.L. Williams.

That would be the first time the insurance industry intervened to complicate Art's plans, but it wouldn't be the last.

By that time, Art was 90% ready to leave coaching anyway. Frank Pearson at ITT offered him a full-time job with a $25,000 a year guarantee. Art was making $10,000 a year coaching and another $15,000 or more selling insurance, so the guarantee would match his income.

Art's cousin Ted recalled the struggle Art's crusade created. "Art was having to make a decision about whether he was going to go into sales full-time or stay in coaching. He could do one or the other, but he couldn't continue to do both. Art was making good money in sales on a part-time basis. He saw a reasonably good future for himself in sales, but he was a very good coach, and he was struggling with the decision. He made a comment to me that he felt he was leaving a secure job coaching to go with something really risky.

"Years later I was at his house, and we were talking about his decision to go into sales, and he said he realized he went from a really insecure position in coaching, where he was working for someone, to a secure position where he was depending on himself."

It was a huge decision. According to Art, "Angela's parents were nervous about us going full-time. My mother, Betty, was very supportive in the beginning, but she was nervous too. It was really tough for Angela's and my family when I went full-time because of the insecurity of it all. Yet when I went full-time Angela said, 'If this is what you want to do, go for it.'"

Art left coaching and jumped into life insurance full-time. His first sale as a full-time agent was to a man named Robert Kelly, Art's assistant coach at the time. He replaced Robert's $10,000 whole life policy with a $100,000 of term.

"When I went full-time at ITT, I made a decision to give it all I had," Art said. "It was my shot. I was giving 1,000 times more because I had an enemy to fight, and something impossible to do. We gave it our all because we felt this was our moment. Our God-given moment."

At ITT, Art's future began to take shape. He was bringing in people part-time and growing a business. But his dream of building it "big" began to show some cracks. About that time, another string of fortuitous things happened. John Kostemeir, who was the former president of ITT, had moved on to Waddell & Reed. He called Art to let him know there might be an opportunity there for him. Art hadn't been full-time at ITT even a year but,

remarkably, many of his teammates there were ready to take a new step with him. Mary Walker said, "Randall started at ITT with Art. We would have followed him anywhere. We would follow him without seeing any contracts for a new company like Waddell & Reed. No one else could put together what Art put together because we believed in him so much." Ironically, just six months after Art left, ITT went out of business. The move turned out to be a lifesaver.

It was at Waddell & Reed that Art began to understand the way multiples worked, and that understanding would later help him change the insurance industry and the business world in amazing ways. I remember once we had a full-timer meeting at Unicoi State Park in north Georgia. On the way back, he rode in Virginia's car with Virginia and me. I asked him why he left ITT.

"Because they had another level on the computer, so my full-timers could override, create a secure income, and have a chance to have a career," Art said. Overrides meant recruiting growth. Recruiting meant a secure income. Recruiting meant a better, easier way to create a sale using hot, natural markets. Art needed a better payment system that didn't limit growth, and Waddell & Reed was one step better than ITT. Before long, Art and his team were number one at Waddell & Reed. "The people I recruited were my friends and they believed in me, and I was passionate about becoming financially independent myself and with them. I got a vision and a plan. In most companies in corporate America, you are stuck behind a manager. You can't go above them or around them."

The discontent at Waddell & Reed continued to grow. "At W & R, I saw things that disturbed me, things I disliked about corporate America," Art said. The additional pay levels were a plus, but Art realized that, despite the money and the ability to sell term, something was missing. He still didn't have control of his future.

Art faced typical corporate bureaucracy and small thinkers. Art knew growth only came with promotions. Stifling people stifled sales and income. In 1976, Art had worthy people to promote to Division Leader (the equivalent of RVP today), but Waddell & Reed would only budget for a small number of promotions. Art was so frustrated he thought about going back to coaching because promising a great future and not being able to deliver broke his heart, and the hearts of those of us who believed in him.

Virginia Carter recalled their growing frustration at Waddell & Reed in an interview for an early A.L. Williams publication (*The Birth of a Legend, 1990*). "In the southeast region of Waddell & Reed, Art was really running our region almost like a separate company," Virginia recalled. "He continued to do the things he believed would work, and at least had enough OK from the home office to recruit what was then considered large numbers. The sort of thing Waddell & Reed believed in was to hire everyone on a full-time basis, requiring them all to have an insurance license and a securities license, just a lot of typical corporate stuff, in total contradiction with what Art believed." As the company tried to control the whirlwind that was Art Williams, they cut territories, slowed promotions, and generally tried to harness the explosion of activity.

Art was reaching his limit. "I was so frustrated I couldn't stand it," Art says. "I needed to go with a company that would do it my way, that is, by hiring part-timers."

Ginny recalled, "After we got to the point where some of us were making some real money, I think Art was afraid that they would just keep on changing the rules to see that we didn't. We had a confab in Bob Turley's office, and Art said something to the effect that maybe we should put something together and all of us could go at the same time. We were so burned up by so many things they were doing to us by then." The only option left was to go it alone. "It was the latter part of 1976, four months after the St. Petersburg regional convention, that I determined to leave Waddell & Reed so that people could have unlimited promotions, and one day build a company within our company," Art says. "Waddell & Reed was mainly an investment company that happened to sell term insurance...we wanted to be a term insurance company that happened to sell monthly investments so people could invest the difference."

People often think Art's career was meteoric, but that was hardly the case. In 1968, when he was awakened to the truth of term, Art Williams was several years away from forming A.L. Williams.

Art learned about BTID from his cousin and focused on learning about how it worked. He spent two years part-time, 6 months of it at ITT. He spent 4 years at Waddell & Reed.

In February of 1977, Art was 35 years old and had decided that he couldn't stand corporate America anymore. It would never be the answer to his dreams. He had to break away.

The Decision: February 10, 1977

Peter Drucker, an influential thinker on business and management, once said, "Whenever you see a successful business, someone once made a courageous decision." (*Drucker, 2003*) It's important for future generations to know the sacrifices people made in order to bring a company to reality and to build the future they have today. At some point, a grand desire requires that you draw a line in the sand. In 1977, Art was willing to do that, and all our histories have been changed because of it.

"Kairos" is an ancient Greek word meaning the right, critical or opportune moment, the time when conditions are right for the accomplishment of a crucial action when all the cosmic tumblers have clicked into place and the universe opens itself up for a few seconds to show you what's possible. Kairos means 'God's time,' a fleeting instant in which an opening appears that must be driven through with resolute force if success is to be achieved.

February 10, 1977 was our Kairos moment.

That first day, I was sitting at my desk, and I got a phone call from Virginia Carter. She was calling from a phone booth to tell me that Art had resigned from Waddell & Reed. I had been there since June of 1974, along with her and Bobby Buisson and Bob Turley and a bunch of others. Until that point, I knew Art and a lot of the managers were frustrated because you just couldn't get a promotion at Waddell & Reed. Still, the news was shocking. Art had waited to leave until February 10. That was a significant date because that was the day the bonus checks cleared from 1976 and Art knew we all needed those checks cleared before we could leave.

That night, we met at Virginia Carter's home, and Art was telling us how great it was going to be, and how much more success we would have. Then he said he had to make a phone call. He went to Virginia's hall phone, which was about three steps up the stairs and we could hear him saying, "I don't have any insurance apps. I don't have any materials. I don't know how we're supposed to write life insurance without apps." Then he came down and with great conviction told us how great it was going to be. We were all a little stunned thinking, "How can this be so great when we don't even have life insurance apps to write?"

And just like that, Art's grand experiment began.

"When we started A.L. Williams, we felt unleashed, we could really go to town now," Art remembers.

I asked Art once whether he knew what he was getting into when he started A.L. Williams. He said he was prepared; he said he was a crusader and he learned in football that, when the whistle blows, you're in the game and you just do what you have to do to win. He never felt overwhelmed or that the stage was too big for him. He said he was prepared for every situation that came up. "Everything I did in my life was tough, but once you get in there, all you know how to do is fight and fight and fight."

In an important way, that fateful day mirrored the grand experiment of the United States of America. Lincoln knew that if the new nation failed, a government "of the people, by the people, and for the people" would be lost forever. (*Kearns, 2013*)

Art's belief was similar. Could average and ordinary people with no business background create their own company? Could teachers, coaches, housewives, accountants, youth pastors, single moms and other "misfits" accomplish what the "experts" said couldn't be done? Could anyone challenge one of the oldest industries in the country with a completely new philosophy? It was a daring question. The possibility of failure was huge, and the result of failure would be devastating for our families and the families we were committed to serving.

A handful of us left Waddell & Reed on Feb. 10, 1977. Through Bobby Buisson, Art had already recruited Bob Miller and Greg Fitzpatrick in Ft. Lauderdale, Florida. It was me and Ginny

Carter and Frank Dineen. "We didn't know exactly where we were going, but we were going forward," according to ALW leader Lynn Strickland. The day after Art left he handed Lynn a list of 85 people that he thought would be likely to go with him to his new company. He asked Lynn to call several of those people and ask them if they would come to a meeting with Art. It was Lynn Strickland that coined the name "the Original 85."

For several days we didn't even have a name. On February 14th Art came to Bill Orender's house to celebrate Virginia Carter's daughter's engagement. Several people were there, and we were all talking about this new company. We would ask, 'What is the name of the new company?' We didn't want a name that would indicate we had anything to do with the insurance industry because at Waddell & Reed we were getting into a lot more homes because the name Waddell & Reed didn't indicate insurance. One of the guys in my base, Art Burgess, asked Art what his middle name was, and he said 'Lynch.' Art Burgess suggested we call it A.L. Williams after Art. The name stuck. (*A Company of Destiny, 1990*)

Those were the days when the life insurance industry was like the wild, wild West. We took United Investors Life Insurance apps that we'd used at Waddell & Reed, and we cut off the very top with the name on it and made universal apps with no name, and we wrote life insurance policies with those apps. A week later, Art took the apps we'd written and flew them up to Minneapolis/ St. Paul where the company that was going to process our apps was located and they hand-wrote checks for our commissions, which he flew back and gave to us. Is there an executive you know who would do business this way? Meanwhile, Art kept telling us how good it was going to be and how big it was going to be. And crazy or not, we *believed* him, in spite of the evidence that said there's no way that was going to happen.

Rusty Crossland, SNSD and one of the Original 85, recalled how, when it was time for Art to make the decision to leave Waddell & Reed to start ALW, Art went to Rusty's house. In deciding to go with Art to start a new company, Rusty said, "It didn't require much thought. I believed 1000% in Art. He was dependable. He had passion. Waddell & Reed was just a company we put business through. Art was building a movement and Waddell & Reed was running a salesforce."

When Art decided to leave the relative security of Waddell & Reed and go on his own, it was what historians call a "Rubicon moment." The Rubicon is a stream in northeastern Italy that marked the ancient boundary between Italy and Cisaline Gaul. Julius Caesar led his army across that stream into Italy in 39 B.C., breaking the law forbidding a general to lead an army out of his province and so committing himself to war against the Senate and Pompey. The Rubicon was where Caesar made a military commitment. Art had his Rubicon moment when he resigned from Waddell & Reed. We had ours when we resigned and cast all our hopes and dreams on him and his vision. It was doom or domination. Art chose to dominate.

When the ancient Greeks landed their ships to wage war with their enemies, it is said that Greek generals ordered their men to burn all the ships. They knew that, when the men realized there was no turning back, they would fight with a vengeance. It was the motivation of necessity. When Art said, "We will beat Prudential" the final shot was fired. He knew the industry would destroy us if they could. Our boats had been burned. There was no going back.

Planting Our Flag

Art told us, "The slogan in the LA Lakers locker room says: 'Somewhere, someplace, sometime, you are going to have to plant your flag, make a stand and kick some ass.' When that time comes, you do it. When that moment of truth comes, CHARGE! When things haven't worked out, at that moment, CHARGE! When it's impossible, CHARGE! When it seems like you're dying, CHARGE! When you're hurting, CHARGE! When you're struggling, CHARGE! A winner can't ever show doubt."

Art made his stand on February 10, 1977. He did it without wavering or compromising. The insurance commissioner of Kansas said he should capitulate and join the Life Underwriters Association, that by doing so the insurance industry would know that he really was one of them. Like General Anthony McAuliffe who, when the Nazis ordered him to surrender, sent a note back saying, "NUTS!" Art said the same kind of thing to the insurance commissioner.

Few realized how deeply Art cared about those who chose to be in the fight with him. He revered each and every one and considered himself to have been privileged to lead them. The kitchen tables of America were his battlefield where his army fought and beat the largest, fiercest fighting industry of all time and he did it with average and ordinary people, people with a fighting spirit and a will to win that he himself epitomized. It was a supreme struggle for the sake of families across the country. It cannot be stressed enough what Art and his army accomplished.

As Herb Brooks said to his USA hockey team before beating the Russians in the 1981 Olympics, "Great moments are made from great opportunity. You were meant to be here. This is your time. Their time is done. It's over. This is your time. Now go out there and take it." Art was our Herb Brooks. We played our hearts out for ALW.

Why Did We Do It?

People left Waddell & Reed to go with Art because of the vision he had. The fact that people gave up all their security to jump into something that was far from a guaranteed success seems amazing. In hindsight, it seems a miracle that so many people wanted to be part of the new company. It was about having a chance for a better life. Art always said that every piece of flesh, every red-blooded person, wants to be part of something big, life-changing, and important, and it's true. We all had an inner drive that our souls longed for. We felt that this was our moment, our one moment to make a mark on this generation. We couldn't really explain it then, it wasn't a tangible reason, but we could feel it in our spirit. To paraphrase G.K. Chesterton, "A true warrior fights not because he hates the men in front of him but because he loves the men behind him." We found comrades and trench buddies at A.L. Williams, and we became a team. We risked everything because we believed. We risked everything because we knew Art.

"We weren't sure A.L. Williams would be the company to change the insurance industry," Art said, "but we were sure that someone was going to step forward and change the life insurance industry and we kept thinking why shouldn't it be us? We were never sure it would be us, but we gave it all we had. Prudential had 40,000 people to our 85. They were started in 1875 and we started 100 years later. It was probably stupid to think that we could beat them, but we were excited to be in the game." Richie Falcone summed it up "Art said he was going to change America. I thought, 'I'm an American, I can change.' And I did."

There's one story that serves as a great illustration of the kind of belief we had. Trudy White was a secretary in Tallahassee at the Waddell & Reed office there. She had been with them for decades. One of the original seven RVPs with ALW, Frank Dineen, worked with Trudy. Since Art was the Waddell & Reed RVP who had his office in that region, he got into her heart like he did all of ours. Before February 10, Art had been talking to Frank about his discontent and the need to make the move. He couldn't encourage Trudy to be one of the Original 85. He wouldn't ask her to lose her job at her age to go with an unproven company that had very little chance to succeed. It would devastate Art and Angela to ruin the life of such a good person. As sorry as they were, they didn't invite Trudy to join the new company.

Trudy White

Several whirlwind days after Art left, he was running around the state of Georgia connecting with those he thought would most likely share his feelings about a new company. He was exhausted. Art huddled at his home one evening trying to catch a breath. He got a knock on his door, and as he opened it, he was shocked. It was Trudy. Tallahassee was 245 miles from Atlanta. She said, "I'm coming with you." Art was dismayed. He didn't want to worry about Trudy's future. He tried to talk her out of it. But Trudy wanted desperately to be part of Art's vision, crusade and future. Trudy became Art's secretary, and later Virginia Carter's. She answered the phones, did our FNA's and became the glue that kept us grounded. Trudy joined the crusade and found the "make a difference" life she wanted. Waddell & Reed had been her paycheck, but we were her family.

Virginia Carter was 58 years old in 1977 yet signed a 3-year lease on an office. Bobby Buisson, Bob Turley, Rusty Crossland, Frank Dineen, and Fred Marceaux all signed leases with zero assurance that Art's dream would be successful. If it failed, they would lose everything. Art didn't blink and neither did we. Art's real success was not the company he created, but the hearts he won over and the depth of dedication they had to him. Art's approach to business was the antithesis of corporate America where they used people to make money for the company. Art had a new perspective. Instead of using people, he served them. He appreciated others' worth.

Those were the Halcyon Days of A.L. Williams, our most successful, prosperous, and happiest days when we struggled just to exist. Jim Penn, a million-dollar earner, said, "When we had nothing, we did everything." We didn't have all the fancy materials, just a flip chart Art had made up, a yellow pad, and a pen. I tell the story of Art telling us to build our companies with a yellow pad and a map of the U.S. We had no literature, no track record, no credibility, no administrative support, and no home office. But we had Art; we had a crusade, a term product, a Pioneer mutual fund product, and our Fast Start Schools. Plus, we had the fact that we were all broke and didn't want to be. We wanted to get wealthy, right wrongs, and correct injustices. We had a fire in our bellies and a chip on our shoulders.

The Foundation: The Crusade

In 1977 Art had two things that would come to be the fuel behind his success. He had a crusade. And he had a dream of building financial independence for himself and for others just like him. Art had a vision beyond anyone else in the financial services industry. As the saying goes, "He had a clear vision when everyone else needed bifocals." (*Butch Cassidy and the Sundance Kid, 1969*) The crusade that dated back to his mother's struggles to raise two boys on $10,000 of life insurance when she could have had 10 times that much fueled the anger that fueled a determination to make sure that other families knew there was "a better way." The realization that thousands of families had suffered the same fate was infuriating. It was made worse by the fact that the whole life agents didn't own what they sold. Most owned term, which was a fraction of the cost for dramatically more coverage. Art couldn't understand how someone could own one thing and sell another.

Art with his mother and son, Art Jr.

Art passed on his crusade to all of us. We didn't so much join Art in the early days as we joined what he believed. There is a crusader inside each one of us wanting to come out. We are all wired to make a difference, to be somebody that could amount to something, but no one ever told us we could until Art Williams. As someone said about Art, "People heard his beliefs and his words touched them deep inside. Those who believed what he believed took that cause and made it their own. And they told people what they believed. And those people told others what they believed."

The first crusades were fought in the year 1091. Our A.L. Williams crusade started in 1977. Crusades were fought by warriors who participated in the military expeditions undertaken by Christian powers in the 11th, 12th, and 13th centuries to win the Holy Land from the Muslims. Our ALW crusaders participated in a modern-day expedition to win the insurance wars from the insurance giants and capture security and well-being for American families. Those early A.L. Williams crusaders pioneered a new company, a new way of building a business, a new way to treat people. They brought more financial independence to orphans and widows than the one hundred years of social security.

Every army needs a general. The 3rd Army in World War II had George Patton; we had Art Williams. We would have followed Art anywhere.

Art gave us something to believe in. He touched a part of us that was dormant and awakened it. As Andy Stanley said, "Blessed is the man who gets the opportunity to devote his life to something bigger than himself and who finds himself surrounded by friends who share his passion." (*Stanley, 2022*) Art was committed to more than his own life. He was committed to our lives and to the lives of people like his mother. That was his super-power and we believed in his crusade and became crusaders ourselves. As Art would say, "A team has to play with one heartbeat." We had one team, one dream, one resolve, a oneness that gave us power and an unbreakable bond. We had one song, one voice, one enemy, one thought so we had a laser beam focus that proved invincible.

Claude Bristol wrote a book called *The Magic of Believing*. (*Bristol, 1948*) In it he talks of the power of belief. Art's power was that his belief was so strong that *we* believed because *he* believed when he was the only one who could see how big this could be.

Great men are remembered for doing something when others did nothing. "Buy term and invest the difference" wasn't new. There were other companies and agents who replaced whole life with term. Few invested the difference. Most were old whole life agents who sold whole life policies and then replaced them with term. After that, they quit the insurance business altogether. Art created a movement when others just created a temporary income for themselves.

Why were we willing to risk everything? Because we saw our shot to do something special and we believed completely in Art Williams. When Art spoke, his words created deep feelings of bonding and belonging to something. He talked about the crusade and how it would give us the extra ounce of courage that it takes to talk to someone, the extra push to make that phone call. He created in us a strong feeling that we were involved in a war, a battle. It was a battle that required warriors, not salespeople. The inner spirit that came out of us was that "little extra that makes all the difference" as he would say.

Who talks like this in a business? Steve Jobs asked his potential new CEO who was coming over from Pepsi, "Do you want to sell sugar water, or do you want to change the world?" We believed we were changing the world, not doing a "job". We felt like it was life and death to families who owned a whole life policy. Life and death to people like me who had dead-end jobs that would lead to dead-end lives.

Art was a rare breed. As one author says, "A rarer breed of person who not only has what it takes but thrives and rallies at every such challenge and the challenge makes them better than if they'd never faced the adversity at all." (*Forbes*, 2019) The life we desired required a fierce enemy that would bring out the best in us. Obstacles became the stepping stones we had to have to strengthen our resolve and find the guts to do it.

Art's cousin Ted saw the uniqueness of Art's crusade. "There are two things that I think made a difference," Ted Harrison said in the early 1990s. "First, Art stayed focused on the concept of by term and invest the difference. He never lost sight of it, and he never let things distract him. Second, he knew he had to give salespeople an incentive program that would compensate them for selling term insurance." (*Birth of A Legend*, 1995)

To Art, being a crusader meant everyone knew where he stood. If you weren't standing up, taking a stand to right a wrong, you couldn't be a crusader. He believed that, if no one was making fun of you, you weren't showing that you're a crusader. Art knew that "without a crusade, life will take away one vertebra at a time until you have no backbone left." As one leader told me, "No one wanted to be in the life insurance business. We loved it because we were on a crusade."

Art loved a good, righteous fight. He was like William Wallace in the movie *Braveheart* who, when asked on the battlefield in front of his English foes where he was going said, "I'm going to pick a fight." (*Braveheart, 2000*) Art embraced conflict and accepted the role of a rebel to the insurance behemoths. He fought the regulators, he fought the corporate higher-ups, and he fought the elitists that thought they were smarter than him. He fought for us, fought with us, and fought for our right to exist. Art gave us a saying: "fit to fight." He saw our crusade as a war, a war only we were prepared to fight. He worked on our courage, challenged our manhood, and asked us to be in the fight with him, not just fight for him. "We were fit to fight," Art said, "which was one of my favorite themes because of our cause. We were never in over our heads because of our cause." We needed Art's warrior mindset to inflame our souls for that one battle we too were born to fight.

One of the best books he had printed was a book of third-party materials that contained articles by consumer-oriented publications stating how term was right and people should not purchase whole life. The book was appropriately titled, "Nobody Loves Us but The People." That was how we felt.

Art showed us we were fighting for what was right. Art didn't have an opinion. He had a crusade.

A Bigger Vision

Once again, a simple meeting became the catalyst for change. Until now, the crusade had been the driving force. Soon there would be a second element to the vision. "One day I went to see Napoleon Hill, author of the bestselling *Think and Grow Rich,* at a meeting in Atlanta," Art said. "He taught me about the six steps to becoming financially independent. Immediately I began recruiting using my paycheck. I grew up poor and then, suddenly, by using the principles in this book, I was on track to become financially independent." At that moment, in addition to his term life insurance crusade, Art felt a calling to give everyone that same hope and show them the plan. "I saw I could help the same kind of people who came from where I came from and had the same kind of dreams that I had." Art's vision was expanding. It was no longer just about crusading for term insurance, he wanted to show average and ordinary people how to build, not just business success, but financial freedom. His infuriating discovery about whole life insurance had ignited a crusade. Art's amplified dream to show people a way out would ignite a movement.

On February 10, 1977, Art was ready to begin. His dream mirrored the grand experiment of the United States of America, a pursuit dedicated to the proposition that all men are created equal. Art's belief and gamble were similar. Could average and ordinary people with no business background create their own company within Art's company? As Lincoln realized the whole world was watching, realized that dictators and monarchs believed it would fail, the insurance and financial services corporate types didn't believe we could do what they, the elitists, could do. Lincoln believed in democracy. Art believed in the power of self-determination, and they were both right. "Lincoln had translated the story of his country and the meaning of the war into words and ideas accessible to every American." (*Doris Goodwin, 2013*) Art created a business system that made owning your own company accessible to every American.

Art had a dream, and that dream became our dream. The dream of A.L. Williams was so simple, yet so profound. It was simply this:

The dream is that for less than $100 a family can go into business for themselves, start part-time, not go for broke, and have a chance to build security.

The dream is to build a significant income and have a chance to be financially independent.

The dream is a company built for people who are tired of being average and ordinary, tired of just getting by, just making ends meet, tired of having more "month" than "money."

The dream is an opportunity to be somebody, for people to look at you and see greatness.

The dream is to have a goal of greatness, for people to be leaders and build leaders.

The dream is to have a primary job of being a "dream seller," to help people believe in themselves and have confidence that they will win.

The dream is to be a leader and part of a championship team.

Art wanted to change people's lives, and despite all the challenges that came his way, he built a system that changed the fortunes of orphans, widows, retirees, and thousands of business owners who started part-time and went on to make fortunes. He inspired the imaginations of average and ordinary people to accomplish something they were told they could never do.

As the saying goes, "Believe in yourself and there will come a day when others have no choice but to believe with you." (*Cynthia Kersey, 2021*) Art would tell us, "If I can get you to see what I'm seeing and dream what I'm dreaming, we will win." He would tell us that our story could turn out to be something you'd make a movie about. The gift he gave us was that he believed in us. In turn, we believed in ourselves because we were confident that we were right. He was a great salesman. He sold 85 nobodies the dream of beating the iconic Prudential. That's like a junior high team planning to beat the reigning NFL Super Bowl champion. But we had the truth, and we had Art. That combination was spiritual.

He cared about us and how our lives would turn out. We cared about our clients, our people, our families, and our futures. We were that team of destiny Art thought we were, and it was his belief that A.L. Williams was "a company of destiny" that made us more than we were.

Art's beliefs became the stakes with which we planted our flags. At its core, Art's dream was the American Dream. He fed us the American Dream, and we ate it up.

Meanwhile, a spirit was starting to form in the ALW culture. A spirit that said we were the people that could do something special, even though the world couldn't recognize our strength. We were like the search and rescue dogs of 9/11.

The September 11th disaster created a unique program to obtain and train detection dogs to direct the digging efforts of first-responders. An ingenious woman would start a program to train dogs and handlers for such noble work. The interesting aspect of this story is where she found the unique dogs that had the energy, the mettle, the courage, and the tenacity to do the job. (*CBS Sunday Morning*) What rare and special breeds had what it would take? She found them, not in fancy breeds, but in dog pounds just like those in every city. They were what you might call "mutts." She discovered them to have the energy, dedication, and drive that the well-fed and pampered dogs didn't possess.

Art attracted mutts that were locked out of corporate America, who were presumed not to have the intelligence to build a NYSE company and compete with a giant insurance empire. Art saw something special in mutts like us and the crusade changed these mutts into a force for good. It made these mutts otherworldly in their dedication. Unlike the pedigrees, with the "I'm too good to do something like that "mentality, we were willing to do whatever it took, for as long as it took, to commit and never, ever give up. The emergence within his team of strength, guts, mettle, grit, audacity, boldness, and selflessness was something to behold.

Art talked about "people who come from where we come from," but that wasn't an insult. We were people who lived his belief that you win with your heart, not your head. A.L. Williams emerged from the neglected world of "average and ordinary" people and answered the call. We had a score we wanted to even up. We desired to prove the "pedigrees" wrong and had a resolute pride that came with "being involved with something bigger than ourselves." Today, these unknowns and "unwanteds" are some of the highest-paid people in North America with businesses that are legendary.

Chapter 2:
THE INSURANCE WARS

At first, they laughed, then they got mad, and finally they came to believe that the monster that would destroy their expensive insurance products would grow to be a dominant force in the industry. A.L. Williams would ultimately become a tsunami of crusaders. But first, they had to survive a war so fierce that no one could have predicted it.

The insurance industry seemed to have misunderstood who they were fighting against. They thought we were just some kind of "fad" company. They failed to respect our beliefs, crusade, and system. They were confident they could take us out with one shot.

The arrogance of the insurance industry was similar to many industries over the years. IBM didn't think personal computers even had a market. The American auto industry never thought Honda, a motorcycle manufacturer, could become the door opener for Japanese cars. The nation's steel industry never thought that Japan could compete in steel. The insurance industry laughed and labeled us as "a rag-tag army, twisters, termites, pyramid schemers, a bunch of huckleberries who had a hitched trailer on the edge of town." We defied them, and they came after us. The biggest problem was that they were far richer and more powerful than we were. They had 100 years of tradition on their side. They had a goal, not to compete, but to annihilate us.

The "Flat Earth" Industry

Many people once believed in the "flat earth theory." The theory says that the earth is flat and not round, and all the luminaries in the sky rotate around the non-moving flat body. The whole life industry was similar. They believed everything regarding life insurance revolved around them, and any other belief was heresy. Their "the earth is flat" conviction mandated swift and severe punishment to any person or group who would dare argue against their traditional truth distortions. Their beliefs were so pervasive that it was literally the only school of thought allowed.

Virginia Carter was in the whole life industry, as was her father, who ran a whole life agency. Early in her career, Virginia attended a special advanced school at Southern Methodist University for a whole month. They only taught the accepted industry dogma that had no place for the heretical "buy term and invest the difference" concept. It was like term didn't exist.

The industry's highest designations were all based on their whole life doctrine. Designations such as CLU (Chartered Life Underwriter) held that the person was a financial professional with extensive life insurance knowledge. Their own literature proclaimed:

> "CLU - The premier designation for insurance professionals. Launched in 1927, the Chartered Life Underwriter is the insurance profession's oldest standard of excellence. Today, it continues to be the credential for practitioners who desire to provide their clients with the security of life insurance and risk management."

That kind of single-mindedness left no room for another theory, especially one that was cheaper.

When Art and his ALW pioneers appeared on the scene, they quickly felt the fury of the whole life industry. The traditional whole lifers weren't about to give up their powerful hold on the minds of their agents and policyholders, never mind the powerful insurance commissioners, lobbyists, and elected officials who were skeptical of anything other than the 100-year-old whole life culture. They had built a monopoly, and they weren't about to let a group of interlopers without any life insurance experience rain on their very lucrative parade.

Today, our minds cannot get around the size, power, wealth, and political strength the life insurance industry had in this country thirty to forty years ago. To condemn the whole life industry was heresy. Anyone who voiced opposition was a heretic. Until Art, no one dared challenge what they sold.

The opposition was sometimes overwhelming. The "enemy agents" promoted a variety of arguments against BTID (short for buy term and invest the difference). The insurance agents would make fun of Art's part-time concept. They would say things like,

"Would you want a brain surgeon to work on your brain if he was part-time?"

"Would you want your lawyer to be part-time if your life was on the line?"

"Do you want your home builder to be part-time when he's going to be building a house that you have to live in for the rest of your life?"

"Can a part-time 'anything' be valuable? If so, why aren't they full-time?"

The "termites" met with various arguments from consumers who had bought the whole life story — because it was the only story they'd ever heard.

"I own whole life. My grandparents had a whole life policy, my parents had a whole life policy, my whole life agent is on the deacon board of my church and I own a whole life policy."

"Buying term is just renting life insurance."

"Term insurance doesn't give you any money back. With whole life, I get all my premiums back plus a little bit more."

It's hard to underestimate the esteem that the local life insurance agents had in their communities. The culture of the time was that the family insurance agent was completely trusted. When I bought my life first life insurance policy, my mother's Prudential agent came to our house. I was about to get married and my mother wanted to make sure I had a life insurance policy in place. When I was introduced to him, he said his name was Joe. I said, "Hello, Joe." My mother turned to me and said, "He's my Prudential agent and you call him Mr." I bought a cash value policy of $25,000 for $40 a month. With a wife and hopefully a family down the road, the agent "took care of me."

An insurance agent in those days was accepted as family. They were never questioned about the product they sold; it would have been disrespectful. They held an honorable position with dedicated policyholders because life insurance was so entrenched in the culture.

Turning the tide against whole life at the time was like trying to change the rotation of the earth.

A Fight to the End

We faced the most prominent industry of the past 100 years. They had the money, the legislators, the politicians, the media. All we had was a burning desire to do what was right.

Art would tell us, "The enemy can't win." Art knew the math of BTID and how $25,000 of protection versus $100,000 for the same price could never be beaten. We were in the fight for as long as it took to get the job done. As my father-in-law found out when he joined the army in WWII, the length of time he would spend in the service was "the duration plus six months." We were there until we won. The insurance industry thought we were like them. They thought we liked it like them. But Art said, "Those guys in the wrong-colored jerseys don't love it like we do. We don't just like it. *We love it.*"

To them, it was just a job, but to us, it was do-or-die. We fought because, if we didn't, we had nothing to go back to. We had laid it all on the line. That was what made the difference. We had Art as a coach, we had spouses that believed in us, and we had a team of people who quit their jobs, moved their families, leased office space, were mocked, were shunned by people they'd known forever, were disowned by church leaders. We wanted to make history, our own and in the financial industry. The industry had no grit in them. We did. We were fighting for our right to exist, to compete, to be somebody, to make a difference with our lives, and we fought as though our lives depended on it. As Benjamin

Disraeli said, "Nothing can resist a human that will stake its very existence on its purpose." (*Quercus, 2011*)

Art knew how tough it would be, but he knew how to challenge our manhood. He talked about being mentally tough more than how life insurance worked. He fired us up by saying, "I want you to hit them in the morning, I want you to hit them in the evening, and I want you to knock their asses off." With Art believing in us and us believing in Art, we were invincible. He never blinked, and neither did we.

They called us "termites," and we were proud of it. They called us a rag-tag group of non-professionals and we were proud of it. We were outcasts in an industry that had a respectability rating slightly higher than used car salesmen and proud of it. We were not allowed to be part of the most prestigious designation the insurance industry had to offer, the Million Dollar Round Table. We were proud *not* to be invited into their elite group. The same with the industry designation of CLU, Chartered Life Underwriter.

They called us a cult, led by a cult leader. They thought we were liars and lunatics who were attempting to destroy their highly vaunted reputations. In reality, we were exposing them; their own math proved their reputations were shadowed in questionable accounting and misrepresentations. Why else would you call what is a partial refund of a deliberate premium overcharge a dividend? It misrepresented what a dividend was, and they knew it. They wanted it to appear as if clients were receiving part of the profits of the insurance company itself, but that wasn't the case. The reality was that they were a weak opponent that was easily shown to be a shell game of moving numbers.

The fight took its toll, but we learned to counter the opposition. I remember a time in Houston visiting one of my offices there and interviewing a real estate agent. She boldly and condescendingly said, "I've heard a lot of bad things about your company." I replied, "Yes, and I've done all the bad things you have heard our company does." The bad things? We replaced their whole life policies. We cut people's insurance costs and gave them four to five times more insurance. To be thought of as a crook by the insurance industry was a compliment!

Art was a football coach, so he understood how to battle against another team. It's violent, but everyone shakes hands at the end, and many combatants end up playing on the same teams over the years. It wasn't that way with us. Once a whole life agent, always a whole life agent. On very rare occasions some great leaders came from a whole life background, but they were not lifers with our company. Virginia Carter sold it for a while prior to our company. She accepted it as something good for people at that time but converted once she saw the huge difference BTID made.

Art was a renegade who went against the establishment, and they vilified him for it. He was punished because they had a monopoly and weren't going to give it up. They complained about ALW to the Better Business Bureaus, the Life Insurance Agents Lobby, the National Association of Life Underwriters (NALU), the Certified Life Underwriters, their congressmen, and the insurance commissioners in each state in the hope they would help put us out of business.

The War at the Kitchen Table

We would replace a terrible whole life policy with high premiums and low face amount with our better-priced policy with a higher face amount of coverage. These good deeds would cause us to be called "twisters," a term used to designate someone who illegally replaced one policy for another. It was a derogatory, condescending term used to neutralize the truth and hide the untruths. If you didn't have a chip on your shoulder, you hadn't yet had an old agent confrontation where they relished denouncing you as a fraud, a huckster, and a con man for daring to question the rightness of whole life.

The main battlefield of the war was at the kitchen tables of America. It was also the place where the whole life industry's complete control made life difficult for Art's little company. In those days when we replaced a whole life policy with a term policy, we had to pick up the whole life policies, send them off to a third-party company who would do an analysis, which was a minimum two-week turnaround *if* they came back correct. If not, we had to send them back. Then we put the information regarding the policy on "comparison statements;" when we made the sale, the client had to sign them, staple them to our policy application, and mail them to our insurance carrier. They would send a letter to the whole life company stating the client's intention of replacing their policy, and the client would get a call from the agent who would end up saying, "If I knew you wanted term, I could have given you that cheaper than the A.L. Williams price." In two out of ten policies, we lost the client because of this process. We became very good at preparing the client for the enemy agent to come back. Those who didn't learn this skill would soon quit the business.

Think of it like this: Suppose you own a Chevy car. Imagine going to buy a Ford car. Imagine having to fill out forms that must be completed before you purchase a Ford that explains all the benefits of your Chevy car. Imagine having to send that form to the Chevy dealership with an explanation from the Ford dealership that you are intending to replace your Chevy with a Ford, then having to wait two weeks before you can buy your Ford, by law. Now also imagine an immediate call from the Chevy dealership telling you all the reasons you should not buy a Ford. Nowhere in America has this ever happened outside of life insurance.

Art knew the best defense was a killer offense, thus his mantra, "Attack, attack, attack." He knew his job was to keep us marching forward and not losing faith. Art did everything he could think of to keep us motivated during these times. We had an RVP meeting in Atlanta every six weeks to keep the fire and the hope burning. If we had been military, we would have been as tough as the Green Berets or the Army Rangers. Every volley the industry sent would result in us replacing 100 of their policies. One of ours quit, two of theirs quit. Art kept us on our toes. He knew how to challenge us. He talked about being mentally tough more than he talked about how life insurance worked. He created the concept of Fast Start Schools, a key component to our success.

These were weekend events that started on Fridays, 7:00-10:00 p.m., then Saturdays 9:00 am - 5:00, and Sundays 9:00 am-noon. Art had started Fast Start Schools at Waddell and Reed. The first one of A.L. Williams was held at a Hilton Hotel in Tucker, Georgia.

About Fast Start Schools, Art said, "We took the dull world of life insurance and made it fun and exciting." Fast Start Schools bonded us and brought an excitement and unity to our group. They were a great way to counteract the abuse and criticism we experienced from the industry every day.

Frank Dineen was in Albany, Georgia, one of the toughest parts of the country for the ALW business. He constantly felt the ire of the traditional life insurance industry. Frank was living in an apartment. In those days his business mail would come to his apartment mailbox. One time someone took all his life insurance policies in his mailboxes that he was to deliver to clients, tore them up, mixed them with manure, and stuffed them back in the mailbox.

Another time Frank went out to his car behind his office and found all four of his tires flat. There was a sign on the windshield that said, "You can't replace any policies tonight, can you?" It happened again two months later, with only two tires this time. When Frank served on a local school board for the Catholic school where he sent his children, an agent told the parish priest that Frank was a crook and would steal all the school's money if he kept him on the school board. Frank wasn't kicked off the school board, but they took his name off the checking account that he shared with the other board members. His relationship with that school and the priest was never the same. Frank said, "I treated it like it was a war."

Frank said these incidents would give him more resolve to replace more whole life policies.

Bob Tillery, one of the Original 85, recalled what the fight was like.

"In 1976 Rusty Crossland convinced me to try the business part-time, and I signed up with Waddell & Reed in January of '77. A few weeks later, Rusty called to tell me that Art was leaving W&R and invited me to a meeting at Art's office. At the meeting Art explained that he wanted to build a special kind of company with a special kind of people. He said that the odds of us making it were stacked against us but if we did make it, it would be great. He introduced us to our new insurance company, Financial Assurance, a small company out of Kansas City. We were also going to represent a small investment company that would eventually become First American National Securities, or FANS for short.

"Art was more than right about how tough it would be. The competition disliked us; the State insurance departments were suspicious of us. We really didn't have a well-known company to brag about; we had to sell our concepts with no fancy flip charts or glossy magazines. We had a legal pad, pen, and right on our side. With these tools we destroyed the whole life concept and built a strong client base. We began taking our message to everyone, and before long we were seeing our incomes rise. Just two months after the meeting, I left my job as Associate Registrar at Georgia Tech and went full-time with A.L. Williams.

"My buddy, Jay, who was also my doubles tennis partner, was doing great and making a few thousand dollars a month working part-time. He called me one day to say that one of his clients, who just happened to be the captain of our tennis team, was not going to keep his Financial Assurance policy that cost him $80 a month less than his former policy.

"I called the client, and he told me that a fellow from the local insurance department had talked with him and told him that we were a bunch of outlaws and that we wouldn't be in business very long. I called the insurance commissioner's office and asked to speak to the individual and let him know what we had done for our client and what had been done for me and my wife. He didn't want to hear it and told me that he had worked for a top-three life insurance company for over 30 years, and there was no way I could convince him that BTID would work. I called our tennis team captain back and asked him to reconsider, and he said he couldn't do business with a company that was outlawed in over 35 states. Without hesitation, I resigned from his team. I called Jay to let him know, and he made the decision to quit A.L. Williams instead of the tennis team.

"From then on, I talked with everybody about finances and the evils of whole life. I started calling parents of newborns who were listed in our local paper. Chris, my wife, would compile a list of prospects for me, and every Sunday afternoon, I would call and set appointments for the week.

"As we began to have success, the opposition did everything they could to destroy us. One of the largest churches in Greenville was affiliated with a local university, and I had quite a few clients at the university and at this large church. A couple of well-known local life agents went to the minister at this church and told them we were a bunch of crooks and were stealing the cash values out of their clients' policies. The minister's sermons were broadcast on radio, and prior to his sermon he warned his members to beware of our company and to never do business with us. My phone rang off the hook for days with clients wanting to cancel their policies and prospects canceling appointments. Several of my recruits quit, too.

"A new recruit and I had made a sale to the music minister at this church's Christian school. He and his wife were happy with the increased coverage and reduced premium. A couple of days after the sale, the client called me to say that their former agent had told them that he had an investigation done and found that we had 20 counts of fraud against us. I assured the client that it wasn't true and would get with the agent to learn what he was talking about. I called repeatedly and left several messages for this agent, and one evening he called. When I asked him about the 20 counts of fraud, he said that he had found what he thought were 20 mistakes on our comparison statement. When I told him that was a far cry from fraud, he simply said it was a matter of semantics. A few days later, I met with him and blew him away with what we were able to do for his former clients. He even admitted that he owned all term but didn't think his clients could handle term.

"I remember calling Art a few months after opening our Greenville office with concerns about the church mentioned earlier. After telling Art about the pastor's comments, Art said, "As long as you're doing things the right way and doing what's best for the client, you have nothing to worry about." He even said that the terrible comments would eventually become an asset to my business. He was right again. Just a few months later, I called on a business owner who attended that church, and when he heard the name A.L. Williams, he said, 'Oh, yeah, I've heard of that company. You guys must be doing a good job because our pastor mentioned you a few months ago.'

"Days later, two men showed up at my office purporting to represent the ethics committee of the Life Underwriter's Association in our area. They demanded to see all my client files to make sure that we were doing the best job for the clients. After telling them I would gladly oblige if they would give me all their client files for me to review, they left."

"When Bob decided to move to South Carolina, the industry nearly succeeded in ending his business. Bob recalled, "One of my best recruits was from Gainesville, Georgia, and he kept me busy calling on his friends and relatives in the Gainesville area. He and I soon began driving the 170 miles to Greenville, South Carolina to meet with his former coaches and professors at Furman University. We had great success in Greenville, and everybody loved this young man. Around May of 1978, Rusty Crossland asked me if I wanted to move to Greenville since we were spending so much time there. We moved to Greenville on August 1, 1978, when Chris, my wife, was seven months pregnant. I had a non-resident license for South Carolina but had to get a resident license which took almost three months, during which time I could make no sales or sales calls. All I could do was recruit and set up an office. I began interviewing people from 7:00 am-11:00 pm every day.

"We were running out of money and had to sell our washer and dryer to pay bills, and on October 10, our beautiful daughter was born. Then, a Board of Regents member in charge of registrars and admission officers called to offer me my dream job as a registrar at the University of Georgia. Had it not been for my fabulous wife, I would have taken the position, but she knew that things would turn around, and a week later, my South Carolina insurance license came in the mail. I made 14 sales that week and had many more in the pipeline."

That kind of toughness was what made being part of a crusade different.

Art and his company were magnetized by the moral obligation to right the wrongs that were being thrust upon the financially helpless and gullible. Before ALW, they sold products without any opposition.

People today can't imagine how dominant the industry was. They attacked us because we opposed them. Their products were constructed to appear "too complicated" for everyday people to understand.

Every time things seemed to be headed in the right direction, an obstacle intervened. The Georgia Insurance Commissioner, Johnny Caldwell, called Art in for a meeting. It was Art, Bobby Buisson, Kevin King, our attorney, and Harold Tarrer who attended. Insurance commissioners had a lot of power within the insurance world. Walking into the room the atmosphere had to feel more like an inquisition than a meeting. It was an anxious situation. Luckily, Harold had played football in high school with Johnny Caldwell's son. That relationship helped us win Caldwell over to our side – another example that A.L. Williams was a company of destiny. The commissioner dropped his investigation and, five years later, joined A.L. Williams' Board of Directors.

With all this animosity boiling around us, how did we even face the kitchen table for an agent confrontation? At first, it was terrifying, but it became something we relished. Bob Tillery describes it best.

"The fun in the early days? An old agent confrontation. We looked forward to each and every one. We'd lick our lips. We would not win every one at the beginning, but we would learn, and towards the end, we never lost a client. We loved playing mind games with the old agent at a confrontation. We would often bring a tape recorder and have it right on the kitchen table because that intimidated the old agent.

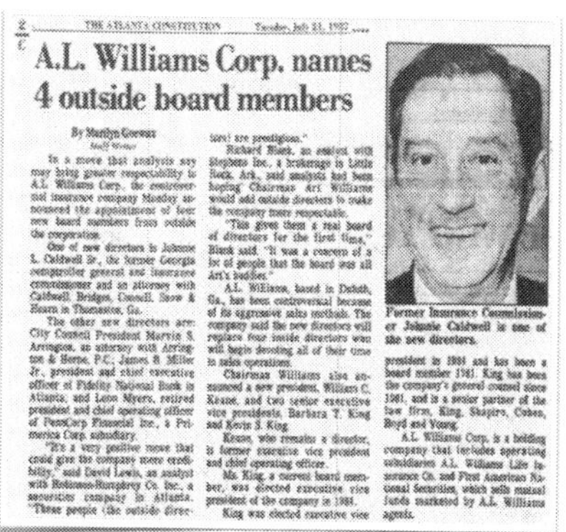

A.L. Williams Corp. names 4 outside board members

Former Insurance Commissioner Johnnie Caldwell is one of the new directors.

Johnny Caldwell announced as Board Member in the *Atlanta Constitution*

"We always brought plenty of third-party materials and copies of our very own policies that we had when we had whole life and how much more we got when we had term insurance, as well as and our personal mutual funds statement. This always led us to question the old agent on what kind of life insurance he owned. It was always funny to see their response when they hesitated, stammered, and got flummoxed. They said, 'Mostly whole life, and I do have a little bit of term.' Then we would say, 'How much term do you own?' They would hesitate some more and would never fully answer the question because they owned mostly term. That was the convincing point for saving a policy during a confrontation.

"Lynn Strickland told me about how he had a long black Cadillac and would always get to the home early. He had a reputation that, when an old agent saw that long black Cadillac sitting in front of the client's home, they would be intimidated. They even gave him a name, 'the undertaker.'

"We all suffered confrontations, but we had a glorious time defeating and deflating an arrogant insurance agent in the home of his good friend and client. We became eager to go on agent confrontations because we knew we were right, and we had the math of BTID. They were unprepared; they thought they were professional, but we believed in what we were doing."

Bob's experiences were shared by all of us. But we fought back. We were the insurance agents' worse nightmare. The kitchen table was like a crime scene to us because that's where the agent sold the client a whole life policy instead of term. The old agent left evidence in the form of the policy that was sold to the family. We used the client's very own policy to prove to them that they had the wrong kind of insurance and not enough protection for their hard-earned money.

The War in the Press

The insurance wars weren't confined to the kitchen tables of America. The impressive success of the little company caught the attention of the whole life industry's supporters in the press. After all, it was unthinkable to the traditional press that the baby A.L. Williams could be legitimately having the success it was having. With some encouragement from the industry, a series of devastating articles began to appear.

Barron's, a giant in the financial press, published a crushing article that painted Art as a huckster, a money-grabbing con artist. The front cover showed our logo as an upside-down pyramid. They were inferring in an intellectually snarky way that A.L. Williams was an insurance pyramid scheme. The title called Art, "the P.T. Barnum of the life insurance industry." It wasn't a compliment.

Another article by the Better Business Bureau came out challenging the legitimacy of the A.L. Williams story. We later came to realize it was paid for by the members of the insurance industry. We discovered that each city has a BBB. Unbeknown to most people, the BBB in each city is paid for by the businesses who pay the BBB franchise owner in order to promote their services and products in the community. It has nothing to do with the approval of the BBB. They don't approve, they just promote. They promoted insurance agents' products and the insurance agents who paid them. Full-page ads from the BBB came out in St. Louis, Chattanooga and Beaumont, TX, saying, "Don't do business with A.L. Williams." They even listed a number to call so people would hear that ALW was outlawed in every state in America. According to Art, "The industry used the BBB to make our lives miserable."

The attacks seemed to come from everywhere. While living outside Atlanta, Art opened his front door one Sunday to find an article on the front page of *The Atlanta Journal* demeaning him and his people as shady felons who were deliberately ruining families' futures by replacing their policies with term policies that would never pay off, thereby "stealing" their money and their cash values. His honor and respect were shattered.

According to Art, "*The Atlanta Journal* article was especially painful because it affected my family. Because it said that my company was under investigation, people in the community would question whether I was doing something illegal. I was concerned that my children's friends' parents looked at my children negatively because the article questioned my character and honesty. The article made people in our small community question whether their friend's daddy might be a crook."

Along with the articles, the whole life industry used other connections. They used professors and writers to push their theories. The phrase "no good deed goes unpunished" summarized how we were viewed and vilified by the industry, industry publications, and so-called experts like Joseph Belth, a professor at the University of Indiana. Another was Ken Young, a Dallas whole life insurance agent with Prudential who saw himself as a warrior who was going to slay the beast called A.L Williams. Some profited by writing and selling brochures that claimed to prove we were wrong. These and other individuals realized they could make a name for themselves by attacking A.L. Williams.

The most shocking display was when Michael Pertshuck, the head of the Federal Trade Commission (FTC) and a strong consumer advocate, was required to meet with members of Congress after the FTC report came out, which supported our position, and was told never to investigate the life insurance industry again. They never did. The insurance "flat earthers" exercised their immense power to influence Congress and avoid giving the American public the truth.

Each time an article appeared, it inflicted business and personal damage. Friendships were lost, families were fractured, neighbors questioned our honesty and integrity, and clients canceled their policies. How many families lost the protection they needed and later suffered?

The industry expected us to fold, but we didn't. We didn't mind being compared to P.T. Barnum. Did you ever see the movie *The Greatest Showman*? It celebrates the birth of show business and tells of a visionary who rose from nothing to create a spectacle that became a worldwide sensation. He was a man who said, "The noblest art is making people happy." Barnum amassed a group of people from diverse backgrounds and treated them as equals. He brought them respect, dignity, and gave them a voice, and so did Art.

The orchestrated attacks in the press only made Art and all of us more determined. They had gone too far. If they wanted a war, this provided the "bulletin board material" for Art to use. Average people would be broken and beaten with articles like we got, but Art only used these to inflame his army and do more than ever. Art never wavered and called upon us to fight back and "hit them harder, pick up more policies, recruit more people, plant your flag and never back down."

For most of us, A. L. Williams had started as a job, but it became a dream and ended as a quest. We couldn't give up until we won.

According to Art, "Every bad article made me determined to beat them, and then, in the heat of battle, I never thought of the mess we were in. My determination was that nothing was going to deter us. The crusade to beat cash value and build financial security for our families kept me going."

The Battle Gets Tougher

People can never realize the extent of our battle against the insurance industry: 2,000 companies, 450,000 agents, 52 insurance commissioners, thousands of Better Business Bureaus, and only one or two insurance companies that would dare bet on us to take our business. Art must have become numb from overcoming so many obstacles.

During the height of the insurance wars, we had reps whose tires were slashed, whose jobs were threatened, and whose meetings were disrupted by whole life agents trying to "expose" us. At one point, Art Williams wore a bullet-proof vest because of the vitriol of the industry.

Art had to pave new roads without blueprints, footprints, or welcome prints. All he had was the truth, hope, and the responsibility of those who believed in him and our crusade. We took pride in being different. We became hope to orphans and widows and to frustrated people locked into a corporate life they didn't choose or embrace. Art created a vessel of hope for all our new associates and financial hope on a scale never seen for a generation of "nobodies" who "wanted to be somebodies so bad it bordered on being an obsession."

Pretty soon, as we suffered the worst the industry could dream up, it was all of us who were obsessed, just like Art. We had one goal: to beat the industry and win for the consumer.

We were outnumbered, but we didn't accept defeat. This wasn't "just business" to Art and all of us. We met the industry toe to toe and the war continued. We attacked their core beliefs. We attacked their character. We went into the homes which were the trenches of our war. We were armed with truth and unveiled the myth that the industry perpetuated. Art used to say that if World War III was happening and a bomb was coming down on his head, he would be out replacing whole life insurance. So, when you ask what kind of warrior it took to dethrone the most powerful industry in the world, the answer is a warrior filled with anger, stubbornness, truth, a missionary zeal, and an army that volunteered to fight the good fight beside Art.

Art had a chip on his shoulder the size of a giant redwood. Imagine if your father died with $10,000 of life insurance when he could have been sold $100,000 for the same premium; imagine you went into the term insurance business and did a great job for people, but you were threatened by your school administrators because the insurance men in your city said terrible things about you; imagine you woke up at your home in Snellville, GA to an article besmirching your character for every neighbor to see; imagine if your fellow agents had tires slashed; imagine if you had been called a twister (a person who illegally replaces whole life insurance), and a termite; imagine if you lost good people because the old agents lied about their character and honesty. How big a chip would you have?

Titans are targeted because they disrupt the status quo, and that described Art.

The ALW Board of Directors became aware of a significant number of threats against Art. They took extreme action to protect Art and his family. A security company was hired to give round-the-clock protection. Security personnel had to be placed around Art's home. The ALW logo was taken off Art's plane. Art was even encouraged to wear a bulletproof vest. When Art spoke, a security guard stood off to the side. Before Art used his yacht, the security people donned wet suits to examine the hull for devices. Art's children felt uneasy with the guards nearby, so Art eventually decided to discontinue security. This lasted one-and-a-half to two years.

When Titans disrupt the status quo, people get upset, but courage and right won out.

Art and the termites loved exposing whole life insurance and its supporters. He was a disrupter for a greater good. He was a force to be reckoned with. The opposition didn't stop Art's crusade.

Far from it. As an admiral in the Japanese Navy said after the attack on Pearl Harbor, "I fear all we have done is to awaken a sleeping giant and fill him with a terrible resolve." (*Yamanoto, 1941*)

Einstein said, "Great spirits have always encountered opposition from mediocre minds. The mediocre mind is incapable of understanding the man who refuses to bow blindly to conventional prejudices and chooses instead to express his opinions courageously and honestly." (*Einstein, 2011*)

Art was that giant that had his soul stirred and his resolve solidified.

David and Goliath

In the battle between David and Goliath everyone roots for David, but that was not the case for Art and his "experiment." It's called the "Goliath Principal." Nobody roots for Goliath, supposedly, but America did. The song "You and Me Against the World" by Helen Reddy should have been Art's theme song. The Goliath was the entire insurance industry with its billions of dollars, its insurance executives, its 400,000-plus agents, its 100 years of customer indoctrination, and the millions of customers whose agents were fellow churchgoers, Elks club brothers, mayors of small towns and so on. They had the big-name companies and the financial control. The Goliath had the hearts of the policyholders because they thought insurance agents knew it all, and blue-collar people trusted them. Unfortunately, the agents had been brainwashed and perpetuated that indoctrination onto financially ignorant families.

Along comes Art Williams with a big cause created from his own mother's hardship. That "big cause" created Art's statement, "I made it my mission to replace every whole life policy in America." The "David" emerged with rock in hand, and the battle began. The rock Art had was the math of BTID. All the "Goliaths" had were labels (termites, twisters), condemnation ("ALW works from a trailer on the edge of town"), and innuendos suggesting we were about to be banned for being illegal.

But remember who won the battle? David! Art had the rock of truth and an army of crusaders. The insurance industry lost ground year after year. Today you can hardly find an insurance agent anywhere, and the Goliath companies are merging just to maintain their block of business. You could almost hear the "thud" as they fell.

The war with the insurance industry was bloodless, but it was war, nonetheless. The obstacles that Art and Angela and the ALW army overcame could never be understood without understanding the dominance of the insurance industry. The biggest obstacle was the force of tradition. Tradition is an inherited, established or customary pattern of thought, action or behavior. "We've always done it this way," was the refrain. The pride Art and all of us felt came from a die-hard boldness and resolve concerning the truth of Art's philosophy.

It was a crusade that was more than words. It was in our DNA. We could take the heat because we were doing the cooking. Looking back, all the attacks created something beautiful. Just like a pearl is the result of a grain of sand irritating an oyster, the industry created an unintended consequence that enabled game-changing value for all Americans.

Happy to Pick a Fight

Art didn't start the life insurance war. Others had fought before him but would retreat and settle. Art never backed down. Art never settled. It has been said that Art Williams was only part of the "buy term and invest the difference" revolution.

Nonsense! He ***was*** the buy term and invest the difference revolution. Sure, there were plenty of agents selling term in the US. Dozens of companies like Firemen's Fund, Waddell and Reed, Kemper, First Life of Oklahoma sold a term product used to replace whole life. The agents at other companies were all salespeople who were believers in BTID, but their agenda was only to make sales. They had no strong crusade to upend an entire industry. Art was the first term person to want to build an army and was more than happy to pick a fight. Maybe it was his resolve to make the world a better place. Maybe it was his crusade for "buy term and invest the difference" and financial freedom for ordinary families. Maybe it was his destiny to answer "the call"?

No matter: he didn't invent BTID, but he pioneered the revolution that made his mark on the insurance industry and turned it right side up.

We could have pleased the insurance gods, but our integrity wouldn't let us. Art wouldn't let us. He taught us that if we didn't watch ourselves "almost" could become a way of life. You "almost" do it right. You "almost" do enough. You compromise long enough, and you end up bowing. We were in the insurance business, but our integrity was our ultimate insurance from becoming just another company and people who just passed through the portals of life and arrived safely as nobodies at the end of our lives. The saying, "How you do anything is how you do everything" applied to us and what we stood for, how we worked and who we attracted. We stood for what was right and our reputations took a hit. The insurance agents degraded us, accused us, and slandered us. But when we paid a death claim of $300,000 that, before ALW, would have been $50,000 of whole life for the same premium, our integrity paid off.

Art Unleashes "The Animal"

Every time you turned on a television or opened a newspaper in the '80s, you would see the cola wars, the burger wars, even the copier wars.

It was a natural opening for Art to declare, "The War is ON!!" He had already been at war with the traditional life insurance industry, of course, but Art decided it was time to take it up a notch. This time, Art was going on the offensive, rather than fend off unwarranted attacks from the competition.

The sales force had long been in the trenches, fighting the enemy across the kitchen table on a nightly basis. That was never going to change.

This time, Art decided he needed someone on the inside to help him lead the charge. He knew he already had the perfect man for the job on his team.

A former award-winning sportswriter who had joined the team a couple of years earlier, Mike Burroughs was no stranger to controversy himself. Since he was a teenager, Mike was known for taking a stand.

"The only way to not be controversial," Art said, "is to do nothing."

Art had plenty for Mike to do. He turned him loose to research and compile every negative piece of information he could find on the competition. Initially, Art used the material himself, but then he started having Mike appear with him as a guest on ALW-TV.

One Monday morning, Art had Mike on the interview set with Treacy Beyer. Mike was ripping the competition to shreds, when Treacy looked at Art and said, "This guy is a real beast." Art had other ideas. The next day, he called Mike up to his office for their daily meeting and named him "The Animal." The rest is history.

Mike Burroughs with Art

Mike started writing books about the competition:

- *If You Live in Glass Houses, Don't Throw Rocks*
- *Myths & Facts About the Life Insurance Industry*
- *Everything You Always Wanted to Know About Universal Life, But Were Afraid to Ask*

He became a regular guest on ALW-TV and started speaking at major company events, including conventions and Super Seminars, where he once spoke to over 100,000 people one summer.

Art formed the "Attack Team," and "The Animal" starred in a series of videos involving chainsaws, boxing rings and baseball bats – along with then traditional industry icons like Snoopy, the Pink Panther and, of course, the '80s version of "the rock," plus whole life agents "Squiggy" and "Squirmy." Mike also wrote and produced a landmark video starring Art and Bobby Buisson, *Bad Day at Black Rock*. There were also rebuttal videos to the lame efforts of the traditional industry to enter the media business. Mike even became the ghostwriter for two industry legends, Arthur Milton, and Frank McIntosh, who joined forces with Art.

The more National Championships A.L. Williams won, the more fun Art had taking it to the competition. "Being controversial makes you better," Art said, "if you're tough enough."

Along the way, Mike kept his day job and earned several promotions en route to becoming a Senior Vice President, heading the Publications Department and ALW-TV.

We Never Went Backward

We never went backwards. We got knocked down but kept picking ourselves back up and finding a way forward.

However, there were times that seemed so difficult that going backwards was safer than going forward, but we had an animal instinct to survive and go forward. Art was our pilot light whose leadership kept us burning and would not let us rest. He sparked the next step by his "keep calling a play" philosophy.

Freedom must be taken, it must be claimed. Freedom is not simply given. You measure freedom not by what you've had, but what you wouldn't have had. Art always reminded us of where we came from, and we reminded ourselves of what the life we left behind would have been like.

On numerous occasions we would have stops and starts. When Art decided to have us paid on issuance of a policy and not on the writing of it, a financial holocaust ensued. It took three months, but he reversed that decision.

The kind of pressure and circumstances that we endured could either be a forge that fuses or a fire that incinerates a company. Because of Art, his personal charisma, his quality of building relationships and the crusading spirit he infused in us, we grew closer. That's how we survived, believing in Art and our mission. He was the elixir that sustained our sanity and purpose.

It was a war, but we came to love it. We had old agent confrontations in the homes of our clients, and we loved it. We were young, stupid, naïve, but we had a passion to fight, and we had an enemy we wanted to beat. As we look back at those memorable days, they were the best days of our lives because they demanded the best we had to give. We were fired up. We felt invincible. They demanded hard work, commitment, resolve, and fanaticism that most people can't understand. Because we were fighting alongside a leader that comes along once in generations and had a purpose that we knew was making a difference for families, we fought the fight and won the war. If you had been there, you would have loved it as much as we did.

Reckoning

The Art Williams phenomenon brought about the life insurance industry's moment of reckoning. There have been many wars and crusades fought for hundreds of reasons, but this became our war, our crusade, and it was deeply personal.

A moment of reckoning is the time when past mistakes or misdeeds must be punished or paid for; a testing time when the degree of one's success or failure will be revealed.

The moment of reckoning is a time when people are forced to deal with an unpleasant situation that they have avoided until now. The moment of reckoning arrived in 1962 when Art Williams' father died and left Art's mother with unnecessary financial miseries. The moment of reckoning found its crusader in 1967 when Ted Harrison shocked Art with the news that inflamed his soul.

The moment of reckoning was caused by the insurance industry's blindness in not giving families the best coverage for the premiums paid. That moment was cast in stone on February 10, 1977 when Art decided to go head-to-head with the traditional insurance industry. The moment of reckoning had arrived. The American people finally found the crusader born to change the insurance world, to "open the whole sorry mess to the light of day" as Norman Dacey would say. (*Dacey, 1968*) The crusader emerged who would take a hammer to the Rock of Gibraltar depicted in the Prudential insurance company's advertisements.

Cash Value Insurance and Mass Hypnosis

Art's deep dive into BTID became a shining ray of sanity when the industry created a form of mass hypnosis and a sleight of hand regarding cash value insurance.

- You get to borrow your own money.
- You lose your savings if you die.
- You pay for two things and only get one.
- Whenever agents needed to make more money, they would come and sell another policy, over and over and over again.
- When a cash value policy was replaced with term, the industry labeled it as illegal. They called it *twisting*.
- When term was replaced with cash value, the industry called it *conversion*.
- Term insurance is temporary insurance, while cash value is considered permanent insurance.
- The savings in a cash value policy had no stated percentage rate of return.

This mass hypnosis included the BBB, insurance regulators, professors, politicians, Wall Street, banks, and 450,000 whole life insurance agents.

As more people became educated, the condemnations came swiftly from widows with children who suffered the same plight as Art's mom and her children to what could have been a kinder story than the paltry death claims they received from expensive policies.

The industry motto was, "If we sell whole life we cannot sleep and if we sell term, we cannot eat." Art chose to sell an extreme number of term policies so we could eat. They chose to sell a lesser number of whole life policies so they could eat. They made a choice.

The moment of reckoning included Norman Dacey's book, *What's Wrong with Your Life Insurance*; Scott Reynolds' book *The Mortality Merchants*, the government's FTC Report; Norman Dacey's appearance on the Phil Donahue show discussing the FTC Report; *Changing Times* articles; *The Saturday Evening Post* article on Art Williams.

Friends and family members who were recruited by Art's team to inform, educate, replace, and improve policies were met with condemnation, insults, and disparagement by the industry. Instead of improving their products to give the future widows and children their money's worth, they chose the sanctity of their belief system at the expense of those same widows and children and the better life owed to them.

Did the intellectuals at this country's fine and expensive universities rise up? No. Did the consumer advocates rise up? No. The only ones to rise up were Art and his band of 85. The moment of reckoning would start with average and ordinary men and women who stood for something and did something about it. It was part-timers in the form of coaches, firefighters, police officers, housewives, schoolteachers, and nurses who rose up. The ordinary did the extraordinary and brought an overdue reckoning.

The industry has crumbled since 1977. In 1970 1,750 insurance companies were operating in the US. Today there are 773. The agents are old and have become toothless tigers. The growl is there but their moment of reckoning has made them obsolete. The average age of a life insurance agent in the United States is 61, and agents tend to sell to individuals within five years of their own age. Eighty-nine percent of insurance agents quit in their first three years. In 1984 Prudential became number two behind A.L. Williams in total face amount of life insurance sold in one year. Art said, "Our proudest moment as a company was beating Prudential in 1984." Metropolitan Life no longer exists. Many others suffered. The company Art started from scratch is the 16th largest insurance company in America. By the mid-1970s, 72 percent of the United States adult population and more than 90 percent of all husband-and-wife families owned some form of life insurance; today it's 52 percent and 50 percent who own it are *under*-insured. (*Fiona McKay, 2021)*

Unfortunately, the reckoning wasn't as damaging and complete as it should've been or could've been and was deserved; whole life companies still exist today. Everyone else but Art and the "termites" let them have their way to the detriment of the people they encountered.

Art has said, "I can never forgive them for what they did to my mama." The whole life insurance industry had their day. They have been judged; they have been found out. They are irrelevant in America, vanquished, annihilated. They have been "knocked out."

"The enemy can't win" and didn't.

The Scoreboard

A.L. Williams was No. 1 in every category that mattered, and we ran up the score:

#1 Consumer Concept
We sold term insurance 100% of the time, compared to the 13% industry average. The typical cost of our term product - $210 for $100,000 of coverage, compared to the typical industry cash value product of $1,272 for the same amount ($100,000) of coverage.

#1 Lowest Cost to Consumer
Averaging all products sold to the consumer, our cost was $3.33 per $1,000. New York Life - $16.17; Prudential - $18.17.

#1 Average Size Death Claim
Our average death claim: $95,131. Compare to Prudential's at $4,500 and the industry average: $6,000.

#1 Life Insurance Sales
For seven straight years, we out-produced ALL other life insurance companies. In 1988, we produced $92.3 billion, compared to No. 2

New York Life's $46.4 billion and No. 3 Prudential's $36.3 billion - beating their combined total of $82.7 billion.

#1 in Efficiency
We spent less money marketing our product, passing savings to the consumer. Example: In advertising, per policy issued, we spent $0.04 to Prudential's $41.54 and New York Life's $68.50. In office expenses, per policy issued, we spent $149.23 to Prudential' $1,383.64.

#1 Total Business In Force
In 12 short years, A.I. Williams became the industry's "first and only" $300+ billion company, compared to Prudential's $245 billion and New York Life's $208 billion in cumulative face amount, after decades of doing business.

#1 Mutual Fund Sales
We built the largest investment sales force in the world, and helped our clients invest billions of their savings in the best investment vehicle available - mutual funds with IRAs and 401(k)s - an unbeatable combination.

#1 Size of Sales Force
225,000 licensed men and women in our sales force. Prudential was a distant second with only 40,000.

#1 Educating the Consumer
Our financial guidebook, *Common Sense,* sold more than 16 million copies.

#1 Business TV Network
ALW-TV was the largest business television network in the world from Day One - bigger than Coca-Cola, Wal-Mart, Ford, Home Depot...... bigger than ALL of them.

Reprinted with Permission
(COACH The A.L. Williams Story, Williams, 2013)

A.L. Williams — From Dream to Destiny

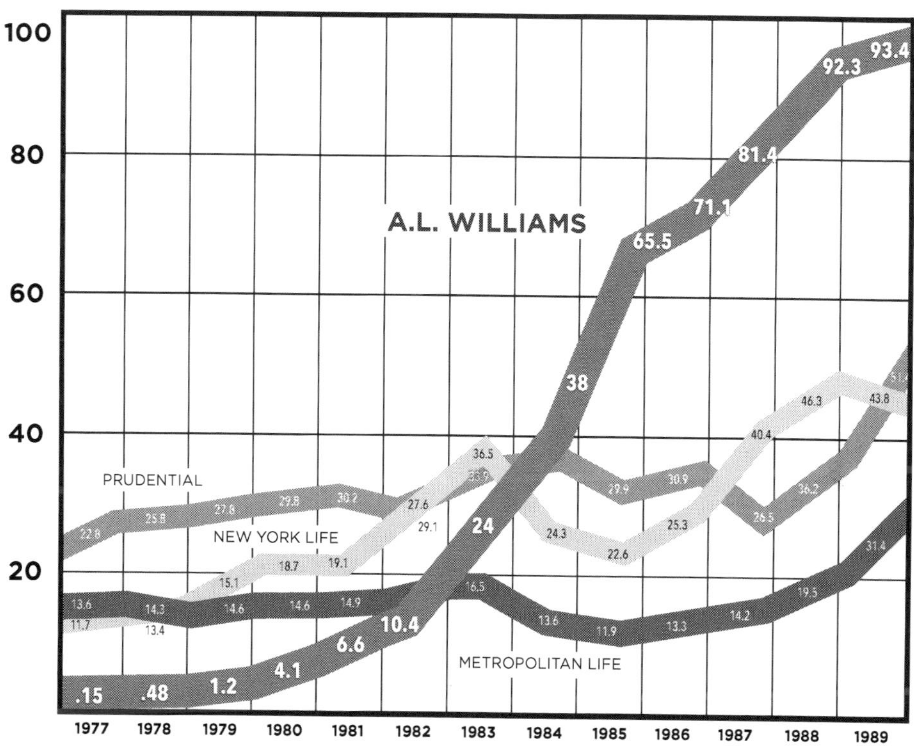

Individual Insurance Issued in 1977-1989

Reprinted with Permission
(COACH The A.L. Williams Story, Williams 2013)

PHENOMENON SPOTLIGHT

Crusaders Die Hard

A die-hard person is strongly or fanatically determined or devoted. The power of a grand Crusade feeds a person's soul.

Both these sentences describe Art perfectly.

A Crusade always means fighting against an established entity. In our Crusade we were led by Art to fight against the largest and most established industry in America, and we became a powerful voice for future widows and orphans. We pushed against the powerful forces of 450,000 life agents.

Art said that "Crusade" was the only word that stuck with him when he thought about how an action was created because of an outburst of passion about what we did. He said the Crusade was the one thing that kept us going and that people fought hard for a Crusade.

"Crusaders die-hard" was Art's rallying cry. The Crusade was Art's star to follow. Art identified that star, and he followed this point of light his entire life.

"I cannot express the shock and awe of the reality of what Ted Harrison told me," Art said. "I saw my mother struggle and it tore me apart. It left her financially devastated, and I couldn't believe the insurance industry let it happen to her. There is nothing like having a personal experience to get your attention, and it was tragic that it had to be my mother. I was a red-hot Crusader after I got my license. I was so passionate it was worse than being fanatical. In the toughest times, "buy term and invest the difference" and the belief that a company should be made up of part-timers kept me going. The crusade to beat cash value and build financial security for our families kept me going," Art said. "You win with passion. BTID, part-timers, and financial independence kept us filled with passion. You can't just like it, you must love it. I loved the fight. I loved the war. I loved the controversy."

Honoring Nelson Mandela, Robert Kennedy said, "Few will have the greatness to bend history itself, but each of us can work to change a small portion of events. It is from numberless diverse acts of courage and belief that human history is shaped. Each time a man stands up for an ideal, or acts to improve the lot of others, or strikes out against injustice, he sends forth a tiny ripple of hope, and crossing each other from a million different centers of energy and daring, those ripples build a current which can sweep down the mightiest walls of oppression and resistance." *(Kennedy, 2013)*

We Were CRUSADERS

- Crusaders live longer and live happier.
- A Crusader is an emotionally motivated spirit.
- A Crusader leads or takes part in a vigorous campaign.
- A Crusade causes the veins around the neck to pop out.
- "Dadgummit" was a battle cry similar to "charge."
- Man on fire: a description of Art's passion.
- A Crusade is missionary zeal.
- Art the Crusader: Everyone knew where he stood.
- If no one is making fun of you, then you are not showing you are a Crusader.
- Art didn't have an opinion, he had a Crusade.
- Art's Crusade spilled out to his people.
- If you are a Crusader, you don't back down.
- What do you stand for? What are you Crusading for?
- Without a Crusade, life will take away one vertebrate at a time until you have no backbone left.
- Are you fit to fight?
- The Crusade made Art a crusader and crusaders change the world.
- If you don't have a Crusade, sooner or later something will knock you out.
- Light yourself on fire with a Crusade and people will come to watch you burn.
- William Wallace (known as "Braveheart") said: "I'm going to pick a fight." Art picked a fight.
- A Crusade transforms people's lives so that they eventually perform good deeds.

What Art taught us, and we experienced, about our Crusade:

- You have to have a chip on your shoulder. A Crusade is that chip.
- A well-lived life is when you don't let down the people who believed in you. Selfish people live miserable lives.
- You only change the world if you have a Crusade.
- Art was a role model. You can tell your influence in life by how many people consider you a role model.
- Because Art was a crusader, the Crusade in him wouldn't let us quit.
- Art never got too far away from us; he never got too big. Don't forget where you came from.
- A Crusade is a deep sense of calling.
- The successful Crusaders lead with their hearts.
- When we show up, our lives matter.
- Crusaders take it personally. "You've got to see yourself involved in something more than just your business," Art said.
- What if you were chosen to do something great, to make a difference with your life?
- A Crusade gives you the extra ounce of courage it takes to talk to people.
- A Crusade gives you the extra ounce of courage it takes to win.

Crusade History

Art never saw this as a business.
A business has no soul, no purpose, no Crusade.
The Crusade put the fight in us.
We rallied around the nobility of the Crusade.

A Crusade was in our hearts and souls. As James 1:27 says, "A pure and genuine religion in the sight of God the Father means caring for orphans and widows in their distress."

Our hearts broke for the many widows who trusted their insurance agents, yet never got a big enough insurance check to take care of their families.

Our purpose was authentic. It came from an indwelling that said, "We are supposed to make a difference with our lives." We could see our purpose completed in providing huge death benefit checks to the widows in financial distress. Who else out there was going to do it?

Art's Crusade became ours and let the record show that when we were called, we ran to the sound of the guns. The guns were the cries of the future widows and orphans that we could save.

Chapter 3:

BUILDING IT BIG

The growth of Art's company after he left Waddell & Reed was like a supernova. The mind-boggling number of new people being recruited and the shocking number of life insurance policies written was something out of a science fiction novel. From 85 people who went with Art (I would say 50 were real devotees), ALW exploded to a record 225,000 plus in a short 12 years. That's like taking the current company at 130,000 representatives and having it grow to 250 million people in the same time frame. From two dots on the map (Atlanta and Ft. Lauderdale), we exploded to having a dot in every major city, and more, across America. Art's company, his message, his beliefs, his "righting wrongs and correcting injustices" stance lit up the life insurance industry and made A.L. Williams brighter than anything the insurance industry had ever seen. We all were caught in an "up" trajectory brought on by the lightning speed of success that whirled around us.

Momentum happens when a moment is captured and can't be stopped. It was our moment. That unique moment found us willing and able. The time of the big insurance companies was over, and their descent was fast because our crusade had a religious fervor that could not be denied. The more they spoke out against us, the faster we grew. The numbers brought many good people and also many folks who were "pieces of work." Some of the egos were something out of Hollywood; there were some "prima donnas" who, as Boe Adams would say, "believed their own 'BS' that they built it" and not the system Art created. These were growing pains, but Art's job became tougher because of these few. Yet as bad as a few of these were, they birthed some of the future giants we have today.

How do you know, when you're in the middle of the fray, that the tide is turning? How do you start to realize that you might succeed after all, maybe even more than you ever imagined?

Angela Williams said it best in an article from 1990. "We started to realize there was no ceiling," Angela said. "When we went through the national expansion, when we moved into Texas and then to Florida and Alabama, and then started spreading into the Northeast, I think that helped me realize that we weren't just going to be a small regional operation. From year to year, we would see the numbers expanding. We had annual conventions, but the first ones came mainly from the Southeast. Even when we went to places like Cloister Hotel outside of Mobile, to me we were still small. From the same standpoint, I guess when we started going to Boca Raton was when I felt that things were really moving.

"But even in those times, I feel like it was two steps forward and one step back because there would always be a major problem or a major obstacle to overcome. Then the competition would come out. We never felt that 'Ok, we are over the hump.'

"The major reason that we've done what we've done was the competition and the controversy, simply because when someone challenges your integrity or tries to put you out of business or make things more difficult for you to achieve, that makes winners fight longer and harder. Without those obstacles, we wouldn't be the company we are.

"If some states had not tried to legislate against the product we were selling and said they were going to run us out of the state, and if we had not lived on the brink of disaster so often, we would never have sent people out of state. Art would never have met Boe Adams. Every surge in the company, every time we experienced new growth, it was because of something that had been cut off, something that was about to get closed in our face and force us to go in another direction. Many times, it proved to be the challenge that took us toward an opportunity to move into another whole arena." *(Birth of A Legend, 1990)*

The Power of Expansion

Art started a company expansion almost as soon as the company was formed. He had recruited Bob Miller and

Greg Fitzpatrick through Bobby Buisson, and they were already in Florida. They both became legends. Larry Weidel came up in the shop of the legendary Bob Turley. Larry went to Greensboro, North Carolina, to build his business and became incredibly successful. He and his RVP team set records that will last for a long time.

The Orender Family moving to Dallas in 1978

Because of the insurance wars, I was forced to leave Georgia when I became an RVP. I went to Dallas, Texas. Jack Shulman, who was from Macon, Georgia, went to Houston; Art Burgess went to New Orleans; Hubert Humphrey went to Denver, Colorado; Mike Tuttle recruited Bill Stewart in Lubbock, Texas who then recruited Doug Hartman and created the entire California explosion. Bob Turley had an organization in Stuart, Florida and one of the guys moved to New England and caused an explosion there. Rusty Crossland recruited people in Washington State and Kansas. The flame was lit in Atlanta Georgia, and it spread across the entire country and into Canada. It could not be stopped.

The Atmosphere Begins to Shift

Even as obstacles continued to pop up, there began to be a subtle shift in the atmosphere. Events occurred that gave us hope that this thing was maybe going to make it.

Gradually, the press coverage began to shift. While the traditional industry still controlled many areas, publications began to notice and report on the incredible business success story that was taking place. Plus, as we got more exposure, we discovered publications that had been around for a few years that had, like A.L. Williams, promoted term but were unknown to us.

The Federal Trade Commission Report

The *Federal Trade Commission Report* was a grenade to the insurance industry. It wasn't an opinion piece; it followed a year-long study of the life insurance industry. For the first time, the whole life industry was investigated, and the results were a nail in their coffin. The federal agency had huge credibility and exposed the fact that, after twenty years of owning a whole life policy, the cash value savings only paid 1.2%. Michael Pertshuck was the head of the FTC. He reported the FTCs findings as unprecedented because the rate of interest was so low. Pertshuck said that many members of Congress commented following his presentation, "I've got one of those policies that I need to look at." The industry exploded in a fury. After the industry's powerful lobby intervened, Pertshuck was informed that a law had been passed to prevent future investigation of that industry. Still, the damage was done and couldn't be refuted. It was the dagger to the heart that we needed, and every A.L. Williams person armed themselves with the FTC report on every appointment.

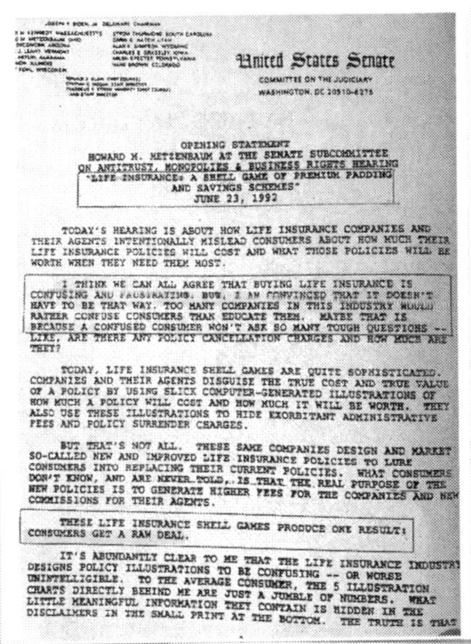

United States Senate

COMMITTEE ON THE JUDICIARY

WASHINGTON, DC 20510-6275

OPENING STATEMENT
HOWARD M. METZENBAUM AT THE SENATE SUBCOMMITTEE
ON ANTITRUST, MONOPOLIES & BUSINESS RIGHTS HEARING
"LIFE INSURANCE: A SHELL GAME OF PREMIUM PADDING
AND SAVINGS SCHEMES"
JUNE 23, 1992

TODAY'S HEARING IS ABOUT HOW LIFE INSURANCE COMPANIES AND THEIR AGENTS INTENTIONALLY MISLEAD CONSUMERS ABOUT HOW MUCH THEIR LIFE INSURANCE POLICIES WILL COST AND WHAT THOSE POLICIES WILL BE WORTH WHEN THEY NEED THEM MOST.

I THINK WE CAN ALL AGREE THAT BUYING LIFE INSURANCE IS CONFUSING AND FRUSTRATING. BUT, I AM CONVINCED THAT IT DOESN'T HAVE TO BE THAT WAY. TOO MANY COMPANIES IN THIS INDUSTRY WOULD RATHER CONFUSE CONSUMERS THAN EDUCATE THEM. MAYBE THAT IS BECAUSE A CONFUSED CONSUMER WON'T ASK SO MANY TOUGH QUESTIONS -- LIKE, ARE THERE ANY POLICY CANCELLATION CHARGES AND HOW MUCH ARE THEY?

TODAY, LIFE INSURANCE SHELL GAMES ARE QUITE SOPHISTICATED. COMPANIES AND THEIR AGENTS DISGUISE THE TRUE COST AND TRUE VALUE OF A POLICY BY USING SLICK COMPUTER-GENERATED ILLUSTRATIONS OF HOW MUCH A POLICY WILL COST AND HOW MUCH IT WILL BE WORTH. THEY ALSO USE THESE ILLUSTRATIONS TO HIDE EXORBITANT ADMINISTRATIVE FEES AND POLICY SURRENDER CHARGES.

BUT THAT'S NOT ALL. THESE SAME COMPANIES DESIGN AND MARKET SO-CALLED NEW AND IMPROVED LIFE INSURANCE POLICIES TO LURE CONSUMERS INTO REPLACING THEIR CURRENT POLICIES. WHAT CONSUMERS DON'T KNOW, AND ARE NEVER TOLD, IS THAT THE REAL PURPOSE OF THE NEW POLICIES IS TO GENERATE HIGHER FEES FOR THE COMPANIES AND NEW COMMISSIONS FOR THEIR AGENTS.

THESE LIFE INSURANCE SHELL GAMES PRODUCE ONE RESULT: CONSUMERS GET A RAW DEAL.

IT'S ABUNDANTLY CLEAR TO ME THAT THE LIFE INSURANCE INDUSTRY DESIGNS POLICY ILLUSTRATIONS TO BE CONFUSING -- OR WORSE UNINTELLIGIBLE. TO THE AVERAGE CONSUMER, THE 5 ILLUSTRATION CHARTS DIRECTLY BEHIND ME ARE JUST A JUMBLE OF NUMBERS. WHAT LITTLE MEANINGFUL INFORMATION THEY CONTAIN IS HIDDEN IN THE DISCLAIMERS IN THE SMALL PRINT AT THE BOTTOM. THE TRUTH IS THAT

The FTC report substantiated what Art had been saying all along – whole life insurance wasn't the superior product the industry purported it to be. It's impossible to overestimate how much the FTC report meant to our business. It gave us the credibility we craved from a source that was unarguable to clients and "enemy" agents.

Money Dynamics by Venita Van Caspel

One of the few people that recognized our "rightness" early on was Venita Van Caspel, a Certified Financial Planner from Houston. Van Caspel was the Dave Ramsey of her day. She was a well-respected authority on idle income investing and building a solid financial house. She wrote a book called *Money Dynamics*. In the 13th chapter of that book, she discussed the right kind of life insurance to purchase. Of course, she determined it was "BTID." Art had met Ms. Van Caspel on several occasions and asked permission for us to duplicate and distribute Chapter 13 of her book. She allowed us to and from that point on, it went with us on every appointment and was left with every client. It was so convincing it seemed like we never (rarely) lost a sale after that. Her book promoted mutual funds, so it was a perfect publication for us. (*Van Caspel,* 1975)

The Mortality Merchants by G. Scott Reynolds

Another person we discovered who advocated for term was G. Scott Reynolds. In 1968 he wrote a book called *The Mortality Merchants,* subtitled *"The Legalized Racket of Life Insurance."* The title alone was enough to put a smile on any termite's face. Obviously, *The Mortality Merchants* wasn't embraced by the traditional industry, so it was not well known. *(Reynolds, 1968)*

Scott Reynolds became an essential part of A.L. William's history. He had met Art, and he knew that Bob Turley was, at that time, fed up with the way the term insurance companies that he represented kept changing his compensation. Reynolds told Bob he *had* to meet Art Williams. Bob later sat down with Art, and Art showed him the override program at A.L. Williams and how he could build a secure income and not have to make a sale every day just to survive. Bob's eyes lit up. He joined A.L. Williams and became one of the absolute "greats" in our business.

"Bullet" Bob Turley

When Bob joined, he brought a credibility that money couldn't buy. Bob Turley was a well-known major league baseball player, mostly with the New York Yankees. He remains the only athlete in history to win all three of these prestigious awards in one year: the MVP of the World Series, the Cy Young Award and the

Hickok Belt. The Hickok belt is presented to the athlete of the year, and Bob had to beat out legends like Wilt Chamberlain, Jim Brown and Arnold Palmer.

In Mickey Mantle's biography, *The Mick,* he said that Bob Turley "was the most financially astute" of all the players he'd ever known. After Bob left baseball, he had a series of companies that went under for various reasons. He believed in BTID and started replacing whole life and selling term insurance.

Bob loved A.L. Williams. When Art met Bob, he told him, "As long as you're a salesperson, you are unemployed every day. We want you to build a business and have some real security." Bob immediately fell in love with our system and eventually built one of the most extensive hierarchies in ALW history.

Bob Turley's 1960 TOPPS Baseball Card

Bob was even more than that; he was a friend to all A.L. Williams people. Art said, "He was unbelievably loyal, a great leader, and one of the giants in our company who is irreplaceable. There will never be another Bob Turley. He was one of a kind."

Bob added so much credibility to our company. We were so proud because of his baseball accomplishments, and to think that he was one of us really brought confidence and hope to all of us who were in the fight. If someone the caliber of Bob Turley was with us, we could accomplish anything.

Bob believed in BTID like we did. Bob was a crusader like we were. Bob believed in recruiting like we did. Bob believed you could build an empire like we did. Bob had been to the top of the mountain in baseball and now he was at the top of the mountain with our company. Just by being himself, Bob automatically gave new legitimacy to A.L Williams.

The Saturday Evening Post

The Saturday Evening Post was a standard in most of the homes in America. It often featured Normal Rockwell paintings on its cover and was the most loved and respected publication in existence. A nasty article about Art in the early years had damaged Art's reputation.

Art was in Atlanta doing a meeting when someone brought him an issue that featured his picture on the front cover. Inside was a powerful, validating article about A.L Williams. Art was overwhelmed. Finally, a major media publication had written something positive. Everybody in A.L. Williams was ready for any form of good news. This news was gigantic. We had the FTC report, we had IRAs, and now the *Saturday Evening Post* article. We were in heaven.

National Religious Broadcasters

Art's own image was slowly moving from "renegade" to "business builder" as the incredible growth of A.L. Williams attracted more interest, and Art's reputation as a speaker grew. In 1987, Jerry Falwell, Chancellor of Liberty University, invited Art to speak at the National Religious Broadcasters meeting in Washington, D.C. Art flew there with Barbara King, EVP of Communications, and Dona Bunch, Publications Director. Art said he wasn't really prepared because his life had been such a whirlwind. He waited until the last minute and decided to give his iconic "Do it" talk at the meeting. It went over exceptionally well. It was a big hit to the A.L. Williams faithful, as well as another feather in the cap of ALW. To date, the presentation has been viewed over one million times on YouTube.

Art gives his iconic "Do It" speech at NRB

What's Wrong with Your Life Insurance by Norman Dacey

One of the first heroes in the press was Norman Dacey, who appeared on the nationally syndicated Phil Donahue TV show in 1979 and took a stand for term. The show had insurance as a topic after the FTC exposed the industry for its false life insurance savings rates and comparisons to the value of term protection.

Dacey's landmark book, *What's Wrong with Your Life Insurance,* first published in 1963, was a scathing expose that cataloged the abuses and deceptions he saw being foisted on an unsuspecting public by the life insurance industry. He ended the book with a quote that spoke to every "termite" on the ALW team. "Where now will the American people find someone with the temerity to stand up to this modern-day juggernaut and cry halt? Who will take up the cause and do it? Will he be found in the halls of Congress or in some obscure Attorney General's office? When he takes the job and does it, he will bring more financial security to the American people than 100 years of Social Security." (*Dacey, 1968)*

It was a breakout moment for Art and our company when it was most needed. We finally had the credibility that we'd fought for. It brought validity to our cause and a fellow crusader that joined us arm-in-arm to stop the juggernaut the life insurance industry had created. The industry might be a Goliath, but we were the David determined to defeat them.

Even the insurance industry began to recognize that A.L. Williams was something new, but not something bad. In *The Art of War,* Sun Tzu said, "A tactic to win battles is to break the will of your enemy by breaking them economically." *(Sun Tzu, 2002)* Many of the traditional agents were stodgy, single-minded people who made their money by going back and back and back to current clients, selling them additional policies. New baby, new policy. New home, new policy. New pay raise, new policy. The record for the greatest number of policies in a household was 36. Agents made money by continuing to draw from the same wells. When we educated people, they educated their parents, friends and relatives and the faucet of easy money for the agents was shut off. When you hit their pocketbooks, and their company's bottom line, they rise in anger. After a while they became demoralized.

In 1979, the company asked me to attend a meeting in Austin, TX, held by the insurance commissioner. At the tail end, a New York Life general agent indignantly asked Lyndon Olson, the commissioner, "What are you going to do about these A.L. Williams people illegally replacing my company's insurance policies?" The commissioner stated, "A.L. Williams and its agents are legally doing business and licensed like every other company in Texas. If you're asking me to have them stop doing business so you don't have to compete, that's not our job. We are here to protect the citizens of this state and not to regulate competition between companies."

Years later, Lyndon Olson served on the board of Citigroup and was appointed as the U.S. Ambassador to Sweden. But at that time, he didn't know the future. He only knew his job, and he didn't take sides.

A New Tax Program Solidifies "Investing the Difference"

In 1981, another bombshell exploded that seemed tailor-made for the A.L. Williams crusade of "buy term and invest the difference." In a tax cut program, President Ronald Reagan included a provision to give a significant tax cut to middle Americans by allowing working people to establish Individual Retirement Accounts (IRAs). Banks, credit unions, and mutual funds were the savings choices permitted and individuals could use those vehicles to deduct contributions from their income taxes for that year. Later, the Roth IRA replaced it, where you couldn't deduct savings, but the money was allowed to grow tax-free even when withdrawn during retirement. (*Washington Post*, June 11, 1981)

Why was this so huge? Because cash value life insurance was the only so-called "savings" program that was NOT allowed. Cash value was not approved as a savings vehicle for this incredible tax break option. Immediately, "buy term and invest the difference" became "buy term and invest the difference in an IRA!" The IRA was the perfect savings vehicle for middle-income families and was an incredible boost to the success of the BTID philosophy. "The IRA gave us the edge and fueled our belief system," Art said.

The Numbers Begin to Climb

As the tide turned in the press, consumers started to believe. The numbers began to climb. A.L. Williams' first problem was convincing clients we were legitimate. The second was how to get business processed once we got it in. The more we grew, the fewer companies were able to manage our business.

Joe Jack Merriman and Bill Atkins were at Waddell & Reed. They were fired in 1976, and Art often said, "If they hadn't been fired, we wouldn't have the company we do today." According to Art, "I believe they wanted retribution against Waddell & Reed, and they were willing to do anything to help us." Joe Jack had started his own company called Financial Assurance Corporation and Bill was his president. They were willing to help. "I was very desperate to find a new company," Art said. "When I got there (to Minneapolis), after we left Waddell & Reed, they agreed to provide two paychecks a week when Waddell & Reed was paying two times per month. We mapped out a plan of action. They helped us develop our compensation plan, as well." They were invaluable to the growing company. "One day I got a call from Joe Jack, and he said, 'Art, this thing has gotten so much bigger than I ever thought. I didn't ever want it to get this big.'" An even bigger company than Financial Assurance was needed.

Big Growth Equals Big Challenges

The more excitement A.L. Williams' growth generated among the sales force, the tougher it was to find someone to process the amount of term we were selling. Funding was extremely important but always a challenge. We needed a lot of money for upfront commissions on the sale of an insurance policy. Art describes the frustration of finding a processing company. "After Waddell & Reed, I met with Providence Insurance. I thought they would be a company we could go with, but they said, 'Art, I have no doubt you will fail. I don't believe in replacing insurance. I believe you have to sell new insurance to make it in our industry. We've been in the insurance industry for 100 years, and your concept cannot work.'"

Many companies we tried to go with had concerns about how the regulators would treat us regarding replacing whole life with term. They were concerned we would create a hornet's nest (which we did) and wanted to stay away from it. Art says, "I interviewed three or four different companies on Wall Street to no avail. Big companies like Fireman's Fund, Provident, and Kemper Insurance all said, 'Not interested.' I thought getting rejection from an insurance customer was bad, but this was a whole new level."

Our most important aspect of growth was also the most difficult. Where in the world of whole life insurance would ALW find a company that would service our business when our numbers were growing faster than anyone imagined? "My biggest obstacle was always the fear of running out of money," Art says. "We could never rest because we knew that, by growing, we would need more money, and it would require a more prominent company to bet on us. But they didn't know us, and they were suspicious. It was rare for a company to understand why part-timers would need advance money; our system was to advance nine months of premium payment commissions to foster the belief that you can make serious part-time money here."

BUSINESS

Football Coach Becomes Insurance 'Maverick'

Art Williams says he's just an average guy. That's hard for both his friends and his critics to believe. Art resigned his job as a high school coach and has become the president of a multi-million dollar insurance firm in virtually unheard of time.

Continued on Next Page

That's when another destiny moment occurred in the form of a person who would take over processing and, by doing so, have an instrumental effect on our future success. His name was Boe Adams. When we were looking to leave Waddell & Reed, Bob

Turley was called on by Boe Adams, who was recruiting agents for National Home Life. Boe had started an insurance company in Denton, Texas, and eventually lost it. Through connections, he met Art DeMoss, the founder of National Home Life. They were looking to expand their life insurance business.

At the same time, Boe had started to hear some interesting rumors about a man named Art Williams who was doing some outrageous things in the insurance world. In 1977, Boe first talked to Art by phone and found that Art's company was looking for a new product company. In January 0f 1978, they met in Atlanta. They talked, and Boe became convinced that National Home should take A.L. Williams' business and that Art Williams was the man to watch in the industry. Boe could see in Art the vision and determination that just might make those "outrageous" ideas work.

Boe's vast experience in creating the inside structures of an insurance company home office was a perfect fit. Without the right administration, Art's distribution system wouldn't function. Boe was the answer. He began to work more closely with Art. He negotiated insurance contracts for Art and recruited Art's home office team. Art knew we needed our own home office, so we wouldn't be lumped with general agents selling whatever. Our own home office was what National Home agreed to. Rusty Crossland recalls Boe coming on the team as the challenges with Financial Assurance grew. "NHL was a Godsend," Rusty remembers. National Home Life was well known, with Art Linkletter as its spokesperson. Art DeMoss figured that selling health insurance through mail order would eventually tap out, and he wanted to build a salesforce.

Treacy Beyer & Boe Adams

According to Art, "We had some problems at National Home getting policies issued and having bank drafts pulled out multiple times. Still, we were set to go to Art DeMoss' house and sign a contract in September of 1979. Art DeMoss died suddenly the Saturday before the meeting. The executives at National Home Life immediately put the company up for sale and National Home gave us six months to find a new home." The search for the right company continued.

The closure of NHL's general agency division brought A.L. Williams some leaders who would become superstars. Boe Adams was a manager for National Home, and he knew many of the general agents who no longer had a company to write business through. This did create a problem with existing reps. They weren't the greenies Art believed in building with. They all had higher contracts than Art's RVPs. They wouldn't come if they had to come in at a rep level and start over. According to Art, "I hated bringing them in as RVPs; it put me in a difficult position with the current ALW people. But it was an opportunity to expand throughout the country quickly. I called the shot, and it turned out to be beyond successful." Bob Safford was the leader of the agency division at NHL. Mike Tuttle, Dick Walker, and Dennis Richardson all made the move to A.L. Williams. Mike Tuttle's hierarchy alone brought all of California to ALW. The company grew fast and far.

That same year, Boe worked with Art to help battle an insurance department that was threatening to pass laws damaging to the company. The bill was defeated, and Boe and Art became increasingly convinced that they were a strong team.

As Art said, "He did things I couldn't do. Boe earned 2% compensation for what he did. He was never the highest-paid person in the company. There were many RVPs making more money than Boe. He offered to give up half of his income to create a National Sales Director position, a position that would create another level of income and a bonus."

"Even when I was still with National Home, I think that Art and I both knew that we'd get together," Boe said. "There was just a special chemistry between us."

Boe was the Roy Disney to Art's Walt Disney. "Walt Disney dreamed, drew, and imagined. Roy stayed in the shadows, forming an empire," wrote Bob Thomas, a Disney biographer. "A brilliant financier and businessman, Roy helped turn Walt's dreams into reality, building the company that bears his brother's name." *(Thomas, 1998)*

Boe was a "how" person; he knew the "how" of building, the actions that would make the dream prosper and grow." Bill Gates may have been the visionary who saw a personal computer in every home, but Paul Allen created the structure that made it happen. Herb Kelleher was able to personify and preach the cause of freedom, but Rollin King came up with the basic idea of Southwest Airlines; Ralph Abernathy was a disciple of Dr. Martin Luther King who had the "how" skills to make the dream actionable and tangible. The "how" types don't want to be out front; they want to work behind the scenes to build the systems that can make the dream a reality." (*Simon Sinek, 2009*) Boe was the Paul Allen, Rollin King, and Ralph Abernathy to Art.

After we left NHL, Stanley Beyer came into the picture. A connection of Boe Adams' suggested he contact Stanley Beyer at PennCorp Financial in Santa Monica, California. Boe handled the negotiations with Penncorp, which would turn out to be the company that would become a true partner to A.L. Williams. Art and his team were still focused on having their own home office.

The Sales Force Finds Its Partner

The move to PennCorp Financial was yet another piece of the puzzle that fell into place. Penncorp had all the appropriate state licenses and the financial wherewithal to finance A. L. Williams. They were big enough to handle the business Art's company was producing and they had a level of infrastructure to handle a large field of agents.

Additionally, that organization introduced A.L. Williams to two men who would become among the most respected leaders in A.L. Williams' history: Treacy Beyer and Stanley Beyer.

Treacy started at Penncorp Financial in California in 1972 and worked his way up the corporate ladder. Treacy was mild mannered and the perfect person to correct the problems we had with operations. He became one of us and eventually moved to Atlanta. Through the years, Treacy held many critical roles at A.L. Williams, and would make a huge impact. "His place in the history of our great company was significant," Art said.

According to Treacy, "My real contribution to ALW was figuring out the financial side, because growing at an astronomical rate required lots of capital. It was a breathtaking amount that was required. My responsibility was to find a group of banks, a consortium, to finance it. At one time we had a half-billion-dollar line of credit. That's equal to at least $1 billion today. My job was to ease the various banks' fears and convince them that our compensation system would not put them at risk. We had banks in New York, Chicago, and Toronto that were huge banks."

Stanley Beyer was the head of PennCorp. Stanley Beyer was keen on finding a big general agency to generate business, and he found it in ALW.

Stanley and Art hit it off immediately and Stanley became like an older brother to Art. Treacy remembers when, in 1982 or 83, Art and Boe met with Stanley Beyer. "When Art and Boe showed up at Penncorp, it was impressive," Treacy recalls.

Stanley loved our company and its people because he had come up in the same kind of sales operation that we had.

When administration problems arose, PennCorp called upon Treacy to fix them. The initial person PennCorp sent to Atlanta to administer struggled in the task. Art would later say that they saw immediate changes with Treacy running administration.

"It was the first time we ever had control of everything. We were the only company to have a 100% "buy term and invest the difference" philosophy. Prudential didn't have 100%, Kemper didn't, no company had 100% but us," Art said.

Still, obstacles arose, not despite the growth but because of it.

According to Art, "I wanted to celebrate our plan for a new home office, which was part of the deal with PennCorp, and we chose to go to Montreal to the oldest hotel in North America. While we were there, Stanley Beyer flew in and said, 'You lied to us. Your persistency is so bad you're about to destroy our company.' Everyone was shocked, but it turned out we had a problem with an organization in Houston that was forcing people to buy the product in order to come to work. They were running amok. In an era before computers, it took a while for Boe's team in the home office to find out. Stanley Beyer sent his people to Atlanta to scrutinize every policy that was written. It was a tense time.

"We were having a meeting in Dallas and Stanley Beyer wanted to come and meet our people eyeball to eyeball and find out what kind of people we really had. "We agreed to take a 17% commission cut and he would pay us back 19% if our quality of business was good. It was the beginning of our persistency bonus to the field. We ended up firing the RVP in question and persistence came back to normal. But we lost a lot of our people, because they could not hold out for the six weeks it took to issue a policy back then, when PennCorp decided to pay after the policy was issued instead of on the application being received at the home office. We found out that the quality of business wasn't as bad as Stanley thought. We kissed and made up and went back to normal, but we lost a lot of managers and people in that three-month period."

The connection with PennCorp Financial proved to be a turning point for A.L. Williams' business processing. Art and Boe could take a breath, knowing that the California company could handle the business. Massachusetts Indemnity and Life Insurance Company (MILICO) would become the product arm of PennCorp, and MILICO became practically synonymous with A.L. Williams.

But that wasn't all. When Art aligned with Stanley Beyer and PennCorp, Art negotiated the necessity of opening ALW's own home office in Atlanta. In March of 1980, the first A.L. Williams Home Office was built in Duluth, Georgia. MILICO had its own space in the vast complex. For Art, it was a dream come true.

Stanley wanted to structure a deal where Art and the A.L. Williams people could participate in the success that PennCorp achieved from the ALW relationship. Stanley wanted to start a reinsurance company that would belong to A.L. Williams, where they would take 50% of the insurance business ALW created and reinsure it. The reinsurance company would take the term insurance ALW was selling and sell it off to a third-party insurance company that backed the policies.

Stanley set a threshold of production goal where that would be enacted, and A.L. Williams reached it quickly. The reinsurance company that was formed was the thing that created the A.L. Williams Corporation. It was a wonderful plan because that 50% was already a profitable business. It became a huge asset because ALWC eventually went public, and when it did, many, many people became wealthy as a result; it wasn't just ALW agents who profited, but many of their family members enjoyed the financial success as well.

Once I talked with an executive from PennCorp Financial who told me that when ALW came on as a general agency for them, they had to hire a new software company to build a whole new program to pay commissions and administer the business. When it came to paying Art, the number was so high that there was no room in the computer program high enough to pay him. They had not accounted for enough zeroes because they never thought anyone could make that kind of money.

How Art Did It: A Real-Life Story

How do you expand from 85 people in one city and one state to 225,000 people in 50 states in just 12 years? Art's plan was to grow through compounding and multiplication.

ALW was built by recruiting best friends. Art believed in building teams, and eventually everyone owning their own team. In 1970, ITT transferred Art from Columbus, Georgia to the Atlanta area to open up an office. Art and Angela chose Snellville, Georgia to live. Art knew no one in Atlanta or the area. He hated cold prospecting. "I'd rather dig ditches than knock on a stranger's door," he said.

Instead, Art gathered up a coach's directory from the state of Georgia. Within a 30-mile radius of Snellville, there were 21 high schools. Art wrote a letter to each head football coach at those schools, introducing himself and saying that he was looking to hire coaches on a part-time basis. Not one coach answered his letter.

South Gwinnett High School was located in Snellville, Georgia, 1/2 mile from where Art lived. Art drove over there one afternoon and introduced himself to Bobby Johnson, who was the head coach and athletic director. Art talked with Bobby about working part-time, but Bobby had no interest. He said, "I threw your letter in the trash and my basketball coach saw it and said he might be interested." The basketball coach's name was Tee Faircloth. Tee had played basketball at Auburn and became Art's first recruit. Tee took Art to meet three of his teammates from Auburn, Bobby Buisson, Bob Miller, and Randall Walker. From that one part-time guy who retrieved a letter from a trashcan and introduced Art to his three friends and teammates from Auburn, Art created 4,000 RVPs, 130,000 licensed people in all 50 states, Canada, and Puerto Rico. Art sent out 21 letters but could only get to 12 of those coaches. From those 12 coaches, he built an empire.

Every time Art recruited a coach, that coach would take him to three or four of his friends, and from those friends, eventually, Art built the greatest part-time sales force in America and the ALW company.

One Team, One Dream

Another uniqueness was our "team" concept. Art was a football coach and knew success required a team effort. Art knew the power of a team, having teammates, being on a winning team, and celebrating with those who fought the fight with you. As the military knows, soldiers will go into battle and stare death in the face because they don't want to let their fellow soldiers down. Activist and Nobel Peace Prize winner Leymah Gbowee said: "You see these individual straws in the broom? Each one of you is like one of those when standing alone. You're ineffective and can't accomplish much. When you stick together, you are so much more powerful." Revolutions are invariably group activities. Rarely does someone start a revolution on their own, let alone at his mother's kitchen table. With teams, they are all trading ideas, egging each other on, and sharing and competing and dreaming, until something radical and entirely new emerges. "Revolutions are birthed in conversation, argument, validation, proximity, and the look in your listener's eye that tells you you're on to something." (*Gladwell*) This passage explains our insurance revolution. Art's army provided him with the emotional backbone, the spiritual encouragement, and the loyalty that he needed. There was joy in bonding together to fight.

"That feeling of alliance with something bigger is the reason we keep wearing the jersey of our hometown sports team even though they've missed the playoffs for ten years and counting. Because how we feel about something or someone is more powerful than what we think about it or them." (*Sinek*) Human beings crave the feeling of belonging. We enjoy the feeling of being part of a group, like when we attend church, attend a parade, or wear the jersey of our favorite team when we attend a sports event.

The early ALW pioneers had a special kind of bond that only comes with a common enemy, with common adversity, and a common leader like Art. We suffered together; we achieved together, cried together, and were victorious together. That's the definition of a team. Art built ALW like a football team, and we were his team. We worked hard to gain his respect and the way we did it was by always staying in the fight.

If you have played basketball you have probably heard the phrase "balls to the wall." It is used at the very end of practice when the coach tells the players to take the basketballs and put them against the wall to begin conditioning wind sprints or gassers. When Art said "balls to the wall" we gave it everything we had.

We loved the challenge. We loved the toughness. We loved the fight. We loved it when "Coach Williams" said "CHARGE!" We loved every old agent confrontation, every negative article, every slur said against us. We lived to tell prospects that a dividend was a "partial refund of a deliberate overcharge," that a paid-up policy was not free insurance, that the worst policy was an endowment policy, that the universal promise of 12% return was not for real, that when you borrow money from your cash values, you are borrowing your own money and at death it is deducted from the death benefit. We lived to see the anger rising up in a client's face when they discovered they'd been lied to; we fought and fought, knowing we had the truth on our side and that there wasn't a whole life policy we couldn't beat.

Each of those who were one of the originals was connected by our shared experience and by the phenomenon of Art Williams.

The Products Change the Game

What's the difference between an ordinary business leader and a business genius? A common leader takes what is ordinary and leaves it ordinary. Art took the ordinary life insurance business and made it something extraordinary. Changing the game from whole life insurance to term doesn't sound so revolutionary. But in just a few years, "buy term and invest the difference" virtually replaced whole life as the predominant product.

Ted Harrison once noted Art's strengths. "First, Art stayed focused on the concept. He never lost sight of it, and he never let things distract him. Second, he knew he had to give the salespeople an incentive program that would compensate them for selling term insurance." (*Birth of A Legend, 1990*)

Art said that competition brings better products, innovation, and better prices to the consumer. The industry didn't want to compete. They wanted to annihilate ALW so they wouldn't have to adapt and provide better products and prices. In the end, they destroyed themselves, as all "standing pat" companies do.

The way the industry had handled term was to make it a secondary product, usable only in rare cases. We went from scrambling to find a product among the few companies that sold term, to eventually creating our own products. When we started out, the only term life insurance available to sell was decreasing term. Waddell & Reed had an annual renewable term that was super cheap, but both those products didn't pay enough commissions for us to make it. While at Waddell & Reed, we sold two term products: a 20-year decreasing term and an annual renewable term (ART). The man who invented annual renewable term was Bill Atkins at Waddell & Reed. W&R was primarily an investment company and wanted a term policy to replace whole life so they could get the cash value to invest. We couldn't make any money selling classic term insurance and we came up with a product called deposit term.

Deposit term saved our life. It became a cornerstone product for us. It took a while for our agents to understand how to sell it. Deposit term required a higher first year premium. It was a 10-year plan. For a $50,000 policy, deposit term required $500 upfront. If the cost was $30 a month in years two through ten, we picked up a check for $530. Most didn't have the $500, but we picked up a check for 1/12th of the $500 plus $30. The 2nd year the premium would drop to $30. The client would receive double the $500, or $1,000 at the end of the 10th year, tax-free growth. It was an excellent product for the customer, and we were paid double what decreasing term or annual renewable term would pay. Now salespeople could afford to give clients a better deal and still feed their own families.

Our goal was to get away from anything else and only have level term insurance.

It was characteristic that, as we grew larger and larger, we had more negotiating strength and more funds. So as we grew, we were able to create the products and systems we needed. Eventually we developed Common Sense Term to 100, which beat any other term product out there. Art said, "When we came up with 20-year term, it killed the competition and got momentum going for us."

We didn't have to rely on other companies to provide products. That was a special form of freedom that we had never dreamed of. Better products, combined with a better investment program with the new IRA, were an unbeatable combination. We felt the momentum shift. We were on a roll.

Keeping the Fires Burning

Keeping a growing sales force of termites excited and facing forward despite all the attacks was no small feat. We needed to stay motivated, and Art needed the support and community we brought him. He fed off our dreams, commitment, sacrifices, and shared passion.

One of Art's most successful inventions was the Fast Start School, which he started at Waddell & Reed before he left, and they came into their own at A.L. Williams. These weekend meetings were designed to be training meetings for newbies. Unlike today, in the early days the sessions didn't teach presentations, reading rate cards, or the system (overrides were still limited, and Art was the only RVP then). Art hung banners that said, "Crusaders Die Hard," "I'm a Stud," and "Be Somebody." These meetings were about selling the A.L. Williams opportunity and winning the hearts and minds of the attendees.

We were feeling our way. A highlight was a young Bobby Buisson sweating, stammering, stuttering and almost passing out speaking in front of the Fast Start School. Art was the M.C. and always gave the crusade talk and amazed everyone with the appalling math of the whole life industry. People from Frank Dineen's team in Albany, Georgia came; they came from Fred

Marceaux's team in Tallahassee, as well as Virginia Carter's, Bobby's and Rusty Crossland's. Bob Miller built his team in Ft. Lauderdale. He drove twelve hours one way every six weeks with a carload of his fellow coaches. Everyone wanted to be there. The atmosphere was electric.

The meeting room was always packed. It was a unique combination of a rock concert and Billy Graham rally. We would love to watch our new people experience this amazing atmosphere for the first time. Imagine entering the locker room of an Alabama national championship team and Coach Bear Bryant is talking to his team.

Our new guests would walk in looking around tentatively, sit down as far back as they could, with arms folded. Their spouse had laser eyes on them with a look that said, "What have you gotten us into?" Their eyes are looking on in disbelief. No smiles on their faces. As the evening moved on their faces would crack with a smile and an occasional laugh. Then Art gets up and talks about the crusade, the passion, and doing something special with your life, being somebody. Their eyes become glued on him. Hearts are tuning in to the message. Their arms are now on the table and their bodies are leaning forward. Their heads are nodding in agreement. Their hearts are now pounding, full of enthusiasm. Their minds are blown. Their hopes and dreams are having an accelerant poured into them as they begin to believe they too can be somebody special. They feel alive for the first time in years. They feel part of something important. They can't remember the last time they had this "Friday night feeling." In high school? There is no "altar call," but they believe, and their hearts become a part of what Art calls a team, a company, an adventure. They are with like-minded people and their core has found purpose. Their doldrums vanish and they come alive. All this may not happen at once, but it starts here, at the first Fast Start School, as something awakens inside of them, a great awakening that awaits all who pursue "a purpose higher than themselves."

The first A.L. Williams Fast Start School was held at a Hilton Hotel in Doraville, Georgia, and later at the Admiral Benbow or the Presidential Inn, both in the Atlanta suburb of Chamblee.

Opportunity meetings were the other regular meeting. They were held weekly. After recruiting at the kitchen table, the husband and wife were invited to an opportunity meeting, where they were shown the "bigness" of A.L. Williams and the concept and opportunity were reinforced. This was a place where part-timers and full-timers came together each week to get rejuvenated. The RVP hosted the meeting and usually had one or two other leaders speak. This weekly meeting kept people motivated, energized and ready to fight.

The Secret Weapon

Throughout the bad times, Art had his own "secret weapon" to keep him motivated. He was never far from his wife, Angela, his partner in every aspect of the business.

Art always told how he and Angela met in the second grade. She often traveled with Art, and her opinion was the one he trusted most. The traditional industry, of course, didn't believe in partnership. That was unfathomable to Art. As he said, "We're committed to husband-and-wife teams being in business together because that is the strongest cause of winning." Most companies prefer the spouse not be involved so their agents can be more dedicated to their jobs. In corporate America, spouses are not valued. They were of value to us, and the backbone of the creation of all hierarchies. At the kitchen table, we wanted to see husband and wife together make the decision to become our client. If one of them was interested in working, we needed the spouse's support to make that happen.

The idea for the official Partner's Program began, according to Angela, when someone asked Art a disturbing question. "You keep saying you have to pay the price, but you never say what the price is!" Art said that Angela knew then that she had to step in and step up.

From then on, every A.L. Williams meeting included sessions for the partners, as well as reps. Angela led seminars and programs that were uniquely focused on the real challenges of having a spouse in the business. One partner said that hearing Angela speak was a turning point in the business for her and her husband. She realized at that time that she wasn't fully supporting him the way Angela supported Art. Things changed after she heard Angela. Angela went on to create a powerful partners organization that highlighted success in both business and family life.

John Roig recalls the effect of Angela on both partners and their spouses. "She was the power behind the throne," John adds. "She kept Art on an even keel. He was a dreamer, and she was a realist. She kept him grounded. She took care of the home and the kids and gave Art the permission and the freedom to be all Art could be, fulfill his dream and affect the lives of so many people. Angela was always in the background. She went to all the meetings and was a quiet reassurance to all of us that he was a solid family man, could be trusted, and had integrity. When Angela talked, you knew it was from her heart.

"One of the first examples Art and Angela showed us was how to have a better marriage. Because we owned our business,

Gloria and I became closer. We worked together and did not live separate parallel lives with her having her job and me having mine, having nothing in common outside of our families. We talked about our business, our futures, our team.

"Angela would say, 'When ordinary people with a common dream come together, they can do extraordinary things.' That's what happened to us in our life.

"While I was out on an appointment, Gloria worked in the office and we worked together, dreamed together. That brought our whole family together. We got close and our family got closer. Art and Angela were our example and we wanted to be examples to our children.

"Gloria was not as excited as I was when I started. She said, 'You can do it part-time, but we've invested many man hours getting you two master's degrees. You've got a job and a career, so don't get carried away with it. You don't even have an office.'" In December 1979, at the ALW convention at Sea Island, Georgia, Angela spoke. She pulled Gloria and the other partners aside and it became the first partner's meeting ever. After she went to Angela's meeting everything changed. Gloria saw that all of Angela's fears were her fears, which gave her encouragement. Art would say, 'You won't be successful unless your spouse buys into what you are doing.'

"When my wife Gloria came out of that meeting, she said to me, 'Let's go for a walk.' While walking, she told me that we could not make our dreams come true unless I was full-time. She was fully onboard thanks to Angela's meeting. I had saved up the money I'd been making on a part-time basis so I could be in a position to go full-time. I went full-time in six months and later opened my own office in Miami. It was June 1980, and in November 1980, I became the 111th RVP in ALW history."

Partnership Was Everything

Art constantly reminded potential representatives, "The spouse is your most important recruit."

While I was working for a steel company we would have many dinners, lunches, and after work get-togethers. Not once were spouses involved. It's as if the message was that I'd be better off without a wife so I could work harder and longer and further my career path.

One of the first things I noticed at Fast Start Schools was that after the end of the Friday night session, there would be a refreshment area stocked with pastries that Angela had organized. She would be next to the tables saying hello to everyone and making everyone feel welcome.

Our spouses were welcome at every meeting. Art and Angela believed in partnership. Art would say, "If you win in business, but it causes you to lose your family, you end up a loser."

We all believed Angela was Art's best recruit. If you look at our history of legendary hierarchies, the power was always partnership. In all the awards, both names would be on plaques, both got tee shirts, jackets, and medals. Both had their names on seating assignments. It was always a partnership. And it made all the difference. On a train from London to Scotland, Art and Angela were surrounded by us as they announced the new Partners Program. We had fun at first saying that when we were broke and struggling, our wives and husbands were spouses, but when we started making a lot of money, the term was changed to "Partner." We laughed but we knew beyond any doubt that without our partners what we had would never have been built. Angela showed that power in partnership creates wisdom, common sense, an extra reason. Family, partnership, and togetherness were vital. The uniqueness of ALW had to start with the unheard-of plan of two family members working as one. It was Art and Angela, Bobby and Red, Randall and Mary, Frank and

Debbie, Mike and Stephanie, Randy and Marcie, Kip and Carol, John and Gloria, Greg and Sharon, Bob and Jane.

Art knew precisely how important Angela was to his business. "I have never lost sight of what Angela did for me," Art says. "I also have not lost sight of the power of the spouse's involvement in building ALW. Angela and I were always totally honest with each other about the business. She knew the business backwards and forwards. I always said the most important recruit in your life is going to be your spouse. The people that stuck with it ultimately had great spouses that stuck with it with them."

Art and Angela never wanted the business to be bad for the marriage. They started and funded an organization called Marriage and Family Resources, where a trained counselor was available to be called on by people in the field. The person even spoke at company conventions on the power of creating a successful marriage, successful kids and a successful business. He taught that success doesn't mean losing one to have the other. It's hard to guess how many marriages and families were preserved that might not have been without the emphasis on partners and families.

It was always clear that Art's priorities were God first, family second, business third. He modeled a life that many of us never saw from our own parents. Art would say, "When you win, you win in all areas of your life, not just business." Many of the same principles that cause someone to succeed in business are applicable to family, health, or spirituality. Things like focus, discipline, time, and goals aren't only for business. To win in all areas requires sorting priorities. Who doesn't want to succeed as a person, a parent, spiritually? Who wants to be a 'dud' as a father, mother, or physically? Art's beliefs were another rarity in the business world. Most corporations only care about your success in the business area; your purpose is to make money for them. Art would call and the first thing he would say was, "How is your family?"

"The competition could never figure out that the invisible warriors in A.L. Williams were our partners," Art says.

The Art of Recognition

Art was a master of promoting excitement in the company. He was also a genius at recognition.

We were anything but a typical company, and the war we were fighting was nothing like the usual business competition. The temptation to throw in the towel was always there, no matter how tough you were. Art had to create new and innovative ways to keep us going. Art knew the importance of recognition, and his awards were fun, challenging, and always interesting. He knew the power of having your name called, of coming up on stage, being singled out for the good things you'd done. At each A.L. Williams convention or meeting, awards night was the highlight of the event.

To the world, the T-shirts looked sophomoric and cheesy, but to the valiant crusaders who fought in the insurance wars they were symbols of the real medals we wore in our hearts. To get a T-shirt from Art was the highest honor. It represented making the team as much as a Little Leaguer at age 12 being given a wool uniform that had the unique smell of mothballs. To make Art's team was just everything.

Later it would be jackets and hats. Once he gave out jogging shorts that had the ALW logo imprinted all over them. They all meant the same. Unless you've stood in front of a mirror and seen yourself with a coveted uniform that made you feel like a million dollars as a 10-11-12-year-old, you wouldn't understand why a two-dollar T-shirt brought tears to the eyes of a grown person. Even the renowned Bob Turley, who pitched in five World Series and won the Hickok Belt yearned for an Art Williams T-shirt.

The T-shirt awards were the earliest awards. They were cheap so several could be given, but they were very effective. Art always said that Angela couldn't believe it when he came up with the idea, explaining that these were grown men and women. No one would care about a T-shirt! They turned out to be our most valuable possessions. Among the most coveted was the "I am a STUD!" shirt. Art also knew that not receiving recognition was more powerful than yelling and screaming to let reps know that he thought they weren't doing their best. Watching others being rewarded was the worst feeling in the world. Art also had a couple of special awards for people who hadn't reached milestones. The "Torn Sweater" award or the tiny T-shirt were a back-handed compliment. It meant that Art had confidence in you, but that you hadn't quite lived up to his expectations.

Andy Young, a giant in A.L. Williams, described the power of the T-shirt award. "We were on a cruise liner in 1987 and I wasn't where I needed to be in the business. Art gave me this baby T-shirt that said, 'I wanna be NSD.' It was smaller than the T-shirts he gave to others. I was so angry I didn't go on another cruise for 25 years. That was a typical coaching method, challenging and seeing if the player responds. I responded. In his monthly bulletins, he would have 'Turkey of the Month' for those who could be doing better. Those two awards – Torn Sweater and Turkey of the Month were two awards you never wanted to get and would work hard to make sure you didn't."

Some of the most elite awards were the championship rings, modeled on the Super Bowl rings of the NFL, which were encrusted with precious stones. Others were Rolex watches with diamonds in place of the numbers and original oil portraits of the leader and their partner, hung on the Wall of Fame at the ALW headquarters.

From his years as a football coach, Art knew the power of competition. He loved to challenge people to "go for it." According to Andy, "At A.L. Williams, Art created an atmosphere and an environment where the hungry people became like gym rats. We loved it. We couldn't get enough of working and winning, but it took a world-class coach to get us to do it. Alabama legendary football coach Bear Bryant had nothing on Art."

For people who felt like Andy, Art's style of coaching and recognition was like a flame, lighting people on fire to win.

All great coaches – and great leaders – know the power of recognition. General George Patton knew that men needed a leader who was tougher than the enemy. Napoleon knew it. He said, "Give me enough medals and I'll win you any war."

Ever the coach, Art had a way of making you uncomfortable, whether it was his praising other people, speaker assignments, the Leader's Bulletin, a phone call, a note that told you that you were special or just overlooking you, which was the harshest degree of discomfort. Art loved us too much and believed in us too much for him to not nudge us constantly toward the life he knew we could have. But as much as his little digs moved us with one hand, he had his other on our shoulder indicating his faith, belief, and warmth toward us. No matter the kind of month, year, or decade you have, a winner strives forward. Because his "butt was always burning" he prodded us, encouraged us, and needled us.

At meetings Art would chastise people for "lollygagging around," coming in and out of meetings. One guy proclaimed that he had won Art's "Hall of Shame Award" for Art's caustic comments toward those that didn't have the same passion, desire, and insanity to win like he did. We all feared being considered a "half-butt" by Art.

But those who learned to be comfortable being uncomfortable became wealthy, built massive businesses, and became the unique men and women Art's system molded us to be. To be a somebody you had to have a somebody recognize you for it to be legitimate. Art qualified.

One of the biggest and best forms of recognition was incentive trips. Those were the real "memory makers." Art would say, "I want to take people to all the great places in the world." Art wanted to travel and wanted his team to travel. He would say, "The day you decide that you and your family deserve better -

Hawaii, Europe, the home of your dreams - that's the day you become a winner."

When Art was at ITT, he was impressed by how the company sent them on nice trips every year. The first airplane ride he took was when he was 27 years old, going to ITT headquarters. That trip made a huge impression.

The A.L. Williams trips started with very humble beginnings at the first company award trip in 1977 at the Admiral Benbow Inn in Point Clear, Alabama. The early pioneers ate hot dogs, but a proud new tradition was born. Art took out a second mortgage on his home to pay for people to attend the first ALW trip. He wanted to make a statement that ALW was for real, that ALW was going to make it. In fact, it was one of four or five times Art and Angela took out a second mortgage on their home to finance the early days of the company.

In the last 40 years, tens of thousands of leaders have gone on these kinds of trips, from Hawaii to Europe to California to Colorado to Cancun to Florida and all points in between.

Art & Angela Williams in Vienna

The dream trips we took etched memories in our minds and hearts. We would never have thought to go to those places or thought we should spend money going there. Art loved seeing us enjoy seeing the world and doing it together. He loved seeing us travel to exotic places we had only read and dreamt about.

When Art and Angela first saw the Boca Raton resort in Florida, Art said, "It blew me away." Art thanked Meetings and Conventions directors Barbara King and Mary Durham for connecting him with Boca.

Art and Boe allocated 1% of the company's contract for meetings and conventions. Travel was one of the most significant pieces of recognition Art and the company offered.

While we were with Financial Assurance Corporation they had a trip to Honolulu, Hawaii. It was the first time any of us had ever been there. We were so broke that we all went on a day trip to snorkel and took a commercial bus because none of us had started making real money yet.

The first major European trip we took with A.L. Williams was to Rome, Italy. Seeing the Vatican, St. Peter's Cathedral, the Sistine Chapel, the Pieta, the grand cathedrals, the Roman Coliseum, and the Roman Forum exhilarated us. That trip caused us to "dream big" and hunger for more. A trip to England followed, as well as Lucerne, Switzerland, Munich, a Rhine River cruise, Florence, Italy, Scotland, and Montreal. There was a television program called *Lifestyles of the Rich and Famous* at that time. Of the top ten resorts of the rich and famous, we counted seven that Art and Angela had taken us to with A.L. Williams.

Nick & Becky Alise in London

We made money. We became financially independent. We traveled the world. We beat Pru. We changed our lives. We made memories that meant more than any of the other accommodations. Art and Angela were our memory makers.

We Had Fun

There's no doubt that there were a lot of tough times. We were constantly hit with some new obstacle. But we had fun, too. We loved being together, and we loved to "blow off steam" with laughter and good times. Fast Start Schools were a great place to mix the business with fun. We loved sharing stories of crazy things that happened.

Original RVP and legend Bob Turley had contracted liver cancer and died at 82 on March 30, 2013, in Atlanta. His friend and downline Andy Young went to see Bob and hold his "Bullet Bob" hand. Andy said, "Every time I went to see him, even in the last days in the nursing home, in the hospice, every time he'd look up, he would say, 'Boy, didn't we have some fun?' Art wanted to build a different kind of company and it included having fun."

In the very early days Virginia Carter's base shop would "roast" a person on their birthday. Dean Martin had a show on television called *Celebrity Roast* where they would make clean fun of a fellow celebrity. An example: "He has the wisdom of an owl, the grace of a swan, and the eye of an eagle. Ladies and gentlemen, this man is for the birds." We would honor a person by making fun of them, which is kind of a man's way of doing it.

Angela especially enjoyed them. One time we went over to their home for a meeting and Angela asked me to roast Art, which wasn't hard to do, as Art had a lot of unique quirks.

In Boca Raton, Art wanted to bring some unity to the various hierarchies, so they started a field day with every different hierarchy having their own special T-shirts for their teams.

There were volleyball tournaments, tug-of-war, three-legged-man races, and egg and water balloon tosses. Another time he had a talent show the night after a meeting.

One favorite story is that, in the early days, we had to get a urine specimen every time we wrote a life app. We would give the client a small gray container with a pill in it, and they would go and void a specimen in the bathroom. We kept telling people, "Make sure you get a urine sample every time you write an app. No questions." One agent was so committed to getting a urine specimen with every app that, after he got his securities license, he still told his clients he needed to get a urine specimen before he could submit the mutual fund application!

Another story that makes me laugh is that one of my agents, Janet Smith, had a confrontation with an old agent. The guy was very arrogant and smug about sitting down with a woman in those days, which was rare in the insurance business. He kept questioning whether she was professional enough to be talking to the client. He kept saying, "I'm a professional. I'm a professional."

Frustrated, she finally said, "You say you are a professional, but so are streetwalkers!"

Art had a laugh that was contagious. His laugh resembled a laugh when a person is being tickled. We loved to hear him laugh and to make him laugh.

The most fun of all was winning, making money, becoming financially independent, building hierarchies, beating Pru and making our dreams come true.

The Spark Becomes a Flame

With the flick of a match, friction occurs and a spark leaps from match to tinder. A small flame burns the edges and grows, getting higher and wider as it spreads. The flame becomes a fire. The match was struck in Atlanta, Georgia and touched every corner of the United States and Canada within 13 years. Whatever the flame touched, lives and the insurance industry were changed forever.

By 1980, we had already grown to over $4,000,000 in face amount of policies in force. Two years later, it was over $10,000,000. Every year the numbers climbed. Some years they doubled. It seemed preposterous when Art first talked about us being an industry leader way back when we didn't even have apps. But Art had a way of making you believe what he said, and we did. When he started talking about beating Prudential, one of the biggest companies in the world, it almost seemed possible. In 1983, Art launched his campaign to beat Prudential with the slogan "I Want Pru BAD!" He had it printed on T-shirts, on banners, on everything. The idea came from Art's coaching days. "Once I had T-shirts made up that said, 'I want Central BAD!' They were the next team we had to beat. I used the same strategy as I'd used as a football coach by talking about the team in the wrong colored jerseys that we had to beat. Prudential was that team." It created an excitement that touched us all. Art's belief was all we needed.

The "I want Pru BAD" campaign was the final shot in the war. We all realized there was no turning back after this direct hit on our nemesis. We had really burned our boats now. The big guns of the industry would never stop hating us. If we failed, they would never let us forget it.

The "I want Pru BAD" campaign built a new fire under us. And that fire turned into an explosion.

In our annual meeting at Boca Raton in 1984, just seven years after forming A.L. Williams, we celebrated the biggest win in A.L. Williams history. The scoreboard told the story:

Prudential, $38 billion of new life insurance; A.L. Williams, $38.3 billion.

We had done it.

A Birthday Message

Written 02/10/1984

We started A.L. Williams because we knew there was a better way to build a company. We just wanted to be real folks, good honest people. We wanted people to feel good about having us in their homes, and we wanted them to believe what we said. We sold a different product – a product we totally believed in – and we sold it in a different way. We found that more people let us into their homes, more bought our product, and we were having unbelievable success. And out of that environment, ALW was born.

In my career in business, I've found that all companies talk a good game. But 99% of the companies don't deliver on their promises. A.L. Williams has delivered. We're doing a job for the American consumer and we're doing a job for our people.

In the last few years, the free enterprise system has been challenged like never before. Most of the companies out there are crying and poor-mouthing and making excuses.

Not ALW. In spite of all kinds of obstacles, ALW has succeeded. We've broken every record for a new company in the largest industry in the world. We're truly one of a kind. There's no doubt that this company is one of the most exciting success stories in American business today.

Yet I believe that ALW is just beginning. We're now in a position to dominate the industry. Today, as we approach our seventh birthday, ALW is the number one producer of term insurance in the nation. What incredible achievements we've made! And what an outstanding group of people made it possible! I'm so proud to be a part of it. When we sit down to celebrate our eighth birthday, I believe that ALW will be the largest producer of individual insurance in the world.

All my life I've wanted to be a member of a national championship team, a group that's recognized as the best in everybody's eyes. A.L. Williams is the champion in the insurance industry.

When you do something great – and ALW has achieved true greatness – history becomes so important. The events, the principles behind them, the traditions, these form the foundation on which we'll build our future success.

Art Williams

Chapter 4:

A NEW ERA OF SUCCESS

The 1984 National Championship gave the whole company a high that we'll never forget. It was a seminal year. After that groundbreaking time, there was nowhere to go but up. Instead of "playing scared," which Art and his followers had always done, we could celebrate how far we'd come.

The numbers continued to climb at exceptional rates. We celebrated our fifth consecutive year as #1 in 1988, producing more individual life insurance in force than any company. There didn't seem to be any competition left.

The sales force was exploding. By 1987, when we marked our first 10 years in business with a massive "10 Years of Greatness" celebration, our seven Original RVPs had become 12,000 RVPs. Just two years later, in 1989, we had over 200,000 sales reps.

The growth was incredible. In A.L. Williams' fourth year of business, we paid $1.5 million in death claims to families. In 1988, we paid $184.5 million.

We now had more individual life insurance in force than any other company through MILICO. There seemed to be no stopping us.

As Art recalls, "The scoreboard showed that our little ragtag army did the impossible. In 1977, the industry sold *90%* cash value and *10%* term, but in 12 short years, the industry only sold 10% cash value." What a legacy!

Out in the field, we were doing better than we'd ever imagined. Our incomes were rising, and financial independence seemed more than just a dream. We made and saved money; we bought our dream homes; we planned for futures that were beyond anything we'd ever dreamed.

The demands of the company prompted Art to purchase his own plane to make the constant trips across the country to

A.L. Williams offices and events more efficient. Nothing excited "termites" more than being asked to "ride with Art" on his plane for one of these trips.

A.L. Williams Goes International

As a new company, ALW only spanned Georgia and Florida. We lived every day in fear that the insurance industry would put us out of business because we were replacing their policies at a record pace. Texas was to be next for expansion, then Alabama. Art was famous for saying, "Have a goal of having offices throughout the United States and Canada." We were happy to be in three states! The thought of being an international company was the furthest thought from our minds. When Canada was opened in 1985, it sent shock waves of belief throughout the company. We were a real company now. We thought, if we could get into Canada, we could conquer the world. Canada brought credibility, pride, respect, and victory to everyone who wasn't sure if we would make it as a company.

The opening of Canada was a landmark achievement. Art sent a small core group of people from the A.L. Williams Home Office in Atlanta, led by Dick Morgan, to begin a whole new era of growth in our neighboring country. Doing business in a foreign country with entirely different rules and regulations was a considerable challenge, but massive effort eventually paid off and we were up and running.

Four years later, Canada was producing $5.5 billion in face amount, and a whole new group of crusaders was growing by leaps and bounds. Art's dream of "building it big" was crossing borders to help thousands of new families.

By the end of the decade, we were doing business in 49 states, D.C. and the U.S. territories of Puerto Rico, Guam, and the U.S. Virgin Islands, plus Canada.

"Art-Sized" Rewards Recognize Producers in the New Era

As production and individual success got bigger, it was only natural that Art would want to "supersize" rewards and recognition.

One of the most desired and envied awards was the $100,000 ring awarded to top producers. It was an exclusive club, and the ring reflected that. The design was patterned on the Super Bowl ring and was encrusted with diamonds and precious gems. It was a conversation starter, for sure, and many sales were made after someone asked an ALW leader, "Is that a Super Bowl ring?" Bob Turley once said that it was hard to take off his World Series ring after he left baseball, but his smile was ear-to-ear when he was awarded his $100,000 ring.

Next were Rolex watches, with diamonds where the numbers would be, kept under tight security in a safe at company meetings.

The Wall of Fame, a late addition, involved an oil portrait of truly extraordinary leaders and their spouses, created by an Atlanta artist and displayed in the A.L. Williams "War Room" at the home office.

Trips likewise got bigger and better, with Hawaii a long-time favorite, but more spectacular venues and eye-popping locations were added each year. Every time a new incentive trip was announced, the competition was on!

The ultimate recognition was to be invited to dinner on Art's yacht, the *Lady Angela*. Art continued to raise our expectations by showing us that "people like us" deserved the best.

Art's rewards were over the top, but it was his way of showing leaders that nothing was too good for those who proved they were "something special."

Launching a Network

In March of 1986, a press conference held at the Waldorf Astoria in New York announced the newest bombshell in A.L. Williams: the soon-to-be-launched ALW-TV. This corporate television network would allow Art to communicate directly with the field from the Home Office. Yvonne Tyson, whose husband Randy was a part-time rep, was in charge of the day-to-day operations of ALW-TV in those early days. Yvonne recalls how it came about, when the network started with only six staff members and six freelance people.

"Barbara King, head of public relations for the company, had been talking to a Chicago advertising group, and they came up with the idea of a TV network and sold the idea to Art," says Yvonne. The Chicago group set up the studio with Barbara. It took three to four months to launch the TV network in 1986. The same group also created the ALW logo. Yvonne explains how, despite the long hours and rushing to learn a new type of communication, everyone rallied to make it a success.

"Everyone put their all into it because they got caught up in a fever for Art's approval like we all did," she says.

Mike Burroughs, part of ALW-TV from the beginning and currently the head of the company's TV division, plus Marketing, Communications and Training, recounts the magic of this new addition to growth.

"Art Williams was a master communicator, yet in 1986 he openly stated that his biggest challenge was communicating with the sales force. Long before the internet and cell phones, there were no magic answers. Fax machines were hi-tech communication tools at the time. A.L. Williams was still sending out printed leaders bulletins and a monthly 'Tape of the Month' subscription program that included the company newspaper and an audio cassette tape.

"The company was bursting at the seams with record growth, and Art knew there had to be a better way. When Barbara King was introduced to the concept of a business television network, Art made a quick decision to go all in. It didn't matter that he didn't know anything about the television business. Neither did anyone else on his team. A.L. Williams didn't even have many videos back in those days. Major company events featured slide shows - minor details, in Art's mind. There was no turning back."

He already had his communications and marketing machine in place. The two leaders who handled all of Art's marketing campaigns, Dona Bunch and Mike Burroughs, had backgrounds in the print world. Not a problem. They immediately became the Executive Producers for ALW-TV's flagship show, *Monday Morning Managers Meeting with Art Williams.*

"We all learned the TV business together," Mike said. "Art called the play and we went with it just like we always did. For our team, it was business as usual, and we kept doing the same things we had been doing with this new cutting-edge communication channel. ALW-TV was an instant success, and it changed the landscape of the company forever."

Barbara moved a few people around, putting Yvonne Tyson in charge of the day-to-day operations for ALW-TV. She brought in some people with TV experience, including a top-notch engineer, a few producers with experience at CNN and local Atlanta TV stations, and a group of young people looking for their start in the TV business. Art's daughter, April, later joined the team for a period of time.

Yvonne said the biggest thing she learned from Art was to believe in herself and to just get the job done.

"All who worked at ALW-TV believed they were bigger and better because of their experience, and they gave all the credit to Art," said Yvonne, who was only skilled in still photography when the network started. "They gave it their all. Art and Angela had the ability to motivate people to work hard by building relationships with them."

From Day One, ALW-TV was the largest private business television network in the world, with more than 1,700 large satellite dishes at the biggest offices across America. Each office had its own large meeting room, which attracted a standing-room-only crowd every Monday morning. Art had solved his biggest challenge.

Every Monday morning – and any other time he wanted to broadcast from the new ALW-TV Studio – Art could go live on the air to speak to the sales force in real-time. It was a game-changer in terms of communication, information, motivation, and education. Once again, A.L. Williams had one-upped the competition with its new vehicle to communicate instantly with the field. A.L. Williams even surpassed the more heralded business TV networks launched by Atlanta-based giants Coca-Cola and Home Depot.

Already a charismatic leader who was very comfortable speaking in front of large crowds, Art became an instant TV star. He could deliver his own message that he decided was the most relevant each week – and he could do it his way. Art hosted every show himself and didn't always have guests, even though he had an interview set in addition to his podium set up so that he could speak to both the cameras and a live studio audience.

At times, he would work with his team to plan special broadcasts. Often there were Sunday night phone calls that led to frantic last-minute work right up until show time. Then there were the days that Art would pull up to the studio 10 minutes before going on air with his own stack of notes. Art's executive producers and the ALW-TV crew didn't always know where Art was going, but they always managed to keep up with him.

John Madden might have been more famous for his work with the telestrator, but Art adopted it early on, drawing up his own plays on the electronic screen. "Put that camera back on me," Art would yell into the camera when he wanted to make a point that only he could make. The telestrator had its limits in A.L. Williams, where there was no substitute for eye-to-eye contact.

Initially, ALW-TV broadcasted live five days a week, a major undertaking requiring long staff hours.

"We did it," Yvonne said, "because we wanted it perfect for Art and Angela. Their name was on it."

It wasn't long before ALW-TV scaled back to a more manageable schedule, but it still provided the sales force with the latest information and training on all product lines. It also marked the company's full-blown entry into the video production business.

Art and his team began to make professional videos to help take the company's marketing campaigns to the next level. These efforts included everything from *60 Minutes*-style investigative report documentaries to features on widows whose lives were changed by A.L. Williams' consumer-oriented concepts and products.

It was the beginning of a new era, and the network is still going strong 36 years later.

Art Is Recognized

In 1987, Art Williams was named "Entrepreneur of the Year." He and Angela went to Southern Illinois University in Carbondale, Illinois to receive the honor. What did the whole life agents think of Art Williams now? It was inevitable that Art's success would be noticed by the business and financial world, and it was clear the tables had begun to turn. As Art would say, "Ain't that something? Ain't that dadgum something?"

Art's Bestseller: *All You Can Do Is All You Can Do*

Art was a prolific writer and was known to outline entire brochures by hand on the back of piece of scrap paper (see attached brochures by Art, center section). Art's first book was *Common Sense,* in which he explained the principles of money in a simple, down-to-earth, "common sense" way that anyone could understand and follow. *Common Sense* became a hit with people

looking for simple but sound financial advice. *Common Sense* was an A.L. Williams best-seller and is still in print today (under the new title *How Money Works*). Over 10 million copies are in print. According to Art, *Common Sense* was his favorite of all the books he wrote.

Next came *Pushing Up People,* Art's rules for "treating people good." Art believed that you win with people, not products, and he wanted to share his methods of bringing out the best in people and leading them towards success. He was at the Pritikin Institute in Miami where he had time to rethink where the company was and what was needed. It was there that he started writing *Pushing Up People.* "Barbara King and Yvonne Tyson encouraged me to do it, and Dona Bunch helped me write it," Art said. "*Pushing Up People* got into the nuts and bolts of A.L. Williams. It was the perfect book to get into the heart of our company. If you push up sales, they'll fall back down again, but it you push up people, sales won't go down."

Art & Dona Bunch

After many requests from the field, Art compiled his principles for building a business into *The A.L. Williams Way,* which outlined virtually every area of the business, from recruiting to applying the multiples to running an RVP office. Art began the landmark book, outlined on the back of a manila file folder, while on an incentive trip to Germany and Austria in 1985.

Art's most famous publication, written in 1988, was called *All You Can Do Is All You Can Do,* in which he shared his secrets to success in business and in life. Published by Thomas Nelson Press, *All You Can Do* spent 14 weeks on the *New York Times* bestsellers list. It introduced thousands of people to Art Williams and became an instant classic.

Art's Company Finds Stability

By this time, A.L. Williams was backed by American Can Company, a Dow Jones Top 30 company and a staple of American business, and Art's little company was producing giant numbers that required considerable administration and financial backing. American Can offered that. For the first time, it looked like we were going to really make it in the big time.

But there was more to come. When the Wall Street giant Sanford Weill, known as the "Wizard of Wall Street," realized our uniqueness, a new level of success seemed possible.

ALW Corporation Goes Public

In 1988, the A.L. Williams Corporation (which included MILICO) was formed. Ultimately, the ALW Corporation and the A.L. Williams Agency would merge into one entity.

In February of 1989, the A.L. Williams Corporation began selling its stock on the New York Stock Exchange. Who would have ever thought, as we sat in Virginia's living room that February night in 1977, that just 12 years later, we would be buying stock in the giant ALWC?

Nothing made those of us from the early days prouder than to see this all-American form of legitimacy. It was a proud and humbling moment. And Art and his "rag-tag" army made it happen.

The End of a Decade

By 1989, A.L. Williams was a juggernaut. The new decade was ushered in with an annual convention unlike any other. Held at the Superdome in New Orleans, a record 37,000 termites celebrated their success and looked forward to the next decade.

In 1989, Sandy Weill purchased the company, providing the administration and financial backing that could provide stability in the years to come. It was Art's way of securing the future for recruits and clients and guaranteeing the company would live beyond him. In January of 1990, Sandy Weill appeared with Art on the *Monday Morning Manager's Meeting.*

It was the final year in a decade of success, but it was also the end of an era.

While we knew Art's heart, it was hard to imagine that he would not be at the helm of the company he created. We just couldn't envision an "A.L. Williams" without Art. Art was the coach we chose to invest our years with. ALW was a sanctuary for people who had unfulfilled dreams, for people who wanted to be somebody. Art was the one person who stood by us because he was one of us. He created the best possible environment. He believed in us, and we believed in him. He was in our corner and would fight for us. His will to win became contagious and became the impetus for our will to win.

We were proud outsiders, and we had an outsider's soul. He wanted to champion our cause, and we won the insurance championship because of it.

Then, in the blink of an eye, it came to an end. Art was gone. Did we expect Art to stay with us forever? He said he would be here until he died, until one day he wasn't.

ALW was our family, and Art was the head of the household. We had fought the war with Art and won. We finally found a company that could afford us. Then the environment changed. A corporation owned us, Art was gone, and we never felt connected working for a big corporation. We were now the tiny fish in their big pond.

The relationships that built ALW got left in the basement as the company became totally corporate. We felt like we had a boss, and we didn't like it.

We had a recruiting and building mindset to build a company within a company. They had a traditional mindset of not recruiting more people but getting more out of the people we recruited. We wanted to conquer the world, now we felt conquered. It would never be the same.

We were coached by Art, so we adapted, and our culture won out, but it took us banding together and keeping the dream Art implanted in us alive.

The company still exists today, and it is a great company, but our Camelot was gone, never to return. Our culture survived, but the glory days of being a David against a Goliath were lost. It was inevitable, but Art's phenomenon exists and will never go away.

Art Considers the Future

He gave full measure for 13 years, from February 10, 1977, to July 1990. On July 1, 1990, he left.

Watching the TV series, *The Crown,* it was stunning to realize that Queen Elizabeth didn't want the burden and the cloistered life of a monarch. I've read that no Catholic Cardinal wants to be the Pope.

As is said, "Heavy is the head that wears the crown." This phrase implies the great responsibilities borne by a king, who worries constantly. This phrase also means a person in charge, or in a leadership role, has to bear many responsibilities, and it is a very tough job.

These leaders could influence people to do the right things, and they, in turn, could make them do the wrong things.

Tired, guilty, sick, and overwhelmed are the consequences of total and complete responsibility. Art had the weight of our futures to weigh him down - all 250,000 agents, 1,000 plus RVPs who put their names on leases, and the insurance companies that went into huge debt to finance our operation. The home office personnel, the shareholders of our stock, many of whom were trusting friends and relatives. Fifty insurance commissioners questioning our every move. Whole life insurance agents wanting us gone, all 450,000 of them. Newspaper people hoping for a juicy story to bring down the empire. Hundreds of RVPs who had gotten old and curmudgeonly forgot where they came from and loved to gripe. Dozens of RVPs who left and were on the hunt to steal people because they were unable to build something of their own. Regulators who strained our compliance department.

Yes, Art got wealthy and had the plane, the yacht, the homes, the admiration of tens of thousands, but also the headaches. He wasn't a vacant suit in an office. This was his creation, and the hundreds of moving parts would overwhelm anyone. The energy, the sleepless nights, the disappointments, the broken relationships that inevitably occur, and the ever-present vigilance all become exhausting. His leadership responsibilities were both a blessing and a curse.

As one RVP from Detroit reminded me, "Art also had to take the ALW logo off of the tail of his airplane when he was visiting all of us state-to-state because of the threats back in the day."

As in the beginning scene of the movie *Gladiator*, Caesar states to Maximus that he had been in power for 20 years, and in 16 of those, Rome had been at war, with only four years of peace. (*Dreamworks, 2000)* He states that he is weary from the responsibilities. Art had fought the insurance wars from 1968-1990, 22 years on the battlefront.

Metaphorically, Art took the proverbial bullet intended for thousands of us. He took the blows, the insults, the ridicule. We "termites," we who dared be so bold as to challenge their right to exist, we who righted their wrongs, we who raised a fist, shook it at them, and did what no other sales organization ever did in history. We "Davids" took on the Goliath and beat them. But Art paid the most considerable price.

As I write this, Art will turn 80 soon. With heart issues, he retired at age 48. His father died at age 48. In fact, his younger brother Bill would die at 45 soon after Art left. Add it all up, and

Art's life was probably saved by leaving the stress and worry behind.

Art Sells His Company

A variety of different factors started coming into play before Art actually made the decision to sell his company to Sandy Weill, who ran Commercial Credit Company.

The encouragement for Art to sell the company was based mainly on these three reasons:

- A desire to secure the future of the company
- There was no succession plan in place
- His health and his family's health history

At 42 years old Art had a pacemaker put in. He had fainted several times, which required him to begin thinking about a plan for the company's future.

It was especially concerning when he fainted in front of 15 people and had to be taken to the hospital in an ambulance. It was considered an athletic heart issue that needed to be treated with a pacemaker, and it worked. Those two events culminated in a wake-up call about something that Art had put off for a long time. "I never thought about a succession plan," he said.

Still, Art's father had died at age 48 from heart problems, and others in his family had died young. It became a major concern.

Executives in the home office, especially Boe Adams, started talking to him about who would take his place. Boe understood the need for a succession plan.

Boe wanted to retire in the next two years, so Art knew he couldn't be counted on to take over. Treacy Beyer was very capable of running the administration because he was familiar with a lot of the company systems that Boe helped put in place. Boe's and Art's relationship was more of a partnership, and that power could not easily be duplicated.

Art had a 45-minute drive to the office every day and loved that time to be able to think. He started getting concerned, after passing out, that he might not be able to drive again. That was always in the back of his mind. The succession plan was the primary reason that Art decided to sell the company. The final straw was Art's reality about his heart issue. He wanted to secure the future of the company.

Boe Adams started encouraging Art to sell. Art recalls, "Boe would say, 'If you die and I'm gone, who will replace us?' I felt confident about Treacy running the company." Art could do the out-front things with the field, but the company needed an inside person like Boe. In reality, both Art and Boe were irreplaceable. Something had to be done.

Many home office executives like Barbara King, Bill Keane, and others kept talking to Art about the dilemma and telling Art that it was a perfect time for him to sell. Selling didn't mean Art giving up control, selling meant that there was a succession of leadership in place so the company could continue and serve the field force the way they needed to be served.

Art didn't think he would live to age 50, even though his body and mind felt good. But the age of 50 was looming. He mentioned to Angela that maybe she could take over, but she quickly dismissed it. A real succession plan without Art or Angela needed to be done.

Sandy Weill wanted to buy ALW because it was bigger than his company, Commercial Credit (which would later merge with Citigroup). Sandy owned the part of the company he bought from Stanley Beyer, but not the agency that Art owned. Art didn't have much confidence in corporate Wall Street types like Sandy. The more Art met with Sandy and his people, the more concerned he became.

All the companies that ALW had been with, starting with ITT and ending with PennCorp, happened before the company officially became the ALW Corporation. All of them struggled to support the growth of ALW.

"All of a sudden, we met Boe who introduced us to Art DeMoss and all these other companies, but they all kept telling us we were too big. Then we needed to have our own headquarters, which we got," Art said. Art started getting really uncomfortable when all these companies began leaving, and he constantly had to struggle to find another company to finance this behemoth.

Art said, "I'm the kind of person who sold to all our people in the company that each company we were with was going to be the last company we would be with."

ITT went out of business. Financial Assurance said we were too big for them. At National Home Life the owner Art DeMoss died, and the board wanted to sell the company.

"All these companies made commitments, and I couldn't believe in them anymore," said Art.

Art wanted ALW to have its own home office for stability. ALW was never in a position to buy a company themselves. One day Stanley Beyer called Art and said, "I want you to meet Sandy Weill, who owns Commercial Credit. I want to sell PennCorp to him and his company." That was unsettling to Art. When Art met Sandy, he thought he was like everyone else he had met from the Wall Street crowd. They couldn't help themselves; they were who they were. But Art and Sandy developed a special bond.

Sixty percent of the profits of PennCorp Financial were from A.L. Williams. If Art didn't support the sale to Sandy, he wouldn't buy PennCorp.

Many of Art's inner circle really pushed hard for Art to sell. Art kept saying, "I don't want to do this." Art remembers, "Boe kept telling me I had to think of all the people out there who owned company stock, the agents out there, the people who had leases on their offices. Boe's heart and mind were in the right place." Art thought of every conceivable option, and finally concluded that none were acceptable.

Art decided to sell the company after considering all the factors, including the urgency that many home office executives understood.

Art went to Sandy's office in New York to sign the contract. Art indicated he has deep regrets about selling the company to

Sandy Weill and Sandy's company, Commercial Credit, which eventually merged with Citigroup.

"I just had a gut feeling that I was making a mistake," Art said, "and every time I didn't follow my gut, I made a mistake. The minute I signed, I knew it was a mistake. There was a lot I felt I still had to do; I had ideas for expanding the company worldwide, more diversified products. I just felt pressure from all the ALW executives to sell to ensure the future of the company. My father, his family and an uncle all died young from heart attacks. And I had to consider all of that."

"The reality of my mistake was when Sandy turned to me and said, 'Art, now the pressure is off for you. I'm so happy for you. Now you can go out and live your life without any of the stress.' When Sandy said that to me, I felt that I had immediately taken a backseat to doing any of that. I sold to Sandy because I wanted a company we could trust. That confirmed I had made a mistake.

"I just could not feel good about what I had done. Every night I was sick as a dog for having signed the company away. It got worse when I went to the first board meeting of the new Commercial Credit Company that now owned the ALW agency, and they never talked about ALW. We were one of the biggest parts of their company, and they never gave us a second thought. All they talked about was raising more money to buy more companies."

Originally Art had a commitment from them that anything over a 12% profit off the ALW agency would be used to pay more commissions and create more income for the field force, but it didn't happen.

"I said to Angela, 'I made a mistake. I didn't want out of ALW. I never felt that I would ever leave the company and I would die on the job.' Angela said, 'But what if you die? What happens to all the people?'"

The issue of Art's heart and succession kept things in perspective. "Succession was a key for me to doubt about keeping ownership. Angela was all in for selling it.

"At that time in my life I kind of gave up. What I had created was no longer in my possession. I didn't want to sell but I had no options. Although Sandy and his corporate staff fell in love with A.L. Williams, it was not the kind of falling in love that I had with the company, because it was different than loving it the way we did. Sandy loved it but could one day sell it to make a huge profit. I didn't sell it to make a huge profit. I stayed another 18 months before I got the call when Sandy said, 'We're making some changes and you are out, Art.'"

Before Art sold the company, he went back to the Stephens company who took ALW public and said, 'I'm being pushed hard to sell to Sandy Weill. I'd like to buy Penncorp myself: they said it would take $1 billion and they could raise the money. They told me, 'We can do that, Art,'"

It tore Art up that he could do it, but he didn't want to have $1 billion of debt and no succession plan. The reality was that, if Art bought the company out, created $1 billion of debt, and then something happened to him, the stock could crash and hurt his beloved people. It was too big a risk to take.

The biggest determining factor to selling was that it took so much money to keep ALW going. Art began to be afraid of companies not understanding how big ALW was and how much money was needed to keep the growth going. How fast we grew scared all companies we were with.

Because growth was so fast, each change to a new company made changing harder. The change of compensation and change in products, all disturbed the ALW field force. The nonstop change was brutal and had the potential to ruin ALW if Art didn't have something permanent.

Everybody from Boe, the home office staff, and people Art trusted the most were pushing hard for Art to sell. Art was getting angry because they pushed so hard. Art trusted them and knew all their hearts were in the right place, but what they wanted was not what Art wanted.

Even at the last second before signing, Art had a bad feeling. "I called all the field leaders about the sale, said all the right things about how this was a huge positive, like I had thousands of times before, but my heart was not in it after that. Art realized he would never have the freedom and the support to do what he thought was needed without being the owner.

Art went to a second board meeting and again they never talked about ALW even once. "My heart was broken. My heart was not in it, but I had to make myself sound like I was all in and was fully supportive of it. I couldn't tell people I thought it was a big mistake. I started playing the "what if" game. What if I had bought Penncorp for $1 billion? But I still might die and have $1 billion in debt; that would not serve the company and our people very well."

Even though Art sold the company, he had to get the ALW Board of Directors' approval. "When Sandy and I went to the Board meeting they asked me to step outside so they could discuss the sale. Sandy and I were outside the office as the Board debated." The Board kept saying they didn't believe Art and Sandy could work together under the arrangement of Art "working for Sandy." The board didn't have its heart in it to agree to Art's desire to sell. Sandy was getting angry and impatient. He thought it was automatic if Art wanted it. Art had to keep going back-and-forth into the Board meeting to talk to them about it. After four hours of debate, Art got frustrated thinking that the decision was made, and everybody was on board. It was a real shocker to Art. He thought that they would agree with his decision because of all his valid reasons to sell. But they hesitated.

Sandy kept saying, "What's the hold up? What's going wrong?" The Board felt like Art. None of them liked the stereotypical New York Wall Street types that Sandy represented. Art went through with the Board all the reasons to do it.

They finally said "Art, if this is what you want to do, we will approve it."

"ALW had four independent outside Board members, and they tried to talk me out of it," Art said. "The four inside members were for selling."

Art's confidantes thought that selling would secure ALW's future. Art put on a happy front, but he never felt good about it.

From what Art said, he went into a massive depression mode for years. Art was battle tested and battle weary, but this was a newfound enemy. He only came out of it when he began thinking of his grandchildren and their need for him. Crises take soul and spirit out of these great men. You can only fight so many wars, take so many punches, use up only so much adrenalin, be so resilient and put out so many fires. Heroes only have so many heroic moments.

After Art was no longer with a company, he and Angela went to their place in Amelia Island, Florida. Art would walk the beach everyday thinking, "How did I screw this thing up so bad when it was so good?" A good friend of Art's was Jerry Falwell. Art asked Jerry to send him some sermons. He was hurting. His baby, his creation, his soul since he came up with the plan, was gone. Jerry sent Art 365 sermons on tape. Art would listen to two or three a day while he was walking. A form of deep depression set in. Art could do nothing to move on. "It was the worst two-to-three-year period of my life. I had a degree of depression that I had never had before, "Art said.

"Angela was my best friend during this three-year period," Art said. "She tried to encourage me every day. She is very religious and reads the Bible endlessly. She was at peace with everything and truly believed it was God's plan for all this to happen."

The downward spiral was really hitting Art hard. Every day he had regret. He looked to other things to fill the void when he left the company. He bought a National Hockey League team; he bought a Canadian Football League team; but none of them could fill the hole in his heart.

"I never really have gotten over it completely. It is a real weakness of mine. When you build something from scratch, devote your life to something, and think it will last forever and then it doesn't, it is a harsh reality. It felt like I had lost a part of me, and it hurt to think I could never get it back."

"Angela said, 'If we had stayed with our company and you had borrowed the $1 billion, I don't think there was any way you could've sustained the pace you were on.'"

After about three years, Art started thinking about his grandchildren and became extremely close to all seven of them. He said, "I can't let them keep seeing me being negative. I've got so much to be thankful for. I've got a lot to be grateful for and that's what I started thinking about."

Art was invited back about three years later to speak to the company at their national convention in Atlanta. All the old-timers had their children in attendance to witness what may have been their last chance to see Art speak. Every seat was filled, and the air was thick with each person's memories and profound reverie.

Eventually, Art started to make peace with everything. Art knew it was over, and he was never going to get his company back. Angela was his backbone during this time.

Art still communicated with the company leadership because he believed that the company would be served by giving its people ownership. Ownership didn't exist anywhere in insurance or financial services. It was and still is revolutionary.

Art flew to New York and presented his idea of ownership to Sandy and his leaders. They agreed that ownership was critical to build the kind of company that would last. Art had two meetings in New York, one at Sandy's house and one at their headquarters. Finally, after six months of talking and giving them his ideas, they agreed to create ownership for this great company and its people.

Years later Stanley Beyer called him from the golf course and said, "Art, let's buy Citigroup. I'm so bored playing golf every day, let's buy it and have some fun." Art told Stanley that he didn't see that as a possibility at that time.

Still, Art missed a great deal about the ALW company in the coming years. He missed the camaraderie with the people he had great relationships with. He missed the times of rallying everyone together and proving everyone wrong. He missed the war. He missed the energy of getting a bad article about his beloved company that fueled him, made him sick, and made him more determined.

Very few people can relate to how much you can love something and not have it anymore. You love it so much you get to a point where you just can't walk away. Most people can't relate to having relationships so strong you have literally loved each other, and they loved you back. It's something a coach could understand.

Unless you build something, you can't understand it. Unless you've given something your all, 100%, had no doubt, loved the fight, you can't relate to something like ALW. Art felt like he was born for a battle and a fight. He loved having an enemy, a team in the wrong-colored jersey. Art says unless you've been attacked, you can never understand. Unless you've actually owned your own company, you'll never understand why Art was so fanatical.

Art had so much left he wanted to do, but what he built will last 100 years and more.

His phenomenon will be felt for generations.

PHENOMENON SPOTLIGHT

Words That Built A.L. Williams

"I want to be somebody so bad it borders on being an obsession."

Art Williams

For Art, his remarkable career started with the desire that obsessed his mind — the desire to "be somebody." His company exploded because he understood that having a desire to be somebody is where it all starts.

"As I look back," Art said. "I believe almost 100% of our people had been screwed and tattooed when they joined A.L. Williams. They were determined to be somebody. Their fight and determination were unbelievable. 'Be somebody' became a motto for the A.L. Williams people. They would fight all day and all night ...and all day the next day."

What Is a Somebody?

It is a primal longing that I am convinced waits to be unleashed within everyone.

Wanting to be somebody is etched in our souls and we can never run away from it. Those with no pursuit of being somebody will be haunted all their lives by mediocrity and wondering "what if?" We are hardwired to be somebody, and we can try to suffocate it, but it keeps resurrecting itself.

A Lack of Wanting to Be Somebody

- A lack of wanting to be **somebody** comes from not having a mission, and when not nourished, it can "corrode the soul."
- A **somebod**y wants to be involved in something bigger than just themselves. There is a yearning to make a difference with their lives.
- Wanting to be **somebody** makes you want to be the best you can be and causes personal growth to fit a person's dream.
- When was the last time, if ever, that you cried because you wanted to be somebody? A **somebody** has tears in their eyes because they want to be somebody so badly.

- A **somebody** is admired and respected; they yearn and work to accomplish that ideal.
- A **somebody** believes that becoming better makes the world better.
- We must understand that we are all created to have meaning in our lives; we are hardwired to do it.
- A **somebody** has an insatiable desire to be great and "amount to something" they can be proud of.

The Opportunity to Be Somebody Is Fleeting

- A **somebody** knows their life and their door of opportunity is fleeting. They feel a constant sense of urgency and have a "do it now" mindset.
- As Art Williams says, "One day, they are going to be patting your face with a shovel."
- Wherever you find winners, you'll find people who understand you have to take advantage of your opportunity before it's too late.
- "I charge you; once you have a dream, decide to begin, and begin right away. Don't wait for anybody to blow whistles for you to start." (*Ayivor, 2022)*
- "I can't believe that God put us on this earth to be ordinary." *(Holtz)*

Art Understood What It Means to Be Somebody

Art said:

- All my life I wanted to be somebody.
- I was put here to be somebody special.
- I want to be somebody so bad, there's nothing I won't do.
- If you are eaten up with being somebody, you can do impossible things.
- Everybody wants to be somebody.
- Winners want to be somebody.
- Winners talk about how great it is to be somebody they are proud of and how they're not like everybody else.

Being Somebody...

- Is not having money, or houses, cars, and yachts, or giving away a lot of money; that's all part of it.

- I think being a somebody is looking in the mirror and saying, "I was all right, I fought a good fight, I did something I didn't think that I could do."
- It's when your spouse looks at you and says, "I'm glad I got you."
- It's when you say to yourself, "I got the best out of my potential."
- It's when your kids look at you and say, "I'm proud of my mom and dad, they were special."
- It's when your grandkids and great-grandkids feel one day that they don't have hope and maybe look through a photo album and say, "Look at my great grandparents, they were studs, I'm so thankful I've got their blood."
- To be somebody, you've got to pitch your tent somewhere.
- To be somebody you can't wimp out or throw in the towel.
- To be somebody, you have to lay it on the line one last time.
- A somebody hates the thought of disappointing anyone. Their standards come from a lofty expectation that achieving is "what they do," and everything they do reflects that. It's not pressure to them but an inner drive they cannot escape because, as Art Williams says, "You are *supposed* to be somebody."
- Everyone is supposed to, but only a few will make the effort to be somebody they are proud of. They are thankful for the drive they have that actually is their blessing.
- A somebody is driven by the thought, "How you do anything is how you do everything." Their 5-star way of life is the lens through which they view life. It's the same view as, "If you are going to do it, do it right the first time." That's how they are wired, and they accept it.
- A somebody is a little crazy. As Herb Kelleher, the legendary founder of Southwest, says, "If you're crazy enough to do what you love for a living, then you're bound to create a life that matters."
- Wanting to be somebody is good for the soul.

Others Knew the Power

- "A somebody is a somebody when no one else knows he wants to be a somebody but them." Richie Falcone, ALW star.

- "I don't know why I can't be satisfied by being average and ordinary. I always wanted to be somebody so bad it hurt."
- "Somebodies are not determined by whether they won or lost. Somebodies are people who go for it with all they have. If you go for it with all you have—not just in the games, but in practice too—you will already be a somebody." *(Dweck, 2006)*
- A somebody has a life of purpose and meaning. Viktor Frankle said, "The will to have meaning and purpose in life is superior to the will to have power or the will to find pleasure. Being human means relating and being directed to something or someone other than yourself." *(Frankle, 2006)*
- Napoleon Hill recommends we each develop our own *Definite Major Purpose Statement* and read it aloud daily. A somebody may not have it written on paper, but it's written on their souls. *(Hill, 1937)*

Art's Words About Being Somebody

"I want to be somebody" was a definitive mindset to those early A.L. Williams people. It ignited a fire in their bellies.

Art said:

- *Everybody thought A.L. Williams was a bunch of "nobodies" that came to town on the back of a truck. Everybody thought we would be out of business in 90 days.*
- *But "I want to be somebody" hit a nerve with the A.L. Williams people.*
- *"Being somebody" became our obsession.*
- *"I want to be somebody" gave us the courage to change, the courage to find a new purpose, the courage to walk a new path.*
- *"I want to be somebody" was more than just five words to all of us. It was a call to arms. It was a way to tell everyone, "I'm sick and tired of being sick and tired!"*
- *"I want to be somebody" announced to the world, "Watch out, I'm ready to be somebody."*
- *Being somebody to us had nothing to do with how much money we made.*
- *Being somebody had nothing to do with what your financial statement looked like.*
- *Wanting to be somebody is good for the soul.*

- *But being somebody has everything to do with how people look at you. It has to do with how they admire you, your passions, your toughness, your honesty, your example.*
- *If you want to be somebody you've got to find a way to help people feel important, to help people feel special.*
- *Being somebody is making a difference with your life. It's investing in people. People are important. Things have no lasting value.*

Always remember:

- Things are temporary, people are forever.
- The most important people are your family.
- Are you somebody important to them?
- The next most important group of people is your team. Are you somebody important to them?
- Being somebody is being an example. Being a doer and doing it. Not just talking and thinking. I want everybody I come in contact with to feel important.
- Where did I get those feelings? Apparently, the coach, the hero that made me feel special. Both my mother and Coach Taylor. I didn't know how special those people were in my life until later.
- Coaches make people feel like they'll do something important with their life. They made me feel: *That I was different. That I was special. That I would make a difference with my life.*
- Nobody accomplishes anything significant on their own. They had somebody who cared about them, who said something special to them, who believed in them.
- I wanted to be that someone in the lives of others. To always be there in the tough times.
- I wanted to encourage them, to fight with them, to push them forward, to never give up on them.
- I wanted to be that someone who was willing to invest the time, one-on-one, build relationships, build friendships, that would last a lifetime.

"Men and women are searching for something exciting, something to feel passionate about, something to connect to." *(Kimbro, 2003)*

And finally...

The only true wealth is becoming somebody that you are proud of and living a life of purpose and meaning.

At A.L. Williams, Art wrote the desire to "be somebody" on our souls, and our lives were never the same. Under Art's leadership, those 13 words built a company that made history.

Chapter 5:

ART WILLIAMS: THE FIRST PHENOMENON

Who or what helped make Art the man who changed so many lives and revolutionized an industry?

People ask me all the time, "What's Art like?" Although there are many videos of Art speaking, nothing compares to meeting Art in person and, even better, having been around in the early days of A.L. Williams and knowing him as a leader and friend. We have bragging rights and we're proud of it.

Art was born in Waycross, Georgia on April 23, 1942. When he was one year old, his parents moved to Cairo, Georgia. Art's father was the head of a pickle factory in Cairo. He had coached for several years before his management job at the factory.

Art spoke about a person of influence in his family's life. "Mr. Roddenberry owned the pickle factory in Cairo. He helped a lot of people move forward in their careers. He paid for my father to get a master's degree in chemistry and my father eventually ran the pickle factory in Cairo. Mr. Roddenberry influenced hundreds of kids in Cairo." Art was always moved by people who helped others to succeed, even from his earliest days.

Cairo was a small town, like Mayberry, the fictional town of the television program *The Andy Griffith Show*. Mayberry is a term that's come to be used for an idyllic town with a wonderful father, cute son, wonderful friends, and quirky people, where everyone cares for each other. It was especially that way with Andy Griffith's TV son, Opie, played by the now legendary director, Ron Howard. Everyone in the town contributed to raising Opie through their personalities and interaction with him. In many ways Cairo, Georgia, had those same elements. It was a small town with one high school. All of us are shaped by our hometowns, and Art was, as well. Art took the lessons from his life and used them to shape his future outlook.

Art's father was a very private person, which was typical of that era, and was reluctant to throw out lots of compliments. It was characteristic of the times. His father came from the depression era when most families struggled just to survive. Art's mother Betty, however, was constantly telling Art how special he was. "I had great parents," Art said. "Many important life lessons came from them."

Art learned a lot of lessons in Cairo that would shape him throughout his life. Art recalled how getting a car in high school impacted his future beliefs. "My father bought me a used car when I was 15," Art recalls. "I learned how ownership is a tremendous motivator. At ALW I wanted people to know they *own* their business." Art's life ultimately took him from Cairo, Georgia to world-altering achievements and international admiration.

Who Were Art Williams' Heroes?

Art's parents were his earliest heroes. When he started playing sports, he found two other heroes that would be long-lasting in his life, as well.

Art explained that everyone needs a third-party person, other than parents, to make a difference in their life. It is expected from the parents but can be life-changing when it's from another adult. That's where Art's coaches came in. They were instrumental in his life.

One of the biggest influences in Art's life was Coach Tommy Taylor.

"I met Tommy Taylor when I was in the third grade. I played all of the sports for him. Cairo was an athletic town. I worked for him in the recreation department in the fifth grade through college."

Tommy Taylor was a coach in Cairo who became a personal life coach to Art. Tommy was a California native and a spectacular athlete. He became a pole vaulter for the University of

Florida and a pitcher for an amateur fast pitch softball team, the South Georgia All-Stars, and was deemed the world's greatest fast pitch baseball pitcher for several years. As the Cairo Recreation Director and the Head Football Coach at Cairo High School, he built a sports dynasty: 14 state championships in football, softball, track, and swimming, receiving 32 Coach of the Year awards. But according to those he coached, his greatest accomplishment was the lives he influenced and changed.

Art said that "Coach Taylor had a gift to see in people things they didn't know they had." Art started working with the coach at a local pool. "He let me know I could do something special with my life. My passion in life was to make kids and others feel like he made me feel. He taught me that you can never give kids and people too much esteem and positivity. He gave me a belief in *me*."

At the dedication of Tommy Taylor Day on May 8, 1993, Art contributed a special passage to a brochure honoring Coach Taylor. He said, "Coach Taylor was like my second dad. He was the most important person in my life next to my parents! I don't know of any coach, teacher, pastor, businessperson, anyone, who meant more or changed more lives than Coach Taylor. He will never know how truly special he was to so many young people and young athletes. What he taught all of us who were fortunate enough to have him be a part of our lives will be passed on to future generations. He was the ultimate coach. He was and is simply the best. Today, I still call him to share my life and ask advice. He continues to motivate and coach me. I love you, Coach."

Tommy Taylor joined Art at Waddell & Reed in 1976 in Tallahassee. Art knew that it would be very risky for Tommy to join ALW because of Tommy's age and health at the time (he'd had heart by-pass surgery). After starting A.L. Williams, Art met with Tommy in a restaurant in Tallahassee and said, "Tommy, I can't let you come with us because the odds are against us making it and you could get hurt. Tommy went into the bathroom and starting crying," Art said. Tommy ended up staying with Waddell & Reed.

Art's other mentor was also a coach. Coach West Thomas was the football coach in Baxley, Georgia from 1951-1954, winning an incredible 117 games, with 38 losses and 11 ties. In addition, he coached girls' basketball, and he served as assistant principal from 1956 to 1972.

He later went back to coaching in neighboring counties and returned to Cairo to coach football in 1976 and became Assistant Athletic Director at Cairo High School from 1979 until his retirement in 1983. He was known for his love of coaching, and his ability to lead young players to become the best they could be. Art revered Coach Thomas as his mentor and teacher and credits the lessons learned from him in helping him achieve success in his coaching and business careers.

Art attended college at Mississippi State in Starkville, MS, where he played quarterback his junior year. He dropped out of football to take an overload of classes so he could graduate in 1964. Lou Miller attended as well. Art later received a Master's in Science from Auburn University. After graduating, Art returned to Cairo, where he began his coaching career. Art felt like he was home. He had never wanted to be anything but a coach, like his dad and Coach Taylor, and he acquired a reputation for being a great one.

In the meantime, Art married Angela Hancock. "I fell in love with Angie in the second grade," Art loved to say. They had two children, April and Arthur L. Williams III. Despite his business success, Art always placed his priorities as God first, family second, and business third.

Art was unprepared for the shock of his father dying suddenly of a heart attack at 48 years of age. The financial and emotional struggle Art's mother had with only $10,000 of whole life insurance to support herself and Art's two younger brothers poured the foundation of a crusade that would later change his life and millions of others.

Art Was Always a Coach at Heart

Art was a coach before he ever heard of "buy term and invest the difference." In Thomasville, Georgia, his first coaching jobs, his talent became obvious, and people noticed.

Art said "I loved Thomasville. We lost in the final state championship game to a school from Atlanta, St. Pius. We beat them with every statistic except on the scoreboard, the only one that matters. After two years I thought I was ready to be a head football coach.

Art achieved that dream when he was only 24 years old. Baxley, Georgia would be his next stop. According to Art, "Their search committee called Coach West Thomas, my high school coach, and he recommended me, and they hired me. It was very unusual to get a head football coach's job after only two years as an assistant coach. Coach Thomas had had the last winning season at Baxley 20 years earlier, so they thought some of his magic had rubbed off on me."

Baxley was a town of just 9,500 people in rural Georgia, but it was a football town. A man named Mickey Lewis was on the coach committee. His wife Jean recalls, "Mickey called me and told me to come home because he had brought the cutest woman with two cute kids with him to their house and her husband was going be the next football coach in Baxley." Jean said that Art could have owned the town because he was successful so quickly. They had not had a winning season in over 20 years. Jean would go on to say, "Angela was a key player. She organized the High Steppers cheerleading group and became very much a part of the community. Art and Angela were very popular. They were highly respected, and Angela was a strong person behind Art as a coach. Art was more than a coach. I am richer today for knowing Art and Angela. They flew in for my husband's funeral. Who they are really shows. Art had a very huge impact on the boys in Baxley and he taught things beyond football; he taught them about life."

Dale Atkins was a receiver and defensive back on Art's Baxley team in 1966 and 1967. In those two years, Art took a team that had not won anything in 20 years and made them winners. Dale said that Art was the greatest motivator he had ever seen. But Art was tough. "For spring practice, he had a goal of getting rid of all the quitters," Dale said. "Art would say, 'We are going to eliminate the quitters and what's left will be winners.' We started out with 90 players and were down to 30 by the time spring practice was over."

Dale especially recalled that Angela was the backbone of Art. "She was the strength behind his program. She was extremely supportive behind the scenes."

Lou Miller was Art's assistant coach at the time. He said, "Art always talked about winning and beating the number one team in the state."

Dale went on to say, "We thought the coach had lost it at this time. He thinks we can be the number one team in the state of Georgia? By game time we believed we could beat them, and we did, 14 to 13. If we had a bad Friday night, that Monday practice would be tough. He was a fanatic at doing it right. We ran plays over and over until they were right. After practice we would do wind sprints to be in better shape and to get us mentally ready. If Art said, 'Climb that light pole,' we believed we could do it." They all could see that Art loved it. In their senior year they beat the number one team in the state.

"Art was famous for saying, 'Give me ten more minutes at the end of practice.' Then he would say, 'Give me 10 more minutes.' When asked if the 10 minutes were up, he would say, 'That's not what my watch is telling me.' We thought, 'This man is crazy. He's a wild man.'"

Dale mentioned that almost all of Art's players had post-high school football successes in life. "He taught them not to quit anything, to work hard and good things would happen. He told them to always be prepared so you can do your job and win. Art taught that life is a game, and the game is to beat the opponent. He would constantly say, 'We are better than they are; never give up.' Art built character in us and told us to always do what is right. We were all fortunate that he passed our way when we were young enough to learn something from it."

"We remember Art telling us that if we got hurt that we would have to run off the field because he didn't want to waste a timeout on us. One time our center broke his leg and had to limp off the field. Another time a linebacker got bitten by a bee and his face was swollen to the extent that he couldn't see or put a helmet on. He said to Coach Art, 'I can't play because I can't see.' Art said 'Put that helmet on. If you can play without being able to see, imagine how good you could play when you can see.'"

Art's team in Baxley had not had a winning season for years, and they were playing the number one team in Georgia, Waycross High School. Waycross had a nose guard on their team who would eventually become an All-American at Florida State University. He weighed 220 pounds and would be going against Baxley's 165-pound center. They had a running back who weighed 195 pounds and was a pure animal. Art and his assistant coach, Lou Miller, went to watch them play the week before. Art said, "Lou, it will be a moral victory if we can just keep it within a 20-point loss." They had eight assistant coaches and Art had one. Everyone thought it was impossible to beat them. But they did.

The same thing happened when Art was at Kendrick High School in Columbus, Georgia. Art's team only had freshman and sophomores at the school, but the other teams were playing seniors. His first year he had a losing record of 4-6.

But Art knew it would be okay because he had some good kids coming up the next year and they went 9-1. The following year, in 1969, they went 12–0 and were one of the final four teams in the state. They ended up playing Valdosta, who had won a national championship the year before. There were 25,000 people in attendance at the game. Valdosta had not been scored on in the eight previous games. Art's team took a 14 -0 lead in the first half, but they would eventually be outmanned and would lose 28 to 14.

All this adversity and struggle as a coach, and all the impossible odds Art's teams faced, prepared Art for the fight of his life — the fight for his company's right to exist. As in ALW, there were a lot of impossible problems that came their way and, like ALW, they eventually won.

Maybe now we can understand why Art said, "I wanted to build a company like I built a football team."

Dale said, "Even to this day if I listen to an Art Williams tape, I get so fired up that I'd like to put on a uniform and play for him again."

Years later Art called Dale and said, "I'm going out on my own and starting my own company." Dale responded, "I don't like life insurance." Today Dale says, "It was a major mistake not joining up."

Art never planned to be anything but a winning coach. He planned to move higher up the coaching chain, maybe all the way to the pros. When he began selling insurance, it was just to make a little part-time income in the summers when school was out. When he discovered he could make more selling insurance than any other way, he began what would become his new passion. But he never thought so at the time. In fact, he wasn't even very good at it early on.

"It wasn't easy," recalls Art. "All I heard the first two years was 'No, no thank you, no, I changed my mind.' It was killing me and keeping me from the crusade. It seemed like my ego was crushed every day. As a football coach, I was esteemed in my community. Once I got into the insurance business, people didn't look at me like they did when I was a football coach. That really bothered me. It took me five months to get my term insurance license and mutual fund license. I didn't want to sell. I wasn't a salesperson. I always thought of myself as a coach. Coaches need people. Living off of commissions is a ball buster."

As quoted in *Locker Room Notes*, Art took the struggle hard. Art recalled saying to himself, "Art, you're such a dud. What's wrong with you? Why did you say the third sentence? It was so stupid. Art, how could you mess it up so bad? Why don't you admit it? People like you aren't supposed to make it. Just throw in the towel. Go back and coach football for a living." Success was far from immediate.

"Victory came tough for me," Art said. "Sales came difficult for me. When people said no, it tore my heart out. When people didn't want to join or they quit, it tore my heart out. I took the business seriously. The first year I was sick, frustrated and eaten up with it. I'd say to myself, 'Art, you are such a dog. You aren't any good.' I spent my whole insurance career before A.L. Williams saying to myself, 'You are such a dud.'"

Art started selling in 1967. "I was at Kendrick high school from 1967 to 1969. I was at ITT from 1966 to 1968.

Art knew his talents. " My gift was motivating people and identifying special people," Art said. That trait, along with his super-sized determination, made him successful, even though he didn't like selling insurance.

"Angela thinks I'm a little OCD," Art said. " When I get into something I don't let go and have a one-track mind. I'm the kind of person who, when I make a decision, I work hard to make it right." Then an event happened that reminded Art of why he had gotten into the insurance business: his crusade.

"Two years after I started, I paid a death claim. I thought, 'This stuff really works,' and I never looked back from that powerful moment." From that point on, Art was committed to the crusade like never before.

Going to a Napoleon Hill seminar was another defining moment in Art's life. "He taught that every successful person did six things to succeed financially. My goal was to have $300,000 accumulated. I thought I could 'kill it' for 10 years and be set for life. That motivated me."

Art's success didn't go unnoticed at his part-time job. "The president of ITT talked to me and really pressed me to go full-time. I was the highest paid person at ITT in Columbus." However, going full-time met with resistance.

"All of my family was frustrated and worried about me going full-time. I was shocked to hear that. They didn't want me to do it. They kept telling me not to throw away my coaching career. I drove down to Cairo and asked Coach Tommy Taylor what he thought I should do. He said that I should try it. With my credibility in coaching, I could always get a job if it didn't work out. That convinced me. Angela never showed disappointment to me. That $42,000 I had made and accumulated was our comfort zone."

Once Art made the decision, he was all in. "I learned some great lessons," Art said. "I learned to live for those who stay and fight. I made up my mind I was going to go for it. I'd been playing small, and I was finished with it. I quit running. I decided, I'm settling right here. I will do it or not do it with A.L. Williams. I am not going anywhere. I was put on this earth to be somebody. I want to be somebody so bad it hurts inside. This is my chance. If I lose, I am going down fighting with A.L. Williams." We realized that going "all in" was the secret for us.

Art Was a Force of Nature

We've all heard that term "Force of nature." It is an idiom. To say a person is a force of nature means that person conveys a very strong personality or character — like a hurricane or a tsunami are also forces of nature — full of energy, unstoppable, formidable, and unforgettable. In short, a person to be reckoned with. Doesn't that explain Art? He'd walk into a room and his personality would fill it. It is best explained in a quote of his regarding stockbrokers and the Wall Street types. He said, "The people who used to intimidate me, I now intimidate," even though, as they wore their three-piece suits and Gucci shoes, Art wore a coach's jogging outfit.

The moment he walked into their auditorium to present the story of A. L. Williams you could almost hear the smugness. When he opened his mouth and out came his South Georgia twang, their eyebrows raised. When he said his first "y'all," you could imagine their thoughts on Art's "hokeyness." Then when he bellowed out his beliefs, his crusade, how he felt about his company, how they would "right wrongs and correct injustices," and the sheer growth numbers, those listening moved from skeptics to believers. They moved from crossed arms, leaning back in their chairs, judging him and his company harshly, to hands on their mouths, sitting on the edge of their seats, mesmerized, and enthralled by what he and his company had accomplished and were prepared to accomplish in the future. His "force of nature" changed the minds of the buttoned-down, bottom-line types to warm, excited listeners who didn't want to miss out on being involved with A.L. Williams. The force of nature changed Wall Street like he changed the coaches, teachers, and average-and-ordinary people he attracted.

Art has been called a "human dynamo." But that's not a good phrase to explain Art. A dynamo is a forceful, energetic individual. It describes a whirling dervish or a Tasmanian devil that has excess energy with no purpose or direction. Art walked fast, talked with a purpose, and acted with a desired outcome. He put in us an engine of his making that sustained us during rejection, fear, frustration, fatigue, and those ever-present chargebacks. That engine took us from a 4-cylinder to an 8-cylinder turbo-charged recruiting and selling blitz.

Art Was an Original

Art was an original in a world of corporate and leadership clones.

In sports, people try to compare one player to another. Art was unrivaled, transcending any examples of leadership I have ever seen. If anything, he was a mix of General Patton, Bear Bryant, Rambo, and Mister Rogers. Yes, Mr. Rogers. He was a "take no prisoners" leader with an ability to connect with his people on a deep level.

As Henry David Thoreau, the nineteenth-century writer, stated, "If a man does not keep pace with his companions, perhaps it is because he hears the beat of a different drummer." *(Walden, 2004)* Art's rhythm, the beat he heard, was more intense than most. This can be seen by his endless writing of letters to us. He called them "go-go letters" because he would sign them "Go-Go-Go! Art". He sent dozens of letters every day encouraging his players to charge forward. To this day when I walk into an office, I see on the wall where people framed every one they received. These became treasures to us because the world is void of encouragement, direction, or praise.

After Art retired, we would get faxes from him with the same encouragement.

He now owns a resort hotel in North Carolina, and he sends letters to all 500 of his "associates," not employees, and once a week he takes cookies to one of his managers. Can you imagine the corporate titans of today doing that?

People look to see what made us a legendary organization. We needed a kick-butt leader like Bear Bryant, but also one that held us in the palm of his hand with tenderness, with an authentic sense that he cared how all areas of our lives turned out. He famously said, "If you win in business but lose your family you are a loser."

Art's words, with his deep Southern accent, sometimes needed subtitles for those not raised in the Deep South, but whatever he said stuck. He wasn't the prototypical CEO of a major NYSE company. He was down to earth, real, and with his blue eyes and ever-present smile, he charmed crowds of 50,000 people. And his laugh! When he laughed, his whole body would shake. No room was big enough to hold his personality. They call it charisma, but we called it passion.

Art Was a Master of Relationships

Art mastered building relationships. As Bill Whittle would say "He put his hand on our hearts and massaged it with his words, recognition and deep caring spirit." Art always said, "You win the heart, and you win the man."

Art loved the famous Vince Lombardi saying, "You win with your heart not your head." His success showed how to build, not a business but a movement. To beat the insurance industry business acumen wasn't needed. What was needed was "heart power." Art gave us his heart and in return we gave him ours.

Art was only truly understood by his people. His unique style appealed to a slice of America that sided with his fervent distaste for corporate America and their elitist way of life. Art built a counterculture away from being yes-men and urged us to think bigger, want to build a legacy for ourselves and not some name on a building. He wanted us to pay the price for our families not some board of directors. He wanted us to fight to be financially independent and not cower to some "suit" who looked down on rebels like us.

I can see him in front of a podium with his tee-shirt that said "BEAT PRU" on it, saying "Hey, hey, hey, y'all listen! HEY"! Then he would take his thumb and seemingly screw it into the podium, twisting it back and forth all the while saying, "You don't want anybody's thumb on you, telling you what to do, deciding your future, deciding where you live and telling you aren't good enough. You've got to fight for what you want." Then came the hammer of his legendary saying: "One day they are going to be patting your face with a shovel and on your tombstone will be DUD or STUD. Hey! Hey! It's your dadgum LIFE! Your dadgum LIFE! You got to want it bad. It's how bad you want it! How much you love it!" His face was contorted, and smoke was coming out of his eyes and ears, and he *electrified* us.

Art could come across as a tough butt. His behavior came across to some people as harsh. But how many people who go on to achieve greatness in any endeavor come across as well-adjusted and completely rational? Art had an edge like few others. He used that edge like the football coach he was.

I remember a scene from Patton when an officer questioned General Patton because the troops never quite know whether he is serious or just acting. Patton responded that it was on purpose, to keep them on the fighting edge they needed to conquer the enemy. Art loved hating the enemy. It gave him material to use to rouse the inner crusade in us. "Us against them" was his forte. He was tough and he was resilient.

We All Needed a Coach Like Art

Art built A.L. Williams in a different way. His approach to building it helped it become one of the largest, most successful companies in financial services. He found that the principles that build a successful team would also work to build a successful business. After all, Art's genius wasn't building businesses - he had never built one before. His genius was building winning teams.

A major influence in Art's life was Winston Churchill. "Winston Churchill was the greatest person in the last 100 years in England. He saved England from Germany," Art said. Art noted that Churchill's passion under fire motivated the British throughout the tough times. "What got me through the difficult times was my passion for what we did," Art said. "I made a lot of stupid calls in my life, but I believed in what we were doing."

Art explains why he loved it so much. "Some of the biggest thrills I've had in my life was taking a group of kids and building a team, bringing out and developing the strengths of each individual and leading them to victory. I used the same principles to build people in business, coaching them and motivating them to believe in themselves, to work on skills to perfection and celebrate their victories, recognizing each individual and making them feel like true winners, in business and in life. Seeing people reach their business goals was what I loved the most. A slogan I always lived by is 'I don't promise you it is going to be easy; I just promise you that it is going to be worth it.' I always look at my life as a coach in football and business as one that built people that had a confidence and knowledge to win big.'"

Art created a company of coaches. His teachings and philosophies are still coaching people today through YouTube and his books. Looking back, all the A.L. Williams leaders can't believe we were lucky enough to have Art Williams as a coach. Everyone needs a coach like Art.

Art Was Intrepid

It was impossible to stop Art. He was resolute, fearless and had the endurance to go all the way. "Don't pick a fight you don't intend to finish." Art said. A.L. Hodge said, "It is easier to find a score of men wise enough to discover the truth than to find one intrepid enough, in the face of opposition, to stand up for it." (*Hodge, 2022*) Art was that person.

BTID was not invented by Art, only discovered. As the above quote indicates, there were other insurance people who believed in it. There were 6-10 companies who were proponents of it, like ITT, Waddell & Reed, and others, but none of them made a stand until Art came along. Can you imagine what it took to shake a fist at the powerful insurance empire with all the money, all the influence, all the lawyers and say, "Your day is over?" That's intrepid.

Art Was Magical

Art was a magical person, truly magical. He loved taking us to magical places and watching our faces as he and Angela introduced us to another world we didn't know existed. When you think of Art, you think of whole life versus term, A.L. Williams, an old football coach. Those who knew him think of him as a person who loved what he did and hated leaving people behind with their dying dreams and hopeless futures. He loved and lived taking people, as he would say, "to places they couldn't take themselves." He said, "I want to take you to travel the world. "And he did.

I remember when we were in Europe on some fancy boat, sitting on an upper deck. One of us said, "Art, isn't it amazing that people like us are on a boat like this?" Art responded, "Let me tell you something. This boat was made for somebody's ass to be sitting on it; it might as well be our asses." That was typical Art. He taught us to believe we *deserved* to have the best.

Art had an unmatched sparkle. He lived his ALW life like a kid in a candy store. He used to say "The NFL, the NBA,

Major League Baseball aren't the big leagues. Your *life* is the big leagues." Art played this game like he coached football.

One of Art's heroes was General George Patton. A quote that explains Art's sparkle about ALW can be compared with the quote by Patton, "Compared to war, all other forms of human endeavor shrink to insignificance. God help me, I do love it so." Art's war was his battle with the insurance industry. Art would say, "You can't just want it, you've got to love it." From February 10, 1977, until he left the company on July 1, 1990, his energy thrived in the hearts and minds of the tens of thousands of people that put on the ALW uniform.

It's a common refrain among his admirers: there was something – an inner light – that came out of Art that made it impossible not to listen to him, and that made him more than the sum of his individual talents. As one person said, "People like him don't come around often, but I'm glad it was during my lifetime." You had to see Art own the audience when he spoke. No speaker touched people where they lived more than Art. He brought you into his mind, his heart, his passion, and his vision. You knew he was the real deal.

Art had what people call the "IT" Factor. It's that "certain something," that nearly indefinable quality that certain people have that, no matter how they look, causes people to be drawn to them. It's a combination of confidence and charisma. Not only did Art have the "IT" factor, but he had an amazing ability to use his charisma to move people to act. We all know someone like that. There's something about them that makes them stand out, "like a bonfire at midnight," and attracts people, seemingly without conscious effort, something that's absolutely magnetic. (*Nerdlove,* 2013) According to life coach Sue Henry, it's more like the "invisible thing a person has that makes them stand out in any crowd." (*Henry 2022)* Her definition of the "IT" factor consists of three main points:

- Confidence with humility
- Genuine interest in others

- A personal mission or "why" that is bigger than them.

Whatever you call "IT", Art had "IT" and then some. Charismatic people are wonderful to be around and tend to lead successful lives. I can't think of anyone that fits that description more than Art.

He Spoke from the Heart

His speaking went to the heart because it came from the heart. Art was a man you could trust. He said what he meant, and he meant what he said. He could often have a tough exterior, but his heart was always tender.

In an industry that had a questionable reputation, Art changed the dynamic. Life insurance salesmen are down at the bottom of the list of respectability, along with used car salesmen. I saw a Gallup survey that looked at different professions in terms of integrity, believability, and trustworthiness. The only ones below insurance agents were Congressmen and car salesmen.

Art changed all that by recruiting quality people who reflected his view.

Abraham Lincoln explained, "In order to win a man to your cause, you must first reach his heart, the great high road to his reason."

Art could be summed up by this observation of Lincoln, "From the beginning to the end, he impressed upon the people the conviction of his honesty and fidelity to one great purpose." *(Goodwin, 2013)*

Art not only spoke from the heart, but his words meant something. Art gave all of himself to those who believed in him. He was a master at speaking and when he spoke the words penetrated. Most people automatically go through life being influenced and not being an influencer. It's easier. Art created an atmosphere and a culture with his talks, passion, crusade, and belief. His talks gave hope to a generation. Many people who joined quit, but they never forgot how they felt after hearing Art speak. For those of us who managed to have dreams that lifted us from the accepted life created for us by others, Art saw greatness in us stemming from the greatness of his cause. His powerful words transported us from accepting "common" to demanding "extraordinary." His passion penetrated so we could no longer not try, not "go for it," not stand back and let the ALW ship go on without us.

When Art spoke, we would feel this passion rising up deep inside. Think Friday night football game, think big basketball game, think tennis match, think your child playing a sport, think how you felt hearing Lee Greenwood sing "I'm Proud to be An American" or hearing a rousing sermon at church. I've seen grown men tear up listening to Art. His passion touched a nerve. His hope-giving message promising a better life was like rainfall to parched ground.

We didn't idolize Art, but we did need his inspiration, his "can do" spirit, his locker room half-time winning talk, his belief. In a world without much encouragement or even positivity, Art's talks were a respite from most people's daily doldrums from dead-end jobs, bad bosses and a life filled with mediocrity. It was like catching lightning in a bottle. Art was an engineer of men's hearts. He saw greatness in people before they knew it themselves.

If you have never experienced dreams of greatness, it could be difficult to understand what this means. However, if you ever caught a glimpse of your life as it could be, Art's talks fed your soul. So many people hunger for that long-gone high school "Friday night feeling," when the future was full of promise, when they thought they could conquer the world, before reality beat them up and left them questioning whether they had what it takes.

Every boy and girl needs an adult to tell them what's possible, and Coach Art was that substitute. Look at the phenomenon Art created and notice how many lives he touched. South Florida's Greg Fitzpatrick tells the story of a real estate manager of over 200 offices that accidentally found Art speaking on YouTube. "At least once a month that manager plays the 'just do it' talk to all of his people."

Greg continued, "Art's iconic statements, 'Be somebody; You are only here for a flicker; I don't know why but my butt's always burning; Everybody wants to be somebody,' became the soundtrack of our lives. They became the power in how we lived our lives, in our decision-making, our choices, how we raised our families, who we chose to listen to and our religious faith determination.

Greg talks about how much we want to be special. "I can't tell you how many times I've sat in an Art meeting with this prayer on my lips, 'Dear God, please let me hear it this time.' I was not alone. It's the old adage, 'When the student is ready the teacher (coach) appears.' But no one is ready immediately; it comes slowly.

"In coaching others, we say, 'If I'm not constantly quoting Art don't listen to me.' His words are definitive for the best life possible. Why? He's the "constant coach" everyone needs.

"When Art speaks it's similar to having a private tutor, mentor, coach, because each word he speaks seems to be customized just for me. Those life-changing words are molded specifically for my dreams, my goals, my legacy, my destiny. That's the architecture of Art's word, to create a vision that morphs into an individualized vision."

This quote sums up Art's heart when he speaks, "I've learned that people will forget what you said, people will forget what you did, but people will never forget how you made them feel." *(Angelou, 2022)*

Art Had Character

Art used to say, "You can spot a phony a mile away." He cautioned us to be our authentic selves. He knew that the right kind of people are smart. They can sniff out a phony. Eventually, they see inside a person, into who that person is. We followed Art because we saw what was inside of him. His integrity, how he treated Angela, how he was aboveboard, and his honesty are all legendary.

One time, I noticed that my pay statement was wrong, and Art had gotten my override. I called his accountant, Ted Harrison. The amount was $500 but, having fun with Ted, I said it was $5,000. Ted called me back and said, 'If you say that's the amount then Art trusts you, so I will send the check.' Of course, I immediately corrected the amount. Art trusted us because we trusted him.

Will you stand up and show us what you are made of? Art didn't specifically say these words, but he implied them when he told us to "Stand for something. Life won't give you what you want, but what you are willing to fight for." Those became fighting words. A battle cry for the superhero inside every person. A call to arms asking us to search our souls to find the fortitude we would need to fight the insurance industry and the demon of discouragement we all possess. It's like he drew the proverbial line in the sand for us to make a commitment to make our lives count. Art said, "The character I most admired in any of the RVPs and managers was honesty, complete commitment, and a positive attitude about handling any decisions or changes we made in the home office from products or compensation or challenges we faced – and we faced a lot of challenges."

"Mensch" is a Yiddish word meaning a person of integrity and honor. That's how Art was. He was a person everybody wanted to be around. Many old-timers would talk about a special moment with Art. When a top RVP in the company retired, he was asked what he would be doing. He said, "I'm going to be Art Williams' friend." It was not uncommon to brag to people that you had talked with Art or if he visited your house you bragged, "Art and Angela slept here." A common joke is, how many RVPs does it take to change a lightbulb? Answer: Three! One to change the bulb and two to talk about how Art would have done it."

Art Was Authentic

Art was authentic. He was a *real* person who never tried to be someone he wasn't. According to Breńe Brown, "Authenticity is the daily practice of letting go of who we think we're supposed to be and embracing who we are." *(Brown, 2020)*

An authentic person is a rare person. E.E. Cummings wrote, "To be nobody but yourself in a world which is doing its best, night and day, to make you everybody but yourself, means to fight the hardest battle which any human being can fight and never stop fighting. 'Staying real' is one of the most courageous battles that we'll ever fight."

What Jesse Jackson said about entertainer Sammy Davis could be said about Art. "Sammy was not the first of his kind," Jackson said. "Nor will he be the last of his kind. Sammy will go down as the *only* one of his kind!" (*Kimbro, 2003)*

The insurance industry could not pigeonhole Art. He could not be defined as they thought he should. He was feisty, unyielding to corporate hogwash; he never kowtowed or pandered to the corporate elite.

There was an executive at Waddell & Reed named Bob who annoyed Art with his superior attitude, always trying to make sure Art knew who the boss was. We were in Panama City, Florida for an event Art had for his region. The story goes that Bob disagreed with Art and told Art so. Art later was in an elevator with Bob's underling and told him to tell Bob "Where to go." Art later said that it was the straw that broke the camel's back. That's when he decided he had to break away and run the show himself. He was authentic and could not be what they wanted him to be if he was in fear of losing his paycheck.

Someone once said, "What a tragedy to climb the ladder of success, only to discover that the ladder was leaning against the wrong wall!" Art had to find another wall, his wall. And A.L. Williams was the way he did it.

Florida pioneer Nick Alise described this well. "My first Art sighting was in 1978. I had just joined ALW, and Bob & Greg had me all psyched to meet the founder of the company. Friday night at 6 p.m. I'm waiting for this 6′ 3″ guy in a three-piece suit, and out walks Art in a bright satin baseball jacket with 'DO IT' across the front! I liked him already, then he started talking, and immediately I knew he was a good guy, and I could trust him. He just sounded like a coach I wish I'd had in high school or college!"

"On another Atlanta trip, we went to Art's home in Monroe, and he and Angela gave us the grand tour of their home, just like Becky and I did when we bought our present home. When we won our first Europe trip, Art invited me to run with him, and as we were walking back to the hotel, Art stops and picks up a penny from the ground. I said, 'Art, I thought I was the only one who did that!' He says, 'I always pick up money laying on the ground.' After Art left the company, I continued to write to him. He would write back immediately, just like the GO, GO, GO, letters he used to send all through the '80s! When Becky's dad died in 1992 (a period when Art was going through his most difficult time) we got a call from Angela, asking if they could come by the house. They drove from Palm Beach to our home and brought a big dish of Angela's homemade banana pudding and spent a couple of hours just sitting and talking. How is that for authentic? They are the greatest ever. I'm tearing up as I'm writing this now."

"Just a few years ago, Art was in Palm Beach and called to ask me to find a local hotel for him to speak at. He and Angela spoke to about 500 or 600 of our top people, and he paid the $2,000 for the room. People flew in just to hear him; then they sat for another hour as each couple, or team of people, came up to get a picture with them. A week later Art called and asked if he could take Becky and me to dinner for organizing the meeting. We took them to our favorite Italian restaurant, five minutes from our house. They couldn't finish all the food and asked for a container to take the leftovers home! Art and Angela have plenty of wealthy Palm Beach friends, but always feel more comfortable with ALW people. We love them, and regularly send them messages telling them how wonderful our life is because of them!"

What Was Art's Superpower? A Stubborn Streak

He built a company his way, and his ways became

timeless to us all. As Mark Batterson would say, "It's a sanctified stubborn streak that doesn't allow us to give up!" (*Houston, 2017*) He planted his flag.

A person's strength can also be their weakness. When Art made up his mind and called a play he never looked back. I remember when he talked about Jimmy Carter and his inability to call a play. He said that as a coach you had 30-40 seconds to call a play. You didn't have the luxury of calling a committee together or taking a poll of the fans to analyze all the variables. That's why Art hated second guessers or Monday morning quarterbacking. He disliked politicians and professors. They criticized businessmen on what they should or shouldn't have done, but never had the courage to strike out on their own or call a play and make it work; he called them "mealy mouths."

As Teddy Roosevelt said, "It is not the critic who counts; not the man who points out how the strong man stumbles, or whether the doer of deeds could have done them better. The credit belongs to the man who is actually in the arena, whose face is marred by dust, sweat and blood; who strives valiantly; who errs, who comes up short again and again, because there is no effort without error and shortcoming; but who does actually strive to do the deeds; who knows great enthusiasms, great devotions; who spends himself in a worthy cause; who, at the best, knows in the end the triumph of high achievement, and who, at the worst, even if he fails at least fails while daring greatly, so that his place shall never be with those cold and timid souls who neither know victory or defeat." *(Roosevelt, 2003)*

Art Could Be Tough

Art was an enigma at times. There were parts of his personality that were tough and angered those who didn't know the real Art. To say it nicely, he could get a bit chippy. Art was a coach and anyone that has ever had a coach worth a darn knows how tough a coach can be. If he was a coach on the field during a timeout, the music being played would need to be loud so no one would hear him "coaching up" his players. No great coaches are warm and fuzzy to the players. The profession demands harsh words and, at times, hurt feelings. For Art it was an overflow of passion. He was incredibly dedicated to the crusade and his enormous responsibility for the lives of all of us who made a huge commitment to follow him. Art was passionate about his mission, and that passion would spill over and could sometimes appear as being mean-spirited. Art was intense and that intensity was not for the faint of heart.

Just as Steve Jobs wanted to make "a dent in the universe" with his life, so did Art. Making that dent put Art into a full coaching mode. It was said about a certain record producer who was such a hard taskmaster, "He was an imperfect perfectionist." Art wasn't a perfectionist the way some look at perfectionism, but he was intense about his people's success and winning the insurance wars. As he said, "Rejection almost got me out of the business until I paid a death claim."

Our business wasn't do or die, but if we didn't, the widow and her kids would struggle unnecessarily.

Art said in *Locker Room Notes,* "Build your strengths, bury your weaknesses." Winning was everything, and it was necessary because failure meant the continuation of the whole life industry. It's easy to criticize leaders when they are tough, gritty and firebrands. Remember, Art was more coach than President and CEO. Presidents are managers who have been handed a business that has already been built. Art was a fighter who had to keep his team fighting with him. He was a general and we were his army. He was George Patton. He was Winston Churchill. As Churchill said after the miracle at Dunkirk, "Never in the field of human conflict has so much been owed by so many to so few." (*Churchill, Wikipedia, 2022)* Art led us, the few, to the glory of "Beating Pru."

Coming late to an RVP meeting was like coming late to football practice. Art would let you know using the necessary coach-speak what he thought. He was kind, generous, a motivator, but he could be tough. One of my RVPs was at an RVP meeting that had microphones set up to ask questions. The old guard knew better than to even think of a question. My new RVP asked a question and Art responded, "That's the dumbest question I've ever heard." My RVP humbly went back to his seat. He smiled and said, "Art recognized me. I'm now in the "Art Williams Hall of Shame." You've not lived until you've been picked on by Art. Tough leaders can be harsh at times, but Art was always fair. His purpose was to make you and the team better.

Someone once said, he was a Boy Scout who knew how to street fight for the sake of his people when he needed to.

Art Was a Misfit

We didn't always believe, but Art believed it with his whole heart, and we couldn't stay away.

Magnetic! Passionate! Mesmerizing! Biting! Honest! And oh, so colorful! When Art spoke, it felt like he was talking directly to the heart of each person. He touched the mind, but especially the soul. He gave hope and direction to accomplish hidden, long-ago forgotten dreams and ambitions. We not only heard him, but we also felt him. His words penetrated and cut through the clutter of beliefs that had invaded us when we were unsuspecting and naive. We loved his straightforward talk that exposed the hypocrisy of the elites of the world, those with big mouths and big opinions.

Art was a misfit, talking to misfits, speaking the language of misfits, and giving his brand of misfits a belief that resonated deep inside of us. With his Southern drawl he was laughed at by Wall Street, maligned by the industry, ridiculed by *Barron's* magazine, banned from joining country clubs, but he relished every moment of his maverick image. Art took pride in being the anti-hero.

He and Angela lived in Snellville, Ga. for a while. His attempt to infiltrate the business world was viewed as laughable until he did it. Art was like the military leader, Napoleon, who didn't fit the prototypical model. But when Art spoke, our worlds moved. He didn't just speak, he captured. His words wrapped around our hearts and minds and etched themselves in our souls. He was the Billy Graham of our crusade. He was the Knute Rockne, and we were his team. He made our hearts race with promise, and our minds imagine a new world for ourselves and others.

He'd say, "Just do it," three words and we knew exactly what they meant. "You know what?" would stir thousands to respond "What?" He was the light, and we were the moths. We would always fight the fight because he fought it with us. We had a special language that we all understood.

He Was Revolutionary

Art's bold vision for our future was grafted into our hearts in ways that will be forever remembered.

"Successful revolutions are inspired by revolutionary leaders. Revolutionary messages are, at their core, always about freedom." *(Hebel, 2011)*

A revolution needs a common enemy, and that enemy was the insurance industry. We wanted to "knock them out," as Art said in his iconic talks. Or as Harold Schultz said, "When you're surrounded by people who share a passionate commitment around a common purpose, anything is possible." *(Schultz, Quotefancy, 2022)*

Art had a compelling ability to talk about getting to the pot of gold at the end of the rainbow. Most people don't know how to follow rainbows, so this was a major revelation to us.

Art's Locker Room Was His Sanctuary

Art surrounded himself with those who were willing to join him in his worthy effort. We made Art proud. He delivered for us, and we delivered for him and the tens of thousands who have followed in his footsteps.

Art's sanctuary was his locker room and Art believed you win in the locker room first. The locker rooms of our company were the Fast Start Schools and meetings. Our presentation flip charts were our uniforms. We didn't even have a company logo when we first started, but ours was the kind that was invisible and tattooed on our souls. Our hearts were his heart, multiplied and unified. He called it one heartbeat. Loners become losers. Followers become financially independent. Art galvanized us into a perfect team. Individually, we struggled. Collectively, we fought an adversary and that made us more than we ever thought we could be.

He constantly talked about "having a goal of greatness." He inspired us to "see ourselves involved in something more than just our businesses."

When Jesus said, "The greatest among you will be your servant," that is what Art preached. Make a difference in the lives of others and, in Art's words, "You will build an empire."

Art Was Our Mentor and Our Lodestar

We all tried to be "little Arts," but we couldn't. Art was our "lodestar." He served as our inspiration, our model, and our guide. He told us constantly that he "wanted to create more financially independent people than any company on earth."

Everybody tries to be like their mentor, hero, idol. But they can't. We go through three stages: We imitate, we emulate, we hopefully equal and surpass.

We raved like him, we said "Dadgummit" like him, we tried to motivate our people like him, we chastised our people like him, we shamed people like him, and it always turned into a disaster. Art had a "cute" way of doing things that had his special never-to-be-copied fingerprints on them. When we said "Hey, hey," we sounded shallow. When we said, "Do you know what?" we got no response.

Art had an uncanny instinct for when and how to motivate that we lacked. Art knew the price to be paid for an outstanding life, a not-average-and-ordinary life, and a be-somebody life.

We owe Art our livelihoods, our legacies, our way of life, our dream-come-true existences. We could feel Art pushing us to be more of who we wanted to be. Like the famous quote from Tom

Landry on what is a coach: "A coach is someone who tells you what you don't want to hear, who has you see what you don't want to see, so you can be who you have always known you could be."

Art was our Mount Rushmore. He started small and evolved into a monument through his passion and relentless spirit. Mount Rushmore was made for immortal giants like Art who built the greatest financial services company in America and changed tens of thousands of lives.

We've all, at one time or another, through notes mostly, told Art how grateful we are for caring about us, having patience with us, bringing us kicking and screaming to a place that we only could dream about. Each note, each word we tried to squeeze in seemed trite because our gratitude could never be fully expressed. Without him where would we be today, what would our lives look like? I shudder to even think about it.

As one person described Art, "He was first thought of to be a star, but he created a constellation."

Art became the symbol on whom some people projected their beliefs, ideas, anger, conceptions, and misconceptions. But he was impervious to it all; he and his army stood steadfast in spite of the bullying we endured. When you know other people are right it's easy to attack them to take the focus off of yourself and what you do. Many in the insurance industry were examples of that by being "outraged" that Art challenged their character and products. We pushed and pushed rendering all those obstacles, all those judgmental words, utterly irrelevant. Art stood on the rock of truth and his convictions.

Art has become the biggest star in all our lives. He has been a superstar to us, and he has allowed us to shine in his afterglow.

Art Made People Feel Good

Art's spectacular life journey was centered on the way he always made people feel. Legendary leader Bill Whittle said that Art could "reach into your heart and massage it."

The one thread that describes Art is his caring spirit. When other business leaders left human carnage in their wake, Art built up men and women by filling a need, by true caring and concern. Art touched a nerve that few touch. Art built people, and a revolutionary business was the by-product.

As was said about Lincoln, "By calling these men to his side, Lincoln had afforded them an opportunity to exercise their talents to the fullest and to share in the labor and the glory of the struggle that would reunite and transform their country and secure their own places in posterity." Art also offered us an opportunity to change the world, to share in the struggle he faced, to fight the battle with him.

Author Walt Whitman said that he fancied that at some commemoration of those earlier days, an "ancient soldier" would sit surrounded by a group of young men whose eyes and "eager questions" would betray their sense of wonder." *(Goodwin, 2013)*

I remember our first ALW company retreat in June of 1977 at Unicoi State Park in North Georgia. After our daylong session, Art sat on a chair, and we surrounded him as Walt Whitman envisioned. We were in awe and wonder, thinking about our future and how our lives would turn out. We were young, had dreams, finally found our purpose, and had the leader to take us there. We were ready to fight and hungry for the battle.

As author John Eldridge said, "A man needs a battle to fight, an adventure to live, and a beauty to rescue." Our crusade through Art gave us that which would "transform our posterity." *(Eldridge, 2022)*

Art captured the spirit of caring. As Mr. Rogers would say, "I see you. You're important. I like you just the way you are." Art Williams said, "See every person as though they have a neon sign on their chest saying, 'Make me feel special.'"

Art endeared himself to thousands because he was not the aloof, above-it-all, distant executive that is unapproachable. Adults crave attention. Adults want to be touched, hugged, made a fuss over. I witnessed grown men cry and weep because Art put his arm around them, made them feel special and touched a deep part of their soul that had not been touched their whole lives. Art always said that recognition was not in the trophy, the plaque, or the award but in the words you say about people during the presentation. Kids cry out to their parents "Mommy, watch me. Look what I can do." They want to know that you think they are special. They ache to hear, "Wow, great job," and so do adults.

I remember the thrill of being in the audience and Art mentioning your name, or having your heart broken when he mentioned someone else. Maybe it's hero worship to need that "atta-boy," but it shows the void we all have, that hole in the heart that shouts out, as Art said, "Do you care about me? Am I important?"

He would say about recognition, "You need to spend three to five minutes saying nice things about people before the plaque is given." He knew plaques will be discarded, but the feelings won't.

Where did he learn caring? He said, "I want everybody I come in contact with to feel important." He learned it from the coach that modeled it and made him feel special, Coach Taylor.

"Coaches make people feel like they'll do something important with their life," Art said.

Art was not only in our businesses he was in our hearts. That was a flame that no amount of money or success could extinguish.

Art Was a Crusader to the Core

Art caused the crusade to be ingrained in the hearts of us all. He was a man who had a job to do and would bear anything to get it done, and he transferred that nerve to us.

Art was not afraid of criticism. He needed it to energize the crusade. Art used it all as "bulletin board material." He couldn't wait for the next article, the next savage condemnation, the next "them are fighting words" attack.

Art and his crusade captured our hearts. This quote from

Simon Sinek's book thoroughly explains ALW's unique feature that caused Art to say, "Capture the heart and you capture the man."

Sinek said, "Southwest was not built to be an airline. It was built to champion a cause. They just happened to use an airline to do it." ALW is the champion for the common man. Now that's a cause. And it's a cause looking for followers. As Sinek said, " Only when the WHY is clear and when people believe what you believe can a true loyal relationship develop." *(Sinek, 2017)*

Art defied the odds because that's what visionaries and crusaders do. Much like the bumblebee was not designed to fly, but still does, Art's plan worked, but no one gave it a chance. The concept was right, recruiting part-timers was right, the crusade was right, but it was funding that was in question. Art needed a deep pocket insurance company to fund us. Our crusade was not in question, the funding was. Those were the odds we fought. But Art defied them all.

Art Was an Opportunist

When his time came, he took it. His opportunity was the leverage of time. He could stay a football coach on one income for 40 years, or recruit and multiply to get thousands of Art clones to override. A similar example is Jerry Baldwin, Gordon Bowker, and Zev Siegl, academic friends who loved coffee and tea. They put their brains together and founded Starbucks. But it was Howard Schultz who saw the gap and realized that coffee "experiences" were the underserved market. Then they built the brand to its undreamed-of potential of 36,220 stores. Now that's leveraging your time.

To an entrepreneur, opportunity isn't a negative thing; instead, it's about paying attention and having the courage to leverage an opening. Entrepreneurs don't just look for opportunity, they notice it when it is hidden to others, and make the sacrifices to leverage it into a business opportunity. Leverage is about using the minimum amount of energy to achieve a maximum amount of return. Entrepreneurs think of it as the push that gives opportunity meaning. *(Harvill, 2022)*

Art uncovered a gap. The gap of low insurance protection, and the gap of not wanting to kill yourself at a job that limits time and money. He created a system that solved both problems and filled both gaps.

Art leveraged the greatest distribution builders that ever lived, builders who were stuck in unrewarding jobs, homemakers, coaches, small business owners, people who were overlooked by corporate America, but found their purpose with Art. He took average and ordinary people, in the world's eyes, and touched their souls with his vision. In unison they became a mighty force. They found their calling and place in this world and brought others just like themselves with them. Big, successful entrepreneurs rarely can take the masses with them to financial success. Art took all who wanted to go with him.

Art Was an Eternal Optimist

Angela would say, "If you spat in Art's face, he would think it was raining outside." Art had the gift and the ability of eternal optimism.

As one author said about being a lawyer, " Law is a jealous mistress, and requires a long and constant courtship." *(michiganbar.org)* The same could be said of an ALW business. It was tough and required immense tenacity. Art was well aware of the strength and determination needed, and he coached constantly. To him it was a football game that had no quarters. You just kept playing "until the job gets done."

Art Was Larger Than Life

That phrase means "the stuff legends are made of." It's a person having an aura of greatness. Art had a way about him. Iconic people are always larger than life to their admirers and Art was definitely that.

If someone is described as larger-than-life, it means that they have a very strong personality and behave in a way that makes people notice them. Who else with a deep Southern drawl would cause even jaundiced stockbrokers to give him a standing ovation?

The phrase describes someone who is so special, famous, well-known, or important that they take on an image of being greater than others of their kind. An example of larger-than-life is an extremely famous band like the Beatles.

Art was full of charisma yet intensely human, brilliant yet amazingly humble. As is said, he did not suffer fools well. Art was a larger-than-life character, whose temperament and intensity were as dramatic as any characters in an epic novel. He was in the same category as many of the fiery modern captains of industry like Jeff Bezos, Steve Jobs and Elon Musk.

General Sherman said of Lincoln, "Of all the men I ever met, he seemed to possess more of the elements of greatness, combined with goodness, than any other." *(Goodwin, 2003)* That's how we felt about Art.

ALW giant Ed Randle said, "If you are fortunate to have at least one person whose influence made you feel special, then you've truly been blessed. He was the one in an enormous number of people's lives."

Art Was an Overcomer

One author said, "Life takes away one vertebra at a time until most people don't have any backbone." Many have a wishbone, wishing and hoping but never doing. Art had a spine forged in steel. He had a quality called temerity, the unreasonable or foolhardy contempt of danger or opposition. He stared down the insurance industry, and they blinked.

Art dared to be great and dared us to join him. Fighting the insurance industry was a bloodless war but it was war, nonetheless. The obstacles that Art and his ALW army overcame could never be understood without understanding the 100-plus years of domination of the insurance industry. They had no rivals. They had no one challenging their math. And the most formidable obstacle was the force of tradition.

Tradition is an inherited, established, or customary pattern of thought, action, or behavior. Grandpa had whole life, all the relatives had whole life, the pastors had whole life, the deacons sold whole life, the school board was dominated by whole life agents. Even when articles were written stating term as superior, people would not change. At best 3 of 10 would change. "We've always done it this way," was the refrain. The pride Art had in his people came from their die-hard boldness and resolve regarding the truth of Art's philosophy.

Art would say, "The enemy can't win. He drove the stake of complete conviction as the mainstay of our business model. It was a crusade of more than words; it was our DNA. We could take the heat because we were doing the cooking. As is said "Wealth is nothing, fame is nothing, character is everything." Art and his army had the character, the guts, and the truth. As in a line from Man of La Mancha, they would "march into hell for a heavenly cause." We had a heavenly cause in our souls.

When life squeezes you what comes out of you? The juice determines the quality of the fruit, and the juice of Art's army was stout, firm and determined.

Art Was Incomparable

When you think of incomparable, you imagine no one to compare to, unequal, matchless, one of a kind. You think of people who no one can be measured against in accomplishment.

Who comes to your mind when you think someone you cannot compare to anyone?

Ordinary men could be viewed as mundane. Not Art. What Art created was incomparable which makes *him* incomparable.

When you heard Art speak, he was unforgettable. In comparison to your average scale, he appeared on a grand scale. McDonald's would call it "super-sized;" 7-11 would call it "Big Gulp." Art was the Mighty Mississippi, the Grand Canyon. Ordinary men could be viewed as mundane, not Art.

An interesting question would be, "What if they asked great home run hitters like Babe Ruth or Hank Aaron to just bunt?" An equal question would be, "What if Art was asked to only be average and ordinary?"

Without Babe Ruth and Hank Aaron, generations of baseball fans would have been deprived of witnessing greatness. Without Art, widows and orphans would have been deprived of countless billions of dollars in insurance claim benefits. Countless retirees would have had to struggle financially for lack of investment choices. Countless thousands of families would not have had the ability to create generational wealth from following Art's business system.

Art Was Our Statue of Liberty

Do you know of any person who has had a greater influence upon the insurance industry and changed the futures of so many people? Richie Falcone summed it up. "Art said he was going to change America. I thought 'I'm an American, I can change.' And I did."

Art was our North Star. A quote about Johnny Cash by Bob Dylan paints many similarities to what Art meant to his ALW teammates and those who for years would follow. "In plain terms, Johnny was and is the North Star; you could guide your ship by him, the greatest of the greats then and now. Truly he is what the land and country is all about, the heart and soul of it personified, and what it means to be here; we can have recollections of him, but we can't define him any more than we can define a fountain of truth." *(Dylan, 2022)*

Art's influencing legacy will live on forever in the hearts of men and women who yearn for the better life promised on the Statue of Liberty:

> *Give me your tired, your poor,*
> *Your huddled masses yearning to breathe free,*
> *The wretched refuse of your teeming shore.*
> *Send these, the homeless, tempest-tossed, to me,*

I lift my lamp beside the golden door.

The reason so many people have journeyed to America is the same reason people desired to become part of Art's company: Freedom. All of us have yearned to feel what it would be to "breathe free".

CHAMPIONS

I EARNED
over
$1,000,000

DO
IT

THE SATURDAY EVENING POST

NOW!

of
A.L. Williams
of
Massachusetts Indemnity
and Life Insurance Company
A.L.WILLIAMS
OPENING
September 1985

20 Fort Lauderdale News, Tuesday, March 4, 1980

Money moves

Successful coaches jump from basketball to business

By Ray Boetel
Staff Writer

When close to half of the area's large school varsity basketball coaches quit in the Great Escape of '78, the names of Phil Linville, Ron Thomas, Jim Dillon and Greg Fitzpatrick were right at the top.

They were the big surprises. They all had been successful coaches who were revered.

Linville's team at Pompano Beach High won their third district championship in four years that season, went on to win the regional and finished 27-7, pushing Linville's career record to 88-28 in four years at Pompano. Thomas' South Plantation High team won more than 15 games for the fifth consecutive year, 18-10. Dillon and Fitzpatrick had competitive programs at Coral Springs and Northeast, respectively. Dillon also had two master's degrees.

But they bolted their jobs, and that was shocking. "It just got harder and harder to put on a good program," said Thomas. But it was also a matter of economics.

Actually, they just traded in their gyms for an office. They're still mapping out game plans but the stakes are greater now. So are the rewards. Three years ago, the four teacher-coaches made between $14,000-$16,000 with coach supplements of another $1,500.

Today, as officers of an investment counseling firm, they're salaries have at least tripled. Fitzpatrick and Bob Miller, another ex-Broward coach, are listed in a company brochure as regional vice presidents. The brochure notes that "Regional Vice Presidents average more than $106,000 a year."

Compare that to winning the big one . . .

* * *

When you are a high school coach, more than likely you have to moonlight at another job to make ends meet.

Linville used to work at summer camp and teach summer school. He also unloaded mail from railroad cars at 2 a.m. during the Christmas holidays.

Thomas used to have a side business going in shark's teeth. He imported shark jaw bones and teeth. "I was known as the 'Tooth Fairy,'" he said. He and his wife cleaned them in the garage and distributed them to retail stores. The Tooth Fairy is out of business.

"We now get to take vacations when we want to," said Fitzpatrick. "I was able to take my wife to Europe for 18 days last year, the first vacation I had in 10 years. As a coach you seldom were able to even get away anywhere at Christmas for a vacation. Even if I did have the time off, I could never afford it. My wife also worked."

Dillon has been in the financial services business for a year and a half, during which he has gone from part-time employment to a position supervising 60 people. Last year, he said, he earned more money than any principal in Broward.

"And that is sad," said Dillon. "I know a lot of those people and they all work hard. I do not want to become 50 years old and make $35,000 a year."

* * *

The change from basketball to business wasn't traumatic, but it was quite a change for these men.

A year ago there was an office rule — a $5 fine for anyone who mentioned basketball and coaching. They are too busy to talk about it now.

"I remember the time when the first thing I picked up every morning was the paper. I turned right to the sports page," said Dillon. "Now it is the business page. I have redirected my talents. We talk about expansion now."

"If some school needed a local businessman to coach a team and I could find the time, I might consider it," said Linville. "But finding the time is the problem."

* * *

The company, A. L. Williams Associates, has found a successful formula in hiring former coaches and educators.

The Broward office has approximately 60, with 45 others either in education now, or formerly in education. In addition to Linville, Thomas and Dillon, Dick Andreska, one-time Chaminade basketball coach, Nick Alisi, a one-time gymnastics coach at Deerfield Beach and John Roig, an assistant football coach at South Plantation, are full-time employees. Fred Conley, who was the head basketball coach at Pompano Beach High before Linville took over, is a district manager in Inverness, Fla., while Jim Savage, former Plantation basketball coach, is working in a North Carolina office.

The firm is based in Georgia but the local office began as a two-man operation based in the bedroom of Miller's house. The company has offices in 35 states.

Staff photo by BOB EAST III

Ron Thomas, once the coach at South Plantation, now can sit back and enjoy the game.

* * *

Not all of the four coaches resigned for the same reasons.

"As a teacher, there was no longer any place for me to go," said Dillon. "That was the main reason why I got out of both teaching and coaching. It got to a point where I could no longer afford education."

Dillon has a master's degree in social studies and another in administration and supervision. He was the head of the social studies department at Coral Springs. He was also working on a doctorate, but he tossed it all away.

"I had never planned to quit teaching when I started working part-time for the company," he said. "But I reached a point where I could not go any higher on the ladder in salary. At one time I wanted to be a high school principal. I also wanted to be a college basketball coach, but I had to give up on both of them. It would take forever to become a dean or an assistant principal in this county and I could just not stay on as a teacher. All I could ever hope to gain was the token raises the teachers receive every few years. It was a hard thing to do, making the break. I was in a very secure position, but I saw the opportunity to be in control of my own future and I took it."

Linville was one of the coaches who knocked the system after leaving it. He gave up coaching first, then decided to leave the system all together. "The system changed," said Linville. "There were no longer any rewards from the community for the kids you coached. The 8th-grade basketball programs, all 9th-grade programs, were eliminated. The gym facilities were poor (six teams trying to get practice time) and are getting worse. My boys' varsity team practiced at 5:30 a.m. every day because of the lack of gym facilities. It was an uphill battle."

* * *

This used to be the time of year you could find Linville, Thomas, Dillon and Fitzpatrick in the gymnasium, getting ready for the playoffs. Now you're not likely to find them in the gym at any time.

But Thomas likes to show up at a big game now and then.

"I look at it from a different perspective now," he said. "I can sit back and enjoy it because I don't have to go out and raise money to buy this or that. I don't have to sell buttons, hold car washes or sell donuts."

And Thomas can be rowdy, if he wants to be.

"Now I can yell at the officials all I want and they can't stick me with a technical."

6A Macon Telegraph & News, Sun., Dec. 24, 1978

'Deposit' Term Life: A Bargain or Ripoff?

From Page 1A

gations of some agents.

Some underwriters, whose policies are being replaced, allege that many agents selling "deposit" term are inadequately trained, don't tell the consumer some of the pitfalls of the product, and prey upon those who own whole life policies.

"The way it is marketed makes you think that your own agent (who has sold you a whole life policy) has lied to you. We object to them saying that whole life is a bad deal," said Charles Heard of Northwestern Mutual Life Insurance Co.

"Deposit" term agents aren't denying that they dislike whole life policies.

"ANYBODY WHO has a whole life product has a problem," said Hatcher. And T. Faircloth, vice president of the company employing Hatcher, confirms that they do tell people to cash in other policies.

"Yes, if it fits into their total program," he said. "I will recommend to a client that he does cancel a whole life policy."

The policy itself is legal, but the methods of sale are sometimes questionable.

"The replacing of whole life with deposit term is strictly legal," said Joseph W. Tasker, chief investigator of the claims and investigations division of the insurance commissioner's office. "Most of the consumer complaints have been from people who feel that they misunderstood the future costs of the policy when it was sold to them.

"And when we have discovered misunderstandings, we try to get their money back. We haven't been 100 percent successful in doing that, but we have been highly successful."

TASKER IS quick to point out that "misunderstandings" do not necessarily mean that the policy was misrepresented, but that there was a breakdown in communications. It is very hard, he said, for a third party to decide where the breakdown occurred.

"We have often found that the agent doesn't understand his own policy," said Gary Jenkins of the commissioner's office, lending some credence to the charge that agents selling "deposit" term may be inadequately trained.

Faircloth said his agents have "no classroom training per se" other than a 3-day training period in Atlanta and various sales and training meetings. Most of the schooling is on-the-job.

Faircloth doesn't feel that formal classroom training is all that necessary. "It is important that you understand your product," he said. But managers are charged with giving the agents help in technical areas.

THE INSURANCE commissioner's office is currently investigating complaints about the marketing practices of some agents of A.L. Williams and Associates of Atlanta, a company with which Faircloth is connected.

Jerry Holbrook, assistant deputy and chief enforcement investigator, would not disclose the names of the agents being investigated because the inquiries are not yet complete. "There have been complaints filed against agents of the A.L. Williams organization and their activities, and that organization extends down into Macon and throughout the state," he said.

Faircloth said he "does not know of a single complaint filed against us by a client." Most of the complaints are filed by other agents, he said.

Some experts feel that complaints about the marketing of the "deposit" term policies are just a small part of a big problem in the state's insurance industry.

"We shouldn't make this into a witch hunt," said Skipper. "The marketing of the product is a symptom that something is wrong with our regulations."

What we need in Georgia, he said, are adequate disclosure laws so the consumer can better decide for himself if one insurance policy suits him better than another.

That, among other changes, would greatly help the insurance industry, he said.

Jenkins agreed that policies could be put into wording that is easier to understand. "We should get rid of some of the technical wording," he said.

And the replacement form that consumers are confronted with when changing policies may be on the road to new changes, he said. "A new form is being considered" that would make issues clearer for the consumer.

"It's going to be a while before we have decent benefit and cost disclosure laws," said Skipper. "I'd say it was at least a decade away here. We can start by adopting what other states have done."

I
WANT

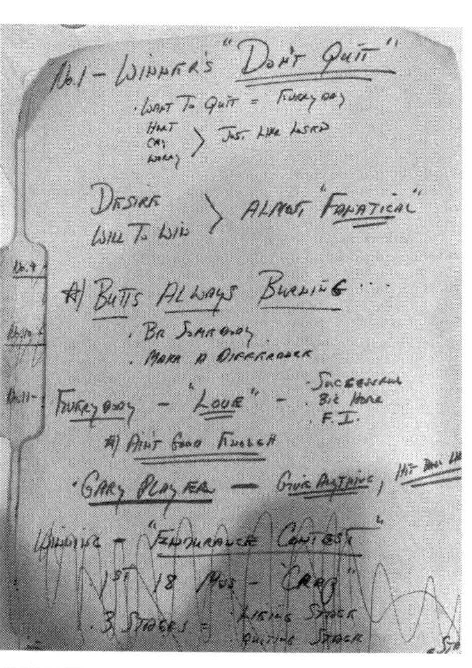
No.1 - Winner's "Don't Quit"
Desire
Will To Win
Almost "Fanatical"
A) Butts Always Burning...
. Be Somebody
. Make A Difference
Everybody - "Love"
A) Ain't Good Enough
Gary Player
Winning = "Endurance Contest"
3 Stages

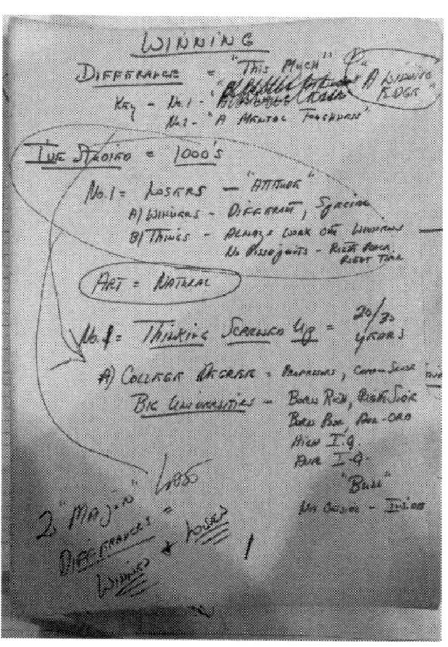
Winning
The Stadium = 1000's
No.1 = Losers - "Attitude"
Art = Natural
2 "Major" Differences = Winners & Losers

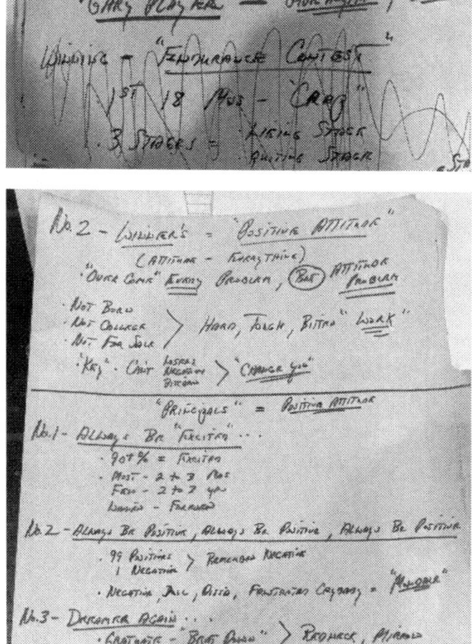
No.2 - Winner's = "Positive Attitude"
No.1 - Always Be "Excited"...
No.2 - Always Be Positive, Always Be Positive, Always Be Positive
No.3 - Dreamer Again...
No.4 - See Yourself = Winning
No.5 - 1st Step - Total Commitment

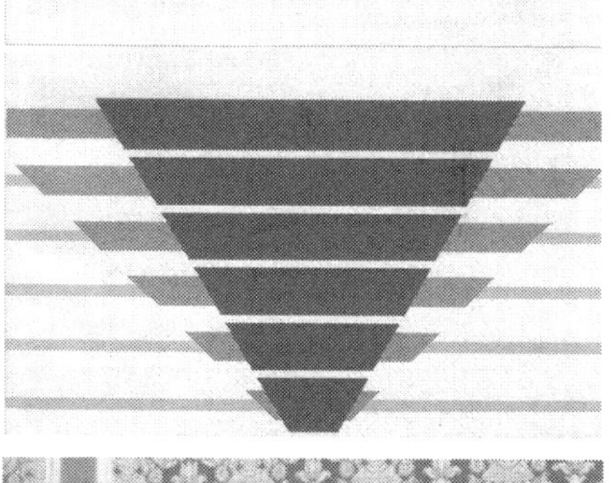
THE
A.L. WILLIAMS
WAY
by Art Williams

IF YOU LOVE AMERICA —
YOU'VE GOT TO LOVE A.L. WILLIAMS

A.L. WILLIAMS'
HEROES

The Boca Raton
Hotel and Club

NETWORK WORLD
THE SATURDAY EVENING POST
TIME
THE WALL STREET JOURNAL
Williams is building an empire
A.L. WILLIAMS
Birmingham Business Journal

A.L. WILLIAMS
1984
NATIONAL CHAMPS

ARTHO
"THE TERM - INATO
THE WAR
IS ON

YOU
KNOW
WHA

DO

Boca Raton
Hotel and Club

DO
NOW

"I AINT NO PANSY!"

BUSINESS

Football Coach Becomes Insurance 'Maverick'

By RALPH HEUSSNER
Reporter, DeKalb EXTRA

Art Williams is one of the most ordinary people you would ever want to look at.

He likes to call himself a "common guy."

"I was always an average student in school and just a little better than average athlete," he says.

But today Art Williams is anything but average. At 38, he is an American success story.

And there is nothing ordinary about A.L. Williams & Associates, one of the fastest growing and most controversial insurance companies in the country.

Williams' background does not suggest that he would become the president of a major national company with 10,000 employees and 188 offices in 35 states.

He was born in Waycross and raised in Cairo, Ga. His father was an educator, and later a chemist. Williams earned a degree at Mississippi State University and went into teaching. He later added a master's degree in educational administration from Auburn University.

Until 1970, Williams was a high school teacher and football coach.

"This was my life," he said. "I was born to be a coach. Growing up, that's what I always wanted to be."

He was well on his way to carving a distinguished career as athletic director and head football coach at Kendrick High School in Columbus. In 1970, his team won its regional championship and was runner-up in the state finals. He was twice named coach of the year.

Williams thought he would follow the career trail

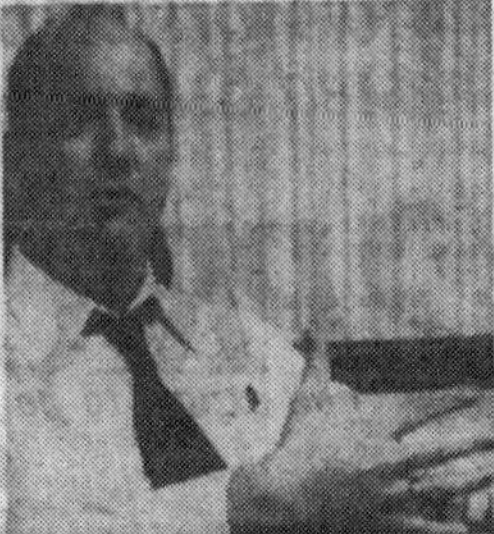

Art Williams says he's just an average guy. That's hard for both his friends and his critics to believe. Art resigned his job as a high school coach and has become the president of a multi-million dollar insurance firm in virtually unheard of time.

of many coaches, going into administration and becoming a principal.

"Things were going well. I liked coaching. I had a lot of security. I was successful. I thought I would be a coach until I died," he said.

Then how did Coach Williams become A.L. Williams, president of an insurance/investment company?

Like many teachers, Williams had a part-time job to supplement his income and help provide for his wife, Angela, and two children.

Continued on Next Page

BUSINESS

Continued from Previous Page

In 1967, Williams received a phone call from a cousin who was a sales representative with ITT Financial Services. "I refused to see him," Williams recalled. "I didn't like salesmen."

But a few months later, they met at a family reunion and the conversation turned to insurance and investments.

"He showed me the value of term life insurance," Williams said. "It was too good to be true. I was scared away. I was an educator and questioned new things. I went to the Bradley Memorial Library in Columbus and read the consumer magazines - Consumer Reports, Moneysworth - and they all said the same thing: whole life insurance is a bad investment.

"A few months later I was selling part-time."

Williams said he had no intentions to leave coaching. In fact, he was embarrassed whenever someone called him a salesman.

"Selling insurance for me was like going off the deep end. I could never see myself doing that. It was a profession not looked upon favorably," he said.

To avoid being stereotyped as an "insurance salesman," Williams decided to do everything different.

"I would never sell on the first visit. I approached people from an educational viewpoint. I would not prospect for clients," he said. "But all of a sudden I found that by taking the anti-approach, I was making more money in my part-time job than in my full-time job. And I felt good about helping people."

In a way, Williams did too well. ITT Financial Services named him a district manager, and in 1970 offered him the job of regional manager, based in Atlanta.

He faced the most difficult decision of his life: he would either have to give up coaching or give up the insurance business.

"It was agonizing," Williams said.

What happened to his life's dream of coaching? "All my life I wanted to do something where I could look back and say I made a difference. I changed something. While I was doing well in coaching, I still felt there was something else. I needed another mountain to climb."

Williams said he knew that the concept of "buy term and invest the difference" had great potential. It is his company's motto.

Williams vividly recalls the day he left coaching. "I gathered my team and told them my decision and we cried together."

* * *

Williams advanced quickly. In 1971, he joined another investment company, Waddell & Reed, as regional vice president.

Continued On Page 57

BUSINESS

Continued From Page 17

But he felt no one in the insurance industry was doing enough to promote term insurance. So he formed his own company.

A.L. Williams & Associates was founded on Feb. 10, 1977, in an office building near Northlake Mall. There were 85 employees.

The growth has been unparalleled. In the first 18 months, the company sold $1 billion in insurance. In less than three years, it has become one of the 20 largest insurance companies in the nation in sales.

Looking to the future, Williams hopes to expand to all 50 states and then become an international company. It is still based in DeKalb County.

The company is controversial because it is openly critical of insurance companies which sell whole-life policies.

Williams has been called a pioneer, a maverick, a genius. The adjectives include lucky, aggressive, unorthodox.

still opportunity today," Williams said. "I'm just a dumb old south Georgia football coach."

New York Stock Exchange, Inc.

Certification of Listing

Be it known that

The A. L. Williams Corporation

Duluth, Georgia

having satisfied in full the listing requirements of the New York Stock Exchange, Inc. is this 6th day of February 1989 authorized for listing and the common stock thereof is hereby admitted to trading on the Exchange.

In Witness Whereof I have hereunto set my hand and caused the Seal of the New York Stock Exchange, Inc. to be affixed.

Attest

Chapter 6:

THE PHILOSOPHIES THAT BUILT A DYNASTY

So much of A.L. Williams is so revolutionary, it's hard to imagine how one man could have so many original and creative ideas. From structuring a salesforce to capturing the power of people, to harnessing the power of belief, Art Williams transformed the way sales organizations worked – and proved its success by the success of thousands of people.

The Holy Grail of A.L. Williams

As our products and crusade became more accepted by the public, another part of our uniqueness was starting to show its worth.

This other game-changer was Art's concept of "a company within a company." He believed that Regional Vice Presidents (RVPs) should build their own companies within A.L. Williams and be the leaders of those companies. Leaders would build success by building for themselves, not building to create success for someone else. By harnessing the "power of multiples," growth could explode. Art created six generations of overrides. He created more financially independent people. He created hope. He created a recruiting explosion that had never been seen in the history of the insurance industry, 250,000 licensed people in twelve years and hundreds of RVPs.

Ronald Reagan once made a famous statement on opportunity. "The American dream of human progress through freedom and equality of opportunity is still the most revolutionary idea in the world today. It's also the most successful." Art understood that idea.

The term "Holy Grail" is defined as an object or goal that is sought after for its great significance. It's something that you want very much, but that is very hard to get or achieve. Art created a

Holy Grail of Opportunity for average and ordinary people. As Art said, "ALW was built for people to make a difference, to do something great and be somebody that they are proud of. Let's change the world; why not us? Let's make a difference in the lives of other people. This company is too great to limit ourselves to small dreams."

Art wanted salespeople to be "king," to be the focus of everything that happened in the company. Art was determined to make it "a different kind of company." Every other company he knew saw salespeople as a necessary evil. It was almost as if their home office thought, "If we could get rid of all those salespeople, we wouldn't have any problems." Even the best companies he could find were all about selling products and making money for the company. Art was about righting a wrong and creating a company that put the salespeople first, not last.

Art understood the basic desire of all of us. Art said, "ALW was formed to give people like me and you a chance at financial independence and a new, prosperous life. It was formed to build security for us and our families and give hope that our lives will get better. It was formed to help us live the kind of lives we want to live." Every person wants to make a difference with his or her life. Every person seeks passion. At ALW we knew that, just because people were not giving us a standing ovation, our lives still mattered. Art created a system where people could be rewarded for their efforts and have their own business. He developed ALW so that we all could build our own "company within a company" and have people in our companies building their own companies. In doing so, his movement would help to bring more widows the life insurance claim checks that would give them financial peace.

The three things the original ALW people wanted were: To be their own boss, to control their own destiny so no one could control them, and to believe passionately in what they did. American companies believed only special people, degreed people and "pretty" people could make it. People who had the right connections, or were the best looking, were the only ones who had a chance to make it to the top. Art said, "Corporations dictate where you live, what you drive, what your children wear, whether or not your wife works, whether or not you will retire in dignity, where you go on vacation, whether or not you'll help charitable causes; they dictate your self-esteem and your self-worth. They do this by how much they pay you." Art saw the RVP system as a way to have unlimited income and a secure income but chiefly "for no one to have their thumb on you."

Art disliked corporate America as much as he did the whole life insurance industry. "What the corporate world has now is discouraging to the person who has a vision, a dream, and a true desire to be somebody." He believed corporate America holds people back, and uses them up, then discards them when they have no more to give, like a used-up battery. He wanted to form a different kind of company where everybody had their shot to own their own company and could get out from underneath corporate America's thumb.

Art wanted us to believe that the American dream was still alive at ALW. He said, "You must believe you were born for this." He wanted us to know that our company was different and that we would deliver for the people who came in and gave it their best. He said, "We build successful businesses by treating people right."

In *The A.L. Williams Way* Art said, "Everyone wants freedom of time and money and the best way to get that freedom is with overrides. We are an overriding company. We are not a sales company." At Waddell & Reed, Art realized he couldn't get that dream when the company limited the number of promotions he could give to qualified people. There was a limit to how many could get their shot.

Art wanted everyone to be in a position to be financially independent. He needed an engine to do that. The only way to be financially independent was to own your own company. People were being held back at Waddell & Reed and he wanted to unleash the power of people getting promoted. The RVP position he created was designed for that RVP to create RVPs who created RVPs, who created RVPs, who created RVPs. He even stated, "We are an RVP company and we run an RVP factory." We recruited people to become RVPs and not be destined to only be salespeople for a financial services company they could never own. When we realized we had access to the only unsaturated market that we knew of in the world, we knew we could recruit the world.

At that time there were approximately 120 million families that needed our services, and you couldn't get to them all without recruiting millions of people. Who is going to recruit them? A person who owns their own company, who could promote unlimited numbers of RVPs in their company, providing the incentive necessary to grow exponentially

Frances Avrett described Art's "Holy Grail" wonderfully. "We must remember that we are the beneficiaries of the most successful visionary business in North America," Frances said. "What Art gave us was an opportunity to recruit unlimited numbers of people, which no other financial services company ever could provide. If people cannot recruit, they cannot have unlimited income and secure income. Recruiting is our uniqueness."

The Holy Grail of Recruiting was recruiting part-timers, which created opportunity. Giving people a system to own their own company catapulted Art's company from 85 people to over 250,000 licensed people in 12 years in all 50 states and Canada, and propelled ALW to be the number one life insurance company in the world. Giving people an opportunity to become financially independent and have ownership was the key. Art coined the phrase "We sell hope, a dream, and an opportunity. Without a dream you're dead, and ALW is a company made for dreamers." Art would say, "We created a monster system. It's a perfect combination of part-time, crusaders, ownership, the right market and BTID." It became magical and a special something that had never been done before in financial services. Those original people wanted to do something big.

The opportunity Art created set off a dream in each of us. It welled up from a dormant place deep inside of us that we had buried. Art gave us hope and fed our aspirations with his simple message. He saw the greatness in us that had not been harvested by mediocre jobs, lack of challenge and an elitist corporate America system. We wouldn't let them break us down. We wouldn't let them decide our destinies. We had found our God-given purpose and had the courage and crusade to pursue it. Eventually we began to feel sorry for them. They couldn't be us and we had abandoned the path they had chosen. Art's system gave us a glimpse of an amazing life. It was the birthplace of a dream for us. ALW offered us one time in our lives to "go for it!" We felt we owed it to ourselves. We saw Art's system as a place to catch the proverbial "lightning in a bottle."

A huge part of the dream was Art. Art was uncommon. As President Herbert Hoover said, "When we are sick, we want an uncommon doctor; when we have a construction job to do, we want an uncommon engineer; and when we are at war, we want an uncommon general. It is only when we get a 'job' that we are satisfied with the common." *(Hoover, 1949)*

The Holy Grail of Opportunity was held together by Art. ALW became "the cure for the common job."

Breaking sales records meant people were beginning to make serious money, just as Art had promised. Bob Buisson was one of Art's first recruits. He and his wife, Red, were models of how to do everything right. Bobby was one of the original 7 RVPs, and one of the first $100,000 earners. Bobby and Red went on to become among the first millionaires outside of Art and Angela.

Art's Masterpiece

The A.L. Williams System and the Power of Three

Art would say there are two things that blew his butt out of the water, the power of the "Rule of 72" and the power of the multiples with people. Art loved and saw the value of compounding, both the compounding of interest and the compounding of people. Albert Einstein called compound interest the eighth wonder of the world. Compound interest and compounding people create the same result, "a little in and a lot out." It's just like a seed in the field. Planting a seed creates a crop, and that crop creates more seed and more crops, which is the gist of compounding. Compounding is rarely taught anywhere in the educational system. Horticulturists, farmers, and beekeepers understand it because, if they don't, they will fail.

There is a story about how the country of Mexico had a literacy problem. They chose a method called, "each one teach one." If a person knew how to read and write, it was their obligation to teach one other person. What if they had said, "each one teach three" and "all three teach three and those three teach three and those three teach three and those three teach three." Imagine how fast illiteracy would've been eliminated in Mexico.

Another example is the story of the dying starfish. The story goes that there were 10,000 starfish that had washed up on a shore and could not get back into the ocean, so they were dying. A young man was on the side of the shore picking one up at a time and throwing it back into the ocean. An elderly man walked by and said, "What difference are you making? There are so many starfish." The young man picked one up, threw it back in the ocean and said, "Well, at least I made a difference for that one." That is a noble thing he was doing, but the reality was that all but a few were going to die with his plan. Instead of doing it one at a time, Art would have recommended that the young man go into the city and talk to three friends about the dying starfish, ask them to tell three of their friends, then tell three of their friends. That's 110 friends who are aware of dying starfish and could help. Now you have an army coming to the shore to throw all the starfish back in the ocean and *save them all*!

As with the starfish, Art needed countless ALW representatives to reach the 120 million people who needed "buy term and invest the difference." BTID had the same math problem that is in the starfish story. Art had to make a decision to save a few or save them all. Art chose to save them all and created his masterpiece to accomplish it.

The Power of 3

The decision to save them all created a need. Art could've been in sales his whole life and helped hundreds and hundreds of people with BTID. Instead, he chose to save the 120 million families that needed to be saved with his BTID concept.

In Art's system, instead of one person helping a client and then going to find another client, Art chose to recruit our clients and have them create three clients and recruit those three clients and take those three clients and do the same thing. Art took the concept of "each one teach one" and added the power of compounding to it. That's how the Art Williams' system went from 85 people to over 250,000 in just over a decade. He created $28 billion in death claim benefits to orphans and widows throughout the history of his company. He didn't save every widow, but he made a massive difference to millions of them.

Thomas Edison perfected the incandescent electric lamp by combining two well-known principles in a new way and changed the way we lived. George Pullman placed beds in railroad coaches, converting them into sleeping quarters. The combination of coaches and beds changed rail travel and made him wealthy.

The reason Art developed the recruiting mentality that is the cornerstone of the ALW company was his own experience in sales. "My biggest fear was setting up appointments, so the solution was recruiting someone and having them set up the appointment," Art said. "That made prospecting easier. I discovered a better way to make a sale. So, the more new associates who joined, the more sales were made, the more people who were overriding others, the more secure income they would have."

Art Williams saw two existing entities. He saw "buy term and invest the difference," and he saw the "power of 3" and the multiples. He married the two to create the greatest financial services company in history.

The day Art realized this was the day he *believed*; it was just like December 17, 1903, when the Wright Brothers' first flight occurred, and they first believed men could fly. Sixty-six years later, a man was on the moon because they combined a glider with an engine.

The day Art decided to combine BTID and the Power of 3 was Art's "Kitty Hawk" moment.

The Brilliance of Part-Time

A cornerstone belief Art brought to the industry was hiring part-timers. According to Art, "The most controversial thing I did was start people part-time at ITT. I had a good feeling that part-timers were the answer. Something inside of me wouldn't let me give up."

Good people with families couldn't afford to quit their job to try something new. Art didn't want people to risk their financial stability to make some extra income. Thanks to ITT, he was able to do it himself, and it was perfect for him at the time. When Art joined ITT, insurance companies didn't hire part-timers. But when they saw Art make huge strides by working part-time, they realized it could be done. Art believed that hiring part-timers in ALW allowed good people with families who couldn't afford to give up a guaranteed income for sales, to try the business and see the success that was possible before they quit their job. Art became the first person in the giant insurance industry to really believe in part-time salespeople.

By championing the cause of part-timers, Art found a way to allow people to explore the business without the stress. It helped us recruit a person who was stable, known in the community, with a family and job.

Art said, "Selling life insurance is nasty and hard, the hardest thing most people would ever have to do. That's why we took the recruiting approach. We recruited our kind of people. Look what happened when we did. We created a monster system."

With part-timers, people sold and recruited their friends

and neighbors. It took some of the sting out of prospecting and recruiting. Plus, we didn't have to spend millions on advertising like most big companies, only to have most quit, as they did in the traditional industry.

Hiring people part-time was just a better way to build a company. Until Art, it was unheard of in the life insurance industry. But Art did it, and he made it work. It is such a simple concept, but with profound results. More proof that Art was always a step ahead of the pack.

"Part of our success," Art said, "was that we had a definite market that we were after with people who were middle-class, and we chose to do it with part-timers."

One Team, One Dream

In classic businesses, there's a lot of talk about building a business, but not much about building a team. What if you could create a team that could withstand tough times, perform beyond their stated abilities, endure the kind of competition most companies can't imagine and achieve the kind of revolutionary success that can transform an entire industry? Art did it, but how did Art "dadgum" do it? He explained it all in one phrase, "One team, one dream."

Art's team had one heartbeat. We heard the phrase, "One Team One Dream," but never understood its truth. Art preached "One Heartbeat" in *The ALW Way*. He talked about it as a key to winning. Remember, Art wanted to build a company like he built a football team, and one heartbeat was a criterion. Art couldn't have everyone playing their own game, going in their own direction, and being caught alone in the torrential downpour of criticism, industry backlash, and the toughness that comes with sales generally.

As Angela would say, "Art has only one speech, but it lasts for two days." Art's message was like a bass drum keeping the beat as the troops marched in unison. Imagine thousands of soldiers marching with their arms swinging the same, their legs striding the same; they look like whirling machine parts. Art wanted us on the same page, his page. To defeat an enemy as large as the insurance industry, the largest industry in the world, it would take a oneness of thinking and acting.

Years ago in college, I witnessed an annual tug-of-war championship. Generally, the team with the strongest men would win. Then a group of scrawny non-athletic types got out a bass drum and were told to pull the rope to the beat of the drum. They won every tug-of-war event for years. Why did we beat the insurance industry at their own game? How did Art lead a team of David's to beat the Goliath's? One heartbeat. Art's heartbeat. Art's crusade. Art's philosophy.

The following explains the science behind Art's thinking: In an article entitled *The Science of the Power of Unity* the author states, "The idea that we are all connected is not some mystical notion. It's science." *(Bailey, 2021)* Research at the Heartmath Institute shows that, at a conversational distance, the electromagnetic signals generated by one person's heart can influence another person's brain rhythms. It also found a mother's brain waves can synchronize with her baby's heartbeat. We are all affected by the thoughts and feelings of those around us. The quality of our relationships impacts how we perceive the world. If one student in the classroom experiences rage and the rest of the class practices composure and empathy, the raging child will calm down. The reverse is also true.

For example, researchers at the University College London Division of Psychological and Language Sciences have found that audiences' hearts synchronize watching live theater. The team monitored the heart rate and electrodermal activity of 12 audience members at a live performance of *Dreamgirls*. The team found that, alongside individuals' emotional responses, the audience members' hearts were also responding in unison, with their pulses speeding up and slowing down at the same rate. "Usually highly effective teammates will actually synchronize their hearts so that they beat in time with each other, which in itself is astounding." (*Bailey, 2021*)

Art didn't know the science, but he knew what a team with one heartbeat could achieve, pulling together at the beat of his crusader's heart. Thus, "You win with your heart not your head" can be expanded to "You win with thousands of people's hearts beating at the same time, at the same pulse rate and fighting the same enemy." Art said, "I truly believe from the bottom of my heart that every team should have one heartbeat."

Pushing Up People

Art put a trailer hitch on his life. Interestingly, you don't see a hitch on the back of a Mercedes or a Maserati or a Ferrari. You only see a trailer hitch on the back of a pick-up truck. Trucks are designed to be a "working" vehicle. Luxury vehicles say, "Don't get dirt on me." Pick-ups say, "I'm here to do the hard stuff." His trailer hitch was intended to pull the rest of us along.

Art never saw himself as an army of one. The old concept of "one for all and all for one" was a belief system that Art had and instilled in all of us. He was a coach and coaches need a team. TEAM? "Together Each Achieves More."

Author Rabbi Daniel Lapin says "God created business to force us to be good to one another. He never designed us to be alone, not needing anybody, not helping anybody, not lifting the load for another person. He wants interaction, and business forces people to interact, and making money forces people to make other people's lives better." (*Lapin, 2014*)

Art believed that if you try to keep pushing up sales, sales always will fall down again. But if you push *people,* sales will stay up. In fact, his cornerstone book is *Pushing Up People*. He was in the people business and not in the insurance or investment business. His legacy was the successful people that "hitched their wagons" to his star.

Art said, "The greatest power in any business is people power. No matter how much potential your business has, no matter how good your product or service might be, the thing that will determine the success or failure of your business is the effort and dedication of the people who make up your business team."

There is a story of Mother Teresa at a fundraising event in the United States. After her talk, a wealthy man came up to her and gave her a check for $1 million. She looked at the check and gave it back to him, saying, "I know you can give more." He ended up donating $25 million. As with Mother Teresa, Art knew the crusade needed more and he needed more of us. He needed us to give until it hurt, and we did.

Art's Coaching Tree

A coaching tree is similar to a family tree except that it shows the relationships of coaches instead of family members. There are several ways to define a relationship between two coaches. The most common way to make the distinction is if a coach worked as an assistant on a head coach's staff for at least a season, then that coach can be counted as being a branch on the head coach's coaching tree. Coaching trees can also show philosophical influence from one head coach to an assistant.

In the NFL, coaches are just about all related. Each coach learns from another mentor within the league, then finds a new team to grow that coaching tree. One coach trains and mentors another who trains and mentors others, etc. For example, both Andy Reid and Jon Gruden belong to Mike Holmgren's tree.

In 2018, an ESPN article showed visually how 28 of the 32 coaches who would serve as NFL head coaches in the upcoming season were connected to head coaches Bill Parcells and Bill Belichick.

What about the Art Williams coaching tree? It started with Art's coach Tommy Taylor. Art said, "My only hero has been Tommy Taylor, my high school coach. When I graduated from high school all I wanted to do was be a coach like Coach Taylor and have the same impact on other young men that I coached." Art was also trained and mentored by West Thomas. "Coach West

Thomas was another important person in my life. He was the head football coach at Cairo High School for 20 years. Art then personally started his own "coaching tree."

He recruited and coached: Tee Faircloth, who led him to Bobby Buisson, who led him to Bob Miller, who led him to the likes of John Roig, Nick Alise, and Greg Fitzpatrick. This is an example of Art's tree. Years after Art started his tree, over 5,000 coaches (called RVPs) can now be counted as descendants of Art's coaching. These coaches are responsible for coaching another 130,000 licensed future coaches in the company Art created, with more incubating. Art trained through his coaching, and he expected us to train others to achieve success and excellence – just like he trained us.

Art's coaching tree is an example of his being a "coffee bean" person. In his book, *The Coffee Bean,* John Gordon explains. "If you put a coffee bean in water, it spreads throughout the water and it changes the flavor. The boiling water doesn't change it as much as it changes the water around it into something better." *(Gordon, 2019)* Art changed everyone around him into someone better; then those people changed everyone else around them into someone better, and on and on. You can tell the artist by his art. The people that sprung from Art's coaching tree became his masterpiece. His tree has become a tapestry of Art's vision, dedication, and legacy.

Was it a Team, a Company, or a Shared Adventure?

Ernest Shackleton was an intrepid explorer. He planned a trip to Antarctica in 1914; he needed crewmen and put this ad in the paper:

> *Men wanted for hazardous journey.*
> *Small wages, bitter cold, long months of complete darkness, constant danger, safe return doubtful.*
> *Honor and recognition in case of success.*

Who would respond to such an ad? The answer? Five thousand people. Applicants showed up in droves.

It reminds me of Art's "We are probably not going to make it, but if we do it will be amazing." People crave to be a part of something big, even if it's risky and the outcome is unknown.

Doldrums is a word that depicts part of the ocean near the equator abounding in calms, where a sailing ship could not sail because of the lack of wind. It also depicts a spell of listlessness or despondency. Doldrums lead to the "dull, disillusioned, dadgum crybaby" life that Art talked about. People hunger for an exciting, adventurous life. They will seek out leaders that offer that life. Art was that leader.

Dietrich Bonhoeffer and Ernest Shackleton understood a community was distinct from what the word "teamwork" has come to mean today. For both these leaders, community meant more than sharing a mission and acting together toward that end. It meant being bound together not only by obligation, but by mutual caring and affection. This caring and affection begins with the leader himself. "The higher the stakes, the more essential it is for the leader to demonstrate ongoing love, respect, and attention to the details — however small — of his followers' lives." *(Bonhoeffer, 2017)*

Art believed in a sense of unity and mutual devotion. A oneness. A band of brothers forged into one heartbeat.

Art, like Bonhoeffer and Shackleton, couldn't have done it alone. He needed the power that this community of adventurers brought him. He fed off their dreams, their total commitment, their belief in him, their sacrifices and shared passion for a cause greater than themselves. His cadre gave up "good jobs," signed leases (Virginia and Bobby signed 3-year office leases with no guarantee they could pay them), traveled long distances to recruit, worked their proverbial fingers to the bone. Why? High adventure and the thrill of it all. They got a thrill at every kitchen table. A thrill when replacing a $100 a month $50,000 whole life policy with a $300,000 term policy on both the husband and the wife, for $75 a month.

Words can't express the fun, the excitement, the effervescence of one of Art's Fast Start Schools. The Fast Start Schools created a spark that caused sleepless nights of wonder, hope and big dreams.

The word "advent" means new and fresh beginnings. It is the genesis of the word "adventure." It reminds us that we don't have to sleepwalk into the future. The Fast Start Schools offered an advent to each person. Most people are ready for a new beginning, tired of working for someone else, anxious to be somebody.

As was said of the polar explorer Ernest Shackleton, "Surely there is no end with such a man as Shackleton: something of his spirit must still live on with us; something of his greatness must surely be a legacy to his countrymen." He had a way of compelling loyalty. One who sailed with Shackleton wrote, "We would have gone anywhere without question, just on his order." (*Worsley, 2003*) Like Shackleton, Art had that same way of compelling loyalty.

The Crusade

"There is something about devotion to an inward vision, the intense desire and concentrated effort to fulfill what you believe to be your mission on earth. This mysterious core is so powerful that it can make the remarkable appear ordinary, so contagious that it can spread like wildfire from one to another in an organization, and so persuasive that it can transform doubt and uncertainty into conviction. This quality burns all bridges behind it, clears all obstacles before it, and arrives at its destination no matter how long it may take, regardless of the sacrifice or cost." (*Kimbro, 2003*)

Art offered a crusade, not a job. He was devoted to that inner vision and was committed, "no matter how long it may take, regardless of sacrifice or cost."

Author Victor Frankl wrote *Man's Search for Meaning*. As a prisoner in Auschwitz and Dachau, his theses as to what makes people yearn to survive carry great weight.

According to Frankl, life is never made unbearable by circumstances, but only by lack of meaning and purpose. "Those who have a 'why' to live can bear with almost any 'how.'" *(Frankl, 2006)*

The crusade was our great meaning. We didn't sell life insurance. We led a crusade for changing the lives of ordinary American families. A crusade is an emotionally motivated spirit. A crusade has missionary zeal. It gives you something to stand for. Art's crusade spilled out to his people. The crusade made Art a crusader and crusaders change the world. If you don't have a crusade, sooner or later something will knock you out.

Being a crusader meant everyone knew where you stood. Art always said, "If no one is making fun or you, then you're not showing you are a crusader." That made all our anxiety about the opposition evaporate. We knew that crusaders don't back down. Art's crusade spilled out to his people, and it made us believe we could change the world. He showed us that when you show up, your lives matter.

The crusade was our *business*. Art never saw A.L. Williams as a typical business. A business has no soul, no sense of significance. The crusade put the fight in us. We rallied around the nobility and significance of the crusade.

Art said, "A crusade gives you the extra ounce of courage it takes to talk to someone." He said, "You have to see yourself involved in something bigger than your business, bigger than yourself." We knew we were different than our competition. They did it for a commission. We did it to right wrongs and correct injustices.

Art taught us that:

- A crusade transforms people's lives so that they eventually perform good deeds.
- A crusade is a deep sense of calling.
- The successful crusaders lead with their hearts.
- A crusade won't let you quit.
- You can only change the world if you have a crusade.

- If Art had believed in just "running a business" would A.L. Williams have become what it did? Businesses don't expect greatness. They don't expect "fight." They don't talk about winning. But a crusade does.
- Crusaders die hard.

The Talk That Calmed Our Fears

When you are on an airplane and there is turbulence, the first thing most people do is look at the flight attendants to see whether or not they are disturbed or fearful. If they have fear in their eyes you realize that something is very serious. If they're smiling and going about their jobs, you remain calm and realize that everything is good. It was the same way with Art.

Art had to be afraid. How could he not? He put his head down on a pillow at night many times thinking that it might be over. He knew that we were unsure because of the competition, the articles, the changing of companies, the state regulators, the administration problems in getting policies issued, and the anger of clients when their bank drafts were mishandled.

In those raw emotion-filled days all eyes were instinctively focused on Art, looking for his flinch, his fear, his body language, his words, the slightest grimace. All we saw was the fierce look of determination and resolve. Art knew we had put it all on the line like he did. We had gone full time, opened offices, and put our names on leases. At times we would have moments of terror, but we never blinked. We reflected Art's courage. If he blinked, if he showed fear, we would have panicked. Like Art, we had the belief and the power of the crusade. It was not just business, it was personal. Fear is a poison that could have caused us to lose focus, lose confidence or lose morale. That's why Art gave us his famous "Knockout" talk. It also seemed like the more that went wrong the tougher his talks would become. The Knockout talk epitomized his method of stiffening our resolve. It went like this:

When Art was a football coach before every game, he would tell his players that he had talked with the referees and told them that he had his nice clothes on he and didn't want to get them dirty, so if any of his players got hurt to just move the ball away from the player and keep playing. He told them didn't want to stop the game for an injured player. He did not want to put doubt or fear in a player's mind and have them overreact to injuries that, most of the time, were minor. Art said he hated when there was an injury on the field and the game would stop. Everyone ran out to the injured player, the player limped off the field, then three minutes later he'd be back in the game.

Art preached to his teams that they were tougher than the competition, the team "in the wrong-colored" jerseys. So, he created a "knockout chart" to show his players how many of the other teams' players they knocked out, while their opponent had none. Of course, if one of his players' injuries was serious, Art would be the first one on the field. It was a way of building courage. The message was clear: His team was tougher than the opposition. The opponents couldn't stand up to his team's strength and courage. The competition didn't want it as bad as his players did.

Art didn't want his players kneeling during a time out. He wanted them standing, leering at the other team's players as they knelt down to catch their breath. His message? "We knock them out, they don't knock us out." One year Art's team knocked out 27 competing players and they had zero knockouts.

Art put that same result and determination in us with the anthem, "The enemy can't win." Art concluded his knockout talk with a battle cry, "We are going to knock their asses off!" Then he would walk off the stage. We all jumped to our feet. That's how Art doused our fear and gave us strength. He gave us a call to arms, "Attack, attack, attack!"

There is a wonderful story of newsman Eric Severeid who was a journalist during WWII. He and other journalists were in a plane that was shot down over Burma six hundred miles from safety. As they all scrambled out of the plane and realized the pilots had died, desperation enveloped them. They huddled under the wing of the plane giving in to the reality that their only hope was to be captured and put into a prisoner's camp to inevitably die. They needed shelter for the night, so they climbed to a cave that they had noticed and fell quickly to sleep. The next morning, they hiked to a stream and ate fruits from some trees. The next night they found another cave. The daily routine of cave for shelter, stream for water, fruit from trees became their routine. Severaide explained that going from cave to stream to cave to stream they somehow journeyed to safety. The thought of six hundred miles seemed impossible. But day by day it was doable. Another way to explain a success journey is, "Inch by inch it is a cinch. Yard by yard it is hard." *(Holtz)*

Art coached his team to stay focused on just today and let tomorrow take care of itself. That kept us from having to eat the whole elephant at one time, but only one bite at a time. We attacked and fought today to attack and fight another day and another and another. Art coached us to win one kitchen table at a time. Our success finally came when we "knocked their asses off," one replaced policy at a time, one recruit at a time, one widow and her children who were better off at a time, one new part-timer who became an RVP at a time, one old whole life insurance agent who kept losing their policies to us one at a time, one new $100,000 earner at a time. That was how we won.

Art Preached a Goal of Greatness

Art would say, "The first goal you should have is a goal of greatness. A life's goal should be to succeed to such a high level that others who are successful are compared to *you*." We were average and ordinary people. Nobody had ever talked to us about a goal of "greatness."

Abraham Lincoln was asked by a friend to visit a church with a great preaching pastor. After the service, he was asked what he thought of the preacher's sermon. Abraham Lincoln replied, "He failed because he never asked us to do anything great."

We admired people who came from nowhere and became somebody from nothing like Abe Lincoln. Art and his people came from humble beginnings, as well.

Mark Twain said, "Great minds will give you a feeling that you can become great too." (*Twain, reddit.com)* That was Art's legacy. His extraordinary desire to do something great overflowed into us.

Art said, "You can be good, or you can be great. We choose great." He also asked, "How do you judge a great leader? By the number of great people they produce. I'm proud to be part of a company that did great things. I just don't want to be a half-butted organization, mediocre, average, and ordinary. I want to do something great. ALW was built for people to do something. To make a difference. To do something great and be somebody that they are proud of."

Author and pastor Chuck Swindoll said, "God is not out of business in picking ordinary, nobodies, not accomplished people to do great things for Him." Art was that special self-made leader who didn't see people as they were, but as they could be. He saw greatness in all of us. We had been locked into a mental straitjacket of mediocrity because the jobs we were in didn't offer greatness. *(White, 2022)*

As author David Foster Wallace wrote, "What I call courageous or effective leaders are individuals who can help us overcome the limitations of our own individual laziness and selfishness and weakness and fear, and get us to do better, harder things than we can get ourselves to do on our own." (*Wallace, 2007)* Few are born great, but most great leaders are thrust into it like Art. He needed people to override others to stay in the business and built a company that "found a better way to make a sale" by recruiting part-timers and promoting people. He was great because he made those around him great.

This explains what it was like to be exposed to Art's coaching. "A leader's true authority is a power you voluntarily give him, and you grant him this authority, not in a resigned or resentful way but happily; it feels right. Deep down, you almost always like how a real leader makes you feel, how you find yourself working harder and pushing yourself and thinking in ways you wouldn't be able to if there weren't this person you respected and believed in and wanted to please." *(Wallace, 2007)*

Art was always saying he wanted to build a company like he did a football team. Most companies have managers, but what they really need is coaches like Art.

Art challenged us because the moment of our "divine appointment" had arrived. "There is always one moment when the door opens and lets the future in," (paraphrased from Graham Green). Art opened that door for us.

Art's teaching and philosophies continue on today, through his books and YouTube, and through the thousands of leaders he coached who are passing his philosophies on to people who will never meet him in person. That's all the proof anyone needs that Art's philosophies not only built an empire and changed an industry but left a legacy of success in business and in life for future generations to follow.

Art's philosophies were unique and controversial, but they have stood the test of time. Over 40 years later, they still work, and they are still branding the hearts and changing the lives of average and ordinary people who desire to be great.

PHENOMENON SPOTLIGHT

The Wisdom of Art: Art Williams' Iconic Quotes

Art wouldn't have been the leader he was without his special way of getting his message across. His iconic quotes are some of the most memorable I've ever heard. A.L. Williams crusaders will be repeating them for decades to come.

Paraphrasing Maya Angelou, "Art is totally contained as a vault of rare gems."

Game-Changing Art Sayings

- Life is just a "flicker."
- Crusaders die hard.
- Attitude is everything.
- Everybody wants to be somebody.
- You were put on this earth to make a difference with your life.
- Life will give you what you are willing to accept. If you accept mediocrity, life will give you that; If you accept average and ordinary, life will give you that; if you accept being broke, life will give you that too.
- You win with your heart, not your head.
- The difference between winning and losing is "this much." (holding up his thumb and index fingers a half-inch apart as he spoke)
- I ain't average! Call me anything but average and ordinary.
- I want to be somebody so bad it borders on being an obsession.
- Nobody will follow a dull, dead, disillusioned, frustrated, dadgum crybaby.

The Big Leagues

- Professional baseball is not the big leagues. The NBA is not the big leagues. The big leagues is **your life**.
- The first step to greatness is total commitment.
- If you want to win, you have to pay the price.
- Your reputation is everything.

- Always play scared.
- The winners do whatever it takes, and a little bit more, and then they talk about how much greater it is than they ever imagined and how great it is to be somebody.
- All you can do is all you can do, but all you can do is enough.
- An ordinary husband and wife working together toward a common goal can do extraordinary things.
- You only have one opportunity to do something great in your life; when your chance comes, take it.
- On your tombstone will be "dud" or "stud."
- You've got to demand and fight for success.

The Dream

- If you want to win, you have to become a dreamer again.
- You have to have a big dream and it has to be important to you.
- You have to see yourself involved in something bigger than just your business.
- I don't know why, but my butt's always burning.
- At ALW we were just tougher than everybody else. We wanted it more. We'd knock your fanny off if you got in our way.
- Our job in ALW is to take "have nots" and show them, teach them, how to be "haves."
- We sell a *dream*.
- The dream is giving people like me and you, who want to be somebody, a chance to go into business for themselves, become a Vice President, make real money, have real financial security and real financial independence and travel all over the world.
- Either you are financially independent, or you are not. There are no "in-betweens."

Pushing Up People

- Treat people good.
- You don't win with systems. You win with people.
- You praise people one million times and criticize them just once, and they'll remember that one thing forever. Just don't criticize. It kills people.
- Your primary responsibility is to make people feel good.
- You must be able to tolerate the imperfections of others.

- Keep selling the dream.
- You do it first.
- Treat everyone as if they have a blinking neon sign on their chest saying, "Make me feel special."
- There has never been a test, and there never will be a test, to determine the heart of a man or a woman.
- Don't lead by intimidation.
- Leadership is everything.

Winners Win and Losers Lose

- Forbidden words: I can't.
- We'll win because the enemy doesn't love it like we do.
- Most people do "almost" enough to win.
- Most people can stay motivated for a day, or a week, or a month, but a winner stays motivated for as long as it takes to get the job done.
- It's time to quit running and quit hiding. It's time to make your stand, to do it or not to do it.
- You've got to get a "mad" on.
- What do winners do? They do it and do it and do it and do it until the job gets done.
- It's almost impossible for a smart person to win in business in America today.
- Always be positive, always be positive, always be positive.

Magnitude

- Understand the AWESOMENESS of this opportunity.
- Feel good about your company, your future, and the MAGNITUDE of what we do.
- Do you really understand the MAGNITUDE of this thing?
- There has only been one person who really understood the MAGNITUDE of this. That man was Art Williams.
- We sell hope, a dream, an opportunity, and a pot at the end of the rainbow.

Do What You Need to Do...Anyway

- People are unreasonable, illogical, and self-centered. Love them **anyway**.
- If you do good, people will accuse you of selfish ulterior motives. Do good **anyway.**

- If you are successful, you will win false friends and true enemies. Succeed **anyway**.
- Honesty and frankness make you vulnerable. Be honest and frank **anyway**.
- The good you do today will be forgotten tomorrow. Do good **anyway.**
- The biggest people with the biggest ideas can be shut down by the smallest people with the smallest pride. Think big **anyway**.
- People favor underdogs but follow only top dogs. Fight for the underdogs **anyway**.
- What you spend years building may be destroyed overnight. Build **anyway**.
- Give the world the best you've got, and you'll get kicked in the teeth. Give the world the best you've got **anyway**.

Chapter 7:

THE PEOPLE EFFECTS OF THE PHENOMENON

The Original 85: The First Followers

Imagine one man who begins dancing by himself while hearing music that stirs his soul (remember those who can't hear the music think the dancer to be mad). Then a few courageous souls join in and are forever known as the First Followers (FF).

This was the core of Art's crusade. Art's First Followers were the courageous people who chose to follow one man with a dream and a crusade, despite the odds.

- An **Initiator** (Art) has the guts to stand above the rest and look ridiculous (the first dancer).
- Then come the **First Followers** (Rusty, Bobby, Virginia, Bob, Frank, and Fred and the Original 85).
- The FF are viciously ridiculed for joining this band of insurance renegades.
- These FF had the guts to join Art's crusade.
- The FF are ridiculed, rejected by their families and friends for joining. They had "good jobs" and were throwing their lives away.
- Author Peter Drucker said, "If anything is done, it is done by a nut on a mission." The First Followers turn the nut (Art), into a generational leader because they follow him. You can only know that you are a leader if you see that others are following. *(Goodreads, 2022)*
- Art was the flint (the material used for producing a spark).
- The FF become the spark (a hot glowing particle struck from a larger mass) that caused more and more sparks (the 85 grew to 225,000 in 12 years).
- Art needed and nurtured the FF or his crusade would dwindle to a mere good idea.
- The FF courageously followed.
- The FF validated Art as the leader by their following.

- A tipping point occurred when the FF recruited the masses and the multiples created sheer numbers. Those numbers created success and the crusade was validated.
- No one now stands out as the FF did.
- No one will ever be ridiculed like the FF were.
- The once-ridiculed now have made others look ridiculous for not joining and becoming wealthy like they did.

Why were the 85 so tenacious? There is a story about General U.S. Grant that explains that tenacity. "It reminds me of a little anecdote about the automaton chess player, which many years ago astonished the world by its skill in that game. After a while the automaton was challenged by a celebrated player, who, to his great chagrin, was beaten twice by the machine. At the end of the second game, the player, significantly pointing his finger at the automaton, exclaimed in a very decided tone, 'There's a man in it!' That, he explained, referring to Grant, was 'the secret' to his army's fortunes." As Grant was the secret to his army's fortunes, Art was the secret to his "rag-tag army." *(New York Times, 1864)*

Art earned a place in our hearts as Lincoln did. "Even Horace Greeley, while holding out for an alternative, acknowledged that the president had earned an honored place in the hearts of his fellow Americans. The people think of him by night and by day and pray for him, and their hearts are where they have made so heavy an investment." *(Goodwin, 2013)*

Like those who signed the Declaration of Independence, we too had the same commitment. "For the support of this declaration, with firm reliance on the protection of the divine providence, we mutually pledge to each other, our lives, our fortunes, and our sacred honor." We wagered it all on this system and Art, that we were right and would fight to the end. As with the Union soldiers we were 'fighting for a holy cause' in a 'righteous conflict.' *(Goodwin, 2013)*

The Original RVPs:

Fred Marceau, Rusty Crossland, Bobby Buisson, Virginia Carter, Bob Turley, Frank Dineen

Fred Marceaux

Fred Marceaux was the kind of crusader that Art's phenomenon attracted. Fred played college football for Bear Bryant at Alabama. He was teaching and coaching football when he was recruited into Waddell & Reed. He joined A.L. Williams when Art started the company. He and another one of the original seven RVPs, Frank Dineen, worked in Tallahassee, Fla.

Fred had that "it" factor. Not the Hollywood "it," not the corporate elite "it," but the"it" that puts everything on the line in pursuit of their dreams, and fights for a cause greater than themselves. Fred had the "it" factor that changed the world. He was one of us and one-of-a-kind. He was a piece of work, a masterpiece of commitment and toughness. Fred epitomized the Art Williams phenomenon because he left the world a better place, using Art's crusade and system. He made his mark on this generation. He was not only an Original Seven RVP, but an original crusader in Art's rag-tag army.

If you would like to know the special kind of crusader that followed Art, who fought the fight with Art, who gave up a "good job" to follow his dream, read this note Art sent out right after Fred passed away:

TO ALL MY A.L. WILLIAMS TEAMMATES. FRED MARCEAUX, ONE OF OUR ORIGINAL 7 RVPS ...WAS A REAL HERO...HE WAS NOT THE SMARTEST OR THE MOST ARTICULATE OR WALL-STREET LOOKING , BUT....HE WOULD....KNOCK YOUR ASS OFF....A REAL CRUSADER....A FIGHTER....A WINNER....I FELT I COULD TAKE FRED AND HE AND I COULD KICK PRUDENTIAL'S ASS ALL DAY AND ALL NIGHT....HE WAS THE ULTIMATE WARRIOR....HE PASSED AWAY LAST NIGHT AT 83....PLEASE PASS THIS OUT TO ALL YOUR STUDS....I LOVED FRED, HE WAS MY FRIEND, HE WAS

MY WARRIOR, HE WAS MY HERO, HE WAS MY PERFECT TEAMMATE AND LEADER, FRED GAVE ALW A CHANCE TO BEAT THE BIG BOYS, PRUDENTIAL, NY LIFE, MET AND ALL THE OTHER CASH VALUE TYPES. I WILL MISS HIM DEARLY….THEY DON'T MAKE PEOPLE LIKE HIM ANYMORE …ART

Could any of us wish for a more moving and meaningful eulogy?

Rusty Crossland

Rusty is one of the Original 7 RVPs that started ALW with Art. Rusty is a multi-million-dollar-a-year earner. He has one of the largest organizations in company history.

Rusty was living in Atlanta, Georgia and working as a basketball coach. Like most people in that era, he only had a $10,000 whole life policy and a small decreasing term policy with Liberty National Life Insurance. Rusty had a friend who called and asked him if he would meet with a friend named Art Williams. It was October 22, 1972. Rusty recalls that Art came in and sat down at the kitchen table.

Art had a small briefcase and the biggest desk calculator I had ever seen. He pulled out a yellow pad and a red pen and explained the difference between cash value and term insurance. He also showed me his mutual fund statement where he had $42,000 saved. I had never seen that much money in one place in my life. I didn't understand mutual funds and I didn't understand life insurance, so it was a real education for me. I was convinced to cash in my policies and buy a term policy with Art. Then he told me that I could make $200 a month part-time. That was all the money in the world, and I could quit my three part-time jobs. Art invited me to the Decatur office of ITT. I didn't do anything until after basketball season, but then I started getting serious. I started making that $200 a month that Art had talked about.

At Waddell & Reed, Rusty was one of the most successful managers we had. Rusty was a real hero there. When Art left Waddell &

Reed, they offered Rusty Art's position. Art called Rusty and gave a 20-minute presentation on his new company. Rusty didn't bat an eye. He said, "I'm in." At ALW we just loved each other and were committed to each other, and it was unbelievable.

"That meant so much to me, Art later said, "Until the day I die Rusty and I will always be buddies; he's one of my dearest friends on earth because of the commitment he made to me."

What attracted Rusty to Art? "I found Art to be super genuine. The same as he is today. No fluff, he was down to earth, he was honest, and concerned about me, my family, and doing what he could to make me successful. That's what coaches do, and Art was doing it."

Rusty liked being coached by Art, but he could be tough, as coaches should be. "I knew to do what coaches asked me to do. Coaches understand being coached. When we didn't do the work we were supposed to do, he would scold us but in a loving way because we knew he loved us.

"I told the Art story. I told people how Art lost his dad and how his mother had to suffer. And how she had to take a part-time job to take care of her children. I told the story of how Art met his cousin and how he did the research on BTID. I told the story of the passion Art had when Art said to me, "This is what happened to my mom. I don't want it to happen to your family and you can change it."

Art's whole approach was passion and change. "I saw what a mutual fund was and how there was an opportunity for me to one day accumulate wealth in a business. As a coach, I could never make my dreams come true. I wanted more for my family. I believed Art when he said, 'If you work hard, work smart, care about people, and do it with passion, you can do it.' Art was our role model for success so we knew we could do it.

I grew up poor. I wanted so badly to get out of the mentality of just being another guy. I had a total belief that this was my only opportunity. I always knew I could be a coach again, a science teacher again, but I didn't want it to be my Plan B."

On building a company within Art's company, Rusty said, "That was an absolute buy-in point for me. Nobody wants to have some company's thumb on you and that rang true for me. I didn't want to punch a time clock and I didn't want to have to work for somebody else. I didn't want to do what a boss told me to do, because I always thought I was worth more."

Bobby & Red Buisson

Bobby was one of Art's first recruits at ITT when Art moved to Atlanta. Bobby and Red Buisson became the models for how to build a great family, a great business and become extremely wealthy. Bobby was one of the original seven RVPs. Bobby became one of the first $100,000 earners. Bobby and Red became one of the first millionaires outside of Art and Angela. Bobby and Red became the first in-house SNSD to work with the field.

According to Bobby, "For many, many years, there has not been a day that goes by that I don't have thoughts and thankful prayers about how I have an even greater appreciation for Art Williams each day than I did the day before. I pray thankfully to our Heavenly Father, Good God Almighty, in the name of Jesus Christ, His son and my Savior, and by the power and mercy of His Holy Spirit for having put Art in my life in 1972, 50 years ago, and in so many other people's lives. Art has had such a positive influence on our families, our clients, our sales force, and so many others who have come to know Art well, and also, to those who have been touched only briefly by Art but have been greatly influenced by him and his work in a positive, practical, and Godly way. The chain of people who have been blessed by his positive influence is countless."

Bobby and Red Buisson have built unquestionably the largest organization in all the company. They have won every award, made the biggest contribution, and have been recognized as the most recognizable and significant couple in A.L. Williams history.

Red is Bobby's wife. Her real name is Marion, but she's known by Red to everybody in the company.

Red said Bobby met Art when he came to their house on a field training appointment. She was nine months pregnant. Red didn't *understand everything because Art kept talking about having an insurance estate of $100,000. No one in her life had $100,000 of anything.*

Red remembers that Art intentionally became best friends with her and Bobby. Not in a manipulative sense but out of a sheer desire for friendship. Art and Angela taught them how to befriend people. They went to the movies and spent all their spare time together. Art and Angela were always inviting them over to be with them. It just didn't happen, it was purposeful. "They taught us how to build relationships and the value of them," Red said.

When Bobby came to work with Art at ITT, he was not a big success right away. He had been in the military and was coaching. They had saved the equivalent of one year's worth of income, so he went full-time right away.

Red and Angela loved going antique shopping. One night they went to an antique auction and bought six kitchen chairs. Red and Bobby had a 1963 Plymouth with the paint peeling off. They were living in Snellville, Georgia at the time and on the way home the chairs were hanging out of the car. It was like they were carnival people with a load. Because the chairs were hanging out of the car, the police stopped them. Red looked at Angela and said, "My sticker's out of date and I don't have my driver's license with me." Angela said, "Quick let's swap places," so they swapped positions and when the policeman came it was Angela who gave him her driver's license. That's what friends do. That's also the kind of person Angela is. She is a 'Let's solve this problem' person." Red said Angela was her best friend, sister and, at times, mother. Angela guided Red and coached her and they created a total bond of trust with each other.

At Waddell & Reed, Bobby had Rusty Crossland and Bob Turley in his base shop. It was evident to Art that he needed to promote Rusty and Bob to what was then a Division Manager position (similar to RVP today) or they would leave. Art came to Bobby and said, "We need to promote them to Division Managers." Bobby agreed. It's an example of what the early pioneers did to make Art's system work and have the company make it. Red said Bobby came home and told me that and said, "Isn't this awesome?" Red said, "That's not awesome, what are you thinking?" But it all worked out well. Bobby and Red built something big because they trusted Art.

When Art started talking about leaving Waddell & Reed and starting his own company, Bobby was committed to go with him. He just needed to know when Art was going.

"Art's character caused all of us to have great loyalty. We felt like Art and Angela were our best friends and would look out for us and our people no matter what. The trust factor was important when Art asked Bobby to come work at the home office and be an in-house NSD. Bobby would be Art's second in command and would handle a lot of the company issues and anything that Art handed to him. Bobby excelled at it because the field force had total respect for him. It was 1980, and Bobby would do it until 1991. Art said,"Bobby this is going to be great, but we can't pay you anything." Red and Bobby's hierarchy were so strong their income never went down.

"Angela was a great influence in Art's business. Art and Angela are both strong willed personalities, but they worked together beautifully. They married young and grew up together."

Red said the reason Angela started the Partners Program was "a lot of wives nag their husbands out of the business." At that time 100% of the people joining were men. She was giving credit to the wives, because their friends and family never had husbands who didn't come home for dinner at night and were on commission income. It was a hard adjustment. The purpose of the Partners Program was to educate and get spouses to understand so they could be supportive. There were a lot of pent-up emotions with the spouses, and they came out at the partner sessions held alongside FSS and company trips. Who wouldn't be emotional? Their husbands had gone full-time, this was a real business and things didn't always go well, plus they weren't sure if this was going to work. The Partners Program was designed to encourage and acknowledge that all the spouses felt the same way at some point, including Angela. Something that she admired in Angela was that, no matter what was going on or how tough it got, Angela never showed doubt.

Red was Bobby's office manager for the first three or four years. She said she loved every second of it because she liked connecting with the guys and seeing them either at the top of the world or in the depths of despair. She did a lot of the paperwork for Bobby and the agents. She loved living their lives with them

She was very proud of Bobby. He had to work at being in sales; he was not a natural. She enjoyed watching him grow, work harder than anybody else because he believed that the person who worked the longest and hardest would win. Bobby was always the first guy there in the morning and the last guy to leave in the afternoon. He was the example that Red wanted her children to see.

Pat Conroy is an author who wrote a book called My Losing Season. He was a graduate of The Citadel and a member of the basketball team that would play Bobby's Auburn team. He is remembered also as the author of The Great Santini, which was made into a movie as well as The Prince of Tides, which starred Nick Nolte. In My Losing Season, Pat Conroy had a chapter about Bobby. At Auburn Bobby excelled and was the Defensive Player of the Year in the SEC. In his book, Conroy said about Bobby, "I followed the rest of Bobby Buisson's career closely. He proved to be as good as I thought. His nickname was 'Bweets,' and Adolph Rupp, the legendary basketball coach at the University of Kentucky, was quoted as saying that Buisson was one of the finest defensive players he'd ever seen. Bobby Buisson, wherever you are, I was an eyewitness to your mastery, the tender wizardry you brought to my home gym. I dedicated the rest of my year to remaking myself in your image. It was an honor to take the court against you. I was no match for you, and for that I apologize. But I took some things from your game that would hold me in good stead."

Rupp was also quoted in the Montgomery paper as saying this about Bobby: "I could win the National Championship every year if I had five Bobby Buisson's on my team."

Bobby brought that kind of spirit to his work in building his own ALW business.

Red says she's most proud of Bobby's work ethic. Red also saw that he had compassion for people, even the ones who were not successful. She said that no matter how successful Bobby was, he did not have an arrogant bone in his body. Everyone in the company would roundly agree.

One thing Red learned from Art was his persistence. She loved the way he influenced Bobby with his honesty, compassion, and work ethic. Art also told Bobby to save money because he was not sure we would make it but, "He said that year after year after year," according to Red.

"Bobby played scared as a basketball player, and he worked scared to death every day building his business. Red said everyone at ALW also worked scared to death. It was how we were trained by Art."

In 1986 Bobby and Red finally started feeling like this was going to work and started enjoying the fruits of their labor, but soon realized it was the people who were more important than the things they were buying.

Neither Red nor Bobby's family thought Bobby had a real job. No matter how much money they made or how successful they were, none of them thought that Bobby could make a living doing ALW. Red is extremely grateful to Art and Angela for the great things they did for them and what they taught them and how they also witnessed them doing it for others.

When Bobby was working in the home office there were some RVPs causing some trouble and Art said to him, "Go out there and 'Williamize' them," meaning teach them the ALW way and show them how things are done. The right way. Art's way.

Red says it seems like the only friends they have in life are their friends in the company. She mentioned that Virginia Carter said she didn't want to retire because she would lose all her friends. Red and Bobby feel the same way. Red said there's a culture here of family and friends that is bolstered by a significant compensation program so that the better your people do the better you do. "There's no envy here, no jealousy here, no backbiting here, no tearing other people down here. Everybody must start at the same level, which creates an instant rapport with all the people in the company. Everyone is in the same boat and everyone, at one time or another, is terrified about whether they will make it. There is a bond here they could never find anyplace else."

If there were such a thing as a "First Family" of ALW, Red and Bobby would be it.

Virginia Carter

Virginia Carter was known as the "First Lady of A.L. Williams." She met Art at Waddell & Reed, then followed him to A.L. Williams. She was a groundbreaker. After attending Agnes

Scott College in Atlanta, Georgia, she served as a U.S. Naval officer in World War II. When she met Art, she was a 53-year-old single mother with four children who was over $50,000 in debt. Her father had sold life insurance, and she followed in his footsteps, but she was barely getting by. At Waddell & Reed, and then A.L. Williams, Virginia had the chance to build her own business, she took it, and she became legendary. She opened a door for women in financial services that did not exist before Art promoted her. She was instrumental in providing leadership to women in A.L. Williams. Her position and influence resulted in an award named in her honor, The Virginia Carter Award.

Art Williams said, "When I saw Ginny, she was everything I thought a superstar should be; she had those characteristics. She was so motivated. She was the first female manager at Waddell & Reed. Yet no one had given her a shot to build it really big until ALW."

At a tribute to Virginia, her daughter Gin said, "I believe that ALW carries the stamp that, in some part, my mother helped to create. She is one of the legends of this great company."

What does it mean to leave a lasting legacy? A note sent by Virginia's daughter, Gin, says everything that needs to be said about the A.L. Williams opportunity, what it meant for families, and how it created legacies that will last for generations.

From the desk of: Gin December 30, 2021

Dear Ones,

As I sent off the final distribution for 2021 last night, I began to muse on the significance of closing out the year with yet another large gift from Virginia Milner Carter. Again, I was struck with the awesomeness of the task of accessing the account that daily registers an income that began somewhere around 1978 and has extended

through the year 2021. And... is expected to extend through my lifetime and possibly through yours, and maybe beyond.
I don't really have words that can capture the waves of energy, emotion, and mind-blowing WOW, that is evident in that one notion. However, I do feel a tremendous reverence and knee-dropping gratitude to my mother, to the circumstances that led her to develop the kinship with the ideas and the people who, along with her, created the framework for the legacy that she left us.

I am hoping that you will take some moments to receive this last gift of 2021 with a focus on what this legacy has meant to you, aside from paying the bills or buying the gifts. Mom dedicated much of her life to creating what she knew would be a legacy to her family. She gave what she wished to other institutions while she lived. But she was clear that the greatest portion of her efforts would be granted to us, her beneficiaries, her beloved family. I know you will accept her gift with the reverence it deserves.

With love to you all,
Gin Sexias Carter
Daughter of Virginia Carter
(With permission)

I am touched by the depth of understanding of what Virginia desired for those that she loved, and how she created something that will last beyond her lifetime. It is said that the goal of life isn't to live forever but to create something that does, and she accomplished that. Her daughter's understanding would make her smile.

A builder friend of mine was complimented as a builder who builds houses that will last 100 years. How many people desire to create an income for their families from a business that will last 100 years as Virginia did?

A good man leaves an inheritance to his children's children.
Proverbs 13:22

Bob Turley

When Bob Turley joined A.L. Williams, it was an amazing thing for us. How could we *not* be a credible company? Bob gave us a confidence and a credibility that we were lacking. And he wasn't a prima donna. He jumped into A.L Williams with both feet and became a superstar in Art's business, too. Besides being a great businessman, Bob was a great person.

Bob had the distinction of being the person who introduced Boe Adams to Art, sparking a business partnership that created amazing growth and true business dynasty. The article below, paraphrased from *Birth of a Legend,* tells Bob's story.

For millions of boys growing up playing sandlot baseball, the dream of success was to grow up and be a big-league pitcher. Especially for the New York Yankees.

"Bullet" Bob Turley, as he was named by the fans, did that. After he graduated from high school at 17, he turned pro, and by the time he was 20, he was in the big leagues. Before the 1955 season, he was traded to the New York Yankees, where he played for eight years, pitching in five World Series.

Turley was a Cy Young award winner, a World Series MVP, and winner of the Hickok Belt for the best professional athlete of the year in all sports. By 32, Bob Turley had already known more success than most people experience in a lifetime.

One day Bob answered an ad from a company that had a plan to sell term insurance. Bob had believed in term for many years, and he went to work with this company. After his sports career was over, Bob worked with several companies, but soon realized something was missing. "I'd work for companies and then they'd drop the term product because of the controversy it created. Suddenly they weren't accepting term applications.

Then Bob met Art Williams, a man who believed in term as strongly as he did. When Art started A.L. Williams, he invited Bob to join him, making him one of the so-called "Original 7."

"The first year in the business I was the number one RVP," Bob said. "I was developing a lot of salespeople, but realized others were flying by me. While I was developing salespeople, they were developing managers. I didn't understand the A.L. Williams concept of management.

"That's the greatest part of A.L. Williams. It's many businesses within a business, always building but never built. It's a new challenge each day. That's what keeps me happy. I call that success."

Bob went on to become one of the giants in A.L. Williams, building a new legacy helping families achieve financial security, just like he'd built one in baseball. (Birth of A Legend, 1990)

Art loved Bob Turley. The strength of the A.L. Williams system gave Bob a financial legacy long after his baseball days were over. "Bob Turley was a major league ballplayer and the most money he ever made in one year was $30,000," Art says. "Scott Reynolds introduced me to Bob.

"When Bob died, he was earning over $3 million a year and had a $137 million a year payroll to his hierarchy. Our company was like a mega-bank where you could build it as big as you wanted and never had to have a personal affiliation with the bank. Nobody on this planet would lend the money to fund $137 million a year in commissions. With our company, you didn't need a line of credit, you just had to recruit a lot of people and the company found the money to fund all your growth. Imagine having over a $1.3 billion payroll over 10 years." Bob Turley was a natural at financial services and Art was proud that he chose to be a part of ALW.

Frank & Debbie Dineen

Frank and Debbie Dineen are members of the Original 7 RVPs in A.L. Williams.

Frank was selling copy machines when he was introduced to Waddell & Reed in 1972. He was at Waddell & Reed before Art even came to that company.

Frank became a believer in "buy term and invest the difference" partly because, before he met Art, he had a stepbrother who had five children and died with five whole life policies for a total of $30,000. This

left his widow in desperate shape and his family struggled financially because of it. Frank said that, like Art, "After what happened my family member, they'd have to kill me to get me out of this business."

Art moved Frank to Tallahassee, Florida to work with Tommy Taylor, who had left coaching and was now part of the Waddell & Reed management team there. Fred Marceaux, another one of the Original 7, was in Tallahassee with Frank and Tommy. Frank hired some people in Albany, Georgia, and eventually moved to Albany in 1975 from Tallahassee.

Frank is originally from Brooklyn, New York. Imagine the cultural conflict in South Georgia, being a person with a New York accent.

All of the "termites" experienced a lot of push-back from whole life agents, but nothing was as severe as what Frank experienced in Albany. His struggles with whole life agents were not the norm throughout the country. It broke Frank's heart that he had a lot of good people who got beat down by the whole life agents, but all it did was create toughness and resolve within Frank and his people.

***True Incidents**: Frank was at breakfast with one of his top people at a restaurant where 10 to 12 whole life agents would eat regularly. Those agents knew who Frank was and what he did. To antagonize and punish Frank, they kept talking louder and louder and saying derogatory things about Frank and his association with ALW. It got so bad that, because the agents were regulars at this restaurant, the owner asked Frank to leave to stop the commotion.*

The next day Frank called up several of his part-timers to take the day off and go to that same restaurant where they began to talk louder and louder about the whole life agents. The owner was concerned and called the sheriff. When the sheriff came and started questioning Frank and his people, he threatened to arrest them for disturbing the peace. After Frank explained everything to him, he backed off.

When Frank married, he asked his wife about her car insurance. He asked Debbie if she had paid the bill, and she said she had not seen any bills. It turned out that Debbie had automobile insurance with an agent in the town who sold whole life as well as auto insurance. When Frank asked the agent about the automobile insurance policy, he found out that the agent had canceled his wife's car insurance policy out of revenge for Frank's position and BTID. The agent said, "What are you going to do, replace my policies?"

He had a police sergeant who had converted a whole life policy with one of Frank's reps. An old whole life agent told the police sergeant that what Frank was doing was illegal. The police sergeant said to Frank, "For the sake of my family, I'm going to keep my whole life policy, because your company is not going be around long to pay the death claim." Every year on the anniversary of the police sergeant deciding to keep his whole life policy, Frank would call him and say, "We are still in business, Sergeant." He did this for 15 straight years.

For Frank it was more than a business; it was a crusade. He felt a strong calling to change the industry that did damage to so many people. Frank felt that he and Art had a common background because of what happened to their families.

Frank said, "My belief kept me going no matter what adversity I was having, Art was having, or the company was having."

Art called Frank up one day and said they were leaving Waddell & Reed and Frank said, "Wherever you're going I'm in." Frank felt great relief when they left Waddell & Reed because he was fed up with the underwriting, the executives in the home office, and the elitist attitudes there. He would have none of it.

On February 10, 1977, Frank left Waddell & Reed with the other 84 people. Shortly after, he was promoted to Resident Vice President, the name for the position at the time.

Frank looked up to Art and Angela as the kind of people he wanted he and his wife to be. He saw how Art treated people and he wanted to be treated the same way. He wanted to find a wife that would be like Angela, and he did with Debbie. Art and Angela were role models in all areas of Frank's life. Frank saw that they believed in the right things. Because Frank and Debbie lived in South Georgia, he got to meet Angela's mom and dad in Cairo. He got to see what their backgrounds were, and the kind of people Art at Angela came from.

How did he find out about Art leaving Waddell & Reed? Art called Frank and Tee Faircloth (an Original 85) a little after February 10 to meet at a crossroads near Albany. Frank and Tee were at the crossroads when Art drove up in his red Audi. Art jumped out of his car and got into the backseat of Frank's car and said, "It hit the fan. We are leaving. You two are going to become RVPs. We have great products. I will be back to you by Friday night." He was there maybe a total of 15 minutes, said Frank. "Art talked so fast we couldn't ask any questions."

Frank said he went to Tee's office in Macon and gave the same talk that Art gave to them. "We're going to have more promotions; we're going to make more money; we have unbelievably better products." We didn't know what else to say, and then I went back to Albany and said the same thing to my own guys."

In Tallahassee, Frank worked very closely with Fred Marceaux and Tommy Taylor. Tommy would tell Frank what kind of player, person and coach Art was. Fred had worked with Art in coaching and would say the same thing. Frank got to know Art better by talking to Tommy and Fred and got to believe in him even more.

Frank and Debbie built a huge hierarchy and have become financially independent because of the phenomenon of Art and Angela and have taken many others with them.

Memories and Recollections

Everyone in A.L. Williams has a story. I've chosen a few to highlight the vast impact Art and his phenomenon had on the lives of so many average and ordinary people who wanted to be part of something extraordinary. Art Williams gave these leaders — and all ALW leaders — that opportunity.

Randall & Mary Walker

Randall Walker was the eighth RVP and one of Art's most trusted colleagues. Randall was a coach, like Art, and Mary was a schoolteacher when the A.L. Williams opportunity was presented to them. Their willingness to lay it all on the line changed their family's legacy forever. Randall passed away in 2005, and today Mary runs the business they built together. Mary tells the story of their journey to success.

Art was living in Snellville, Georgia and had sent out recruiting letters to football coaches in the area with no response. One day he drove over to Snellville high school and talked to Bobby Johnson, the head football coach. Bobby remembered getting the letter and had thrown it in the trash. Bobby had no interest in doing anything with Art but said that the basketball coach saw the letter and wondered what it was about. Art talked to Tee Faircloth, the basketball coach. Tee started part-time and from him came Randall Walker, Bob Miller, and Bobby Buisson. They had all played basketball together at Auburn University. Those four eventually were responsible for 50% or more of all ALW's business. All became mega-wealthy. All had the right stuff and followed Art.

What kind of cloth were the originals cut from? Harvard? Yale? Princeton? Hardly. Randall and Mary Walker started part-time in Carrollton, Georgia. Randall was helping his dad as a cotton farmer and Mary was a business education schoolteacher. In 1972 Tee Faircloth had already been recruited by Art. It turned out that Randall and Mary were the prototypes of the quality of people that built the ALW empire. Mary and Randall had a whole life policy that was replaced by Tee. They had been spending $20 a month for $9600 total of life insurance with four policies. Tee gave them $50,000 on both for $18 a month.

Mary said Art was just a coach. They liked him but they weren't about to change their life because of him, yet. When they first saw Art, he was wearing typical coach's shorts. As Mary explained, "They were tight little stretchy things. Randall wore them too. It made Art seem like one of us. You could always tell a football coach by the shorts he wore."

They started part time and struggled like most people. Randall would occasionally make a sale, maybe once a month. Art had a policy pick-up contest and they picked up 34 sets of policies in a one-week period to win the contest. Mary said of Art," He was a master of contests and recognition."

They may have started slowly because they started part-time. They were only making $13,000 a year in the business which was what Mary was making as a schoolteacher, but it started to work. The 5th year they made $36,000; the 6th year, $70,000; the seventh year (and as a *new RVP), their income jumped to $130,000. Their 12th year they made $270,000.*

Randall started at ITT with Art. Mary said, "We would have followed him anywhere. We would follow him without seeing any contracts for a new company like Waddell & Reed. No one else could have put together what Art put together because we believed in him so much." Other coaches who coached against Art indicated that he was smart, and a borderline coaching genius. He was tough to coach against. Mary said he was the kind of coach that you would do anything to please. She said, "He had the ability to make you believe that he thought you had the most potential of anybody."

Mary indicated that Randall was one of two people in the company that Art consulted whenever he had to make big decisions. "Whenever we had an RVP meeting, everyone would give their opinion. Then Art would ultimately ask Randall what he thought. Randall had not said anything to that point. After Randall was finished speaking, Art knew what he had to do, and the meeting was quickly over. Art knew Randall was fair and didn't have an agenda or a selfish bone in his body. Art knew that Randall saw the big picture and had the future of the company at heart."

Mary and Randall became the eighth RVPs in company history on January 1, 1978. Randall thought it was a compliment to be in the same group as the man who he would follow to the ends of the earth. Mary said, "We believed in him and, even if something didn't work out, we believed Art would fix it and make it better. Doing something that had never been done before necessitated a lot of trial and error."

Art could have his tough moments and get extremely stern. Mary said," Athletes were used to that. Athletes knew that coaches would throw a tennis shoe. Athletes knew coaches would throw a water bottle. Athletes knew that's just part of being a coach, but that's not who they are. Art was the same way. We knew where his heart was, and we let him be the tough coach we needed."

Mary said, "When Art left the company, it broke our hearts. We somehow thought he would be coming back, but he never did."

"We never saw Art as a boss, but as a friend. This wasn't a business to us; it was a family. We rooted for each other and each other's success. Art was our father figure, but that's what you have with a family.

When my son had a terrible car accident and had to go through 12 hours of surgery, Art and Angela came to the hospital. Art spent the entire time holding Randall's hand and talking with him.

"When Randall died of cancer, Art and Angela came to our house and gave us the kind of family love only Art and Angela could give."

Lou Miller

Lou Miller has known Art Williams for almost 60 years. Lou met Art when they were freshmen in college at Presbyterian College in Clinton, South Carolina. "I belonged to a fraternity called Kappa Alpha and Lou joined the same fraternity," Art remembers. Art eventually transferred to Mississippi State where he played quarterback his junior year. Art eventually dropped out of football to take an overload of classes so he could graduate in 1964. Lou would go on to Georgia Southern and play on the golf team.

After Art coached as an assistant at Thomasville he was offered the head coaching position in Baxley, Georgia. He called Lou to work with him as an assistant coach. Lou said, "Art and I were the only two coaches on the staff; that's all they had back then." Art went on to coach at Kendrick High School in Columbus, Georgia. Lou went with him and coached for two years.

Art & Lou Miller

When I asked why Art was such a successful leader, Lou said "Art was a quarterback, and most quarterbacks are leaders. Art was always looking for a competitive edge and always had a positive attitude.

"As we all know, Art was really disturbed when he found out his father could've had more insurance and his mother wouldn't have been left in a financial lurch." Lou said, "Art's mother was his idol, and his mom was a great lady. Because of his relationship with his mom, Art was shaken to the core when he realized

his father could've had much more term insurance. It was the start of Art's crusade."

While Lou and Art were at Kendrick High School, the whole life agents were raising cane with the Kendrick principal. It was at Kendrick high school that Art started part-time with ITT. "Art walked in one day and said, 'Do you have whole life insurance?' I had a $10,000 whole life policy and Art replaced it with $150,000 of term life insurance. I think I was Art's second or third personal sale. It wasn't easy for Art at the beginning," Lou said. "I saw Art struggle."

Lou left coaching for the golf business, but many years later he became an RVP in North Carolina.

"Art is still the same guy he was back when he was a football coach," Lou said. "Success hasn't changed him. He still loves people and cares about people. It goes to the heart and core of who Art is as a person. I saw how Art loved and honored his wife. I saw the time and energy he put into having a great family. He had so much integrity he would never put any of us in a position to compromise on anything. Once a coach, always a coach. The biggest things he taught me were through observing how he lived his life.

"When he believed in something, he became a fanatic. Art believed that every play works at the right time. Art kept calling the plays and if one failed, he just called another play. He taught me that and coached me because that's what Art is, a coach. Sixty years later, he is still coaching me."

Lou went on to say that, for Art, relationships were his priority. He loved people. His biggest influences in life were Coach Tommy Taylor and Coach West Thomas. They were two great role models Art had growing up. According to Lou, "I saw those two men in action every day. Those two men made up the core of who Art is today. Art was a point guard on the basketball team in high school, along with being the quarterback on the football team. But growing up in Cairo was a perfect environment for Art to become the man, the leader, the husband, and the coach he became.

"One of the biggest things he taught me was that it's not about what happens, but how you react to what happens. Art is a touchy-feely person to his best friends. Leaving A.L. Williams left a hole in Art's heart because it was his baby."

Greg & Sharon Fitzpatrick

Greg and Sharon Fitzpatrick are icons in South Florida because of all the success they've had in building their business.

Greg was a basketball coach in the Fort Lauderdale area. As with most coaches and teachers back in those days Greg was paid for only nine months of the year and the summer meant no money coming in. Every summer Greg needed to make $1,200 to make it through the three months. Greg's best friend was Bob Miller, who was his assistant high school basketball coach. Bob had played basketball at Auburn University and was the roommate of Bobby Buisson.

Greg hated teaching summer school, but he had no choice because he needed $1,200. He didn't like sales and never saw himself selling anything or being in the insurance business.

In the spring of 1974 Bob Miller had Art call Greg about being part-time with Waddell & Reed. Art came by Greg's classroom and explained his concepts. Greg immediately liked Art. Art went to Greg's chalkboard and showed him the Theory of Decreasing Responsibility and the Rule of 72. He was only there for about 15 minutes. Greg went to a local library and checked out what Art said about "buy term and invest the difference."

Greg had to talk with Sharon about working part-time. Greg asked Art to come over and talk with Sharon. Art pulled out the traditional method of explaining things to people back then called a yellow pad. Art showed how they could have five times more coverage by buying a term policy. They became clients.

Greg is one of the rare people still around today who was personally recruited by Art through Bob Miller. Art would say, "Greg, you'd be perfect for this." Greg would respond, "But I'm going to be a college basketball coach one day." Greg needed to make extra money, and at least he thought he'd give it a try. Art said, "Let's go see two of your friends and see what they have to say." Greg called his father and his assistant basketball coach and set up the appointments for Art to come by saying, "I just want your opinion on this. "After seeing Art do the *presentation, Greg said, "I can do that." Greg went to a three-day cram course and got his insurance and securities licenses. Soon after, he had two appointments and made $1,200 and didn't do anything again for 11 months. In his first three years, Greg created a total of 12 clients and made $3,600, which was all he needed. He never thought about doing anything more.*

Everything changed for Greg when he had a 7-foot basketball player on his team who was being recruited by an assistant basketball coach at Auburn. The Auburn assistant coach said, "If we don't get this kid to come to Auburn, I'm going to lose my job." That sealed everything for Greg. He could not see himself having that kind of stress-filled life. Greg was one of the Original 85 people, along with Bob Miller, to join A.L. Williams.

When Art called Greg to tell him that he was starting a new company, Art told him, "Now we have an opportunity to recruit as many people as we want, and you can build your own company."

Art was in Atlanta and would come to Ft. Lauderdale occasionally, but he sold Bob and Greg on how great it would be if they could start a scratch operation. The only schools available back then were Fast Start Schools in Atlanta, where Art had a three-day school. Bob Miller filled his car with five other recruits, including Greg, and drove 12 hours to the school. They would leave Thursday night, drive all night, and arrive on Friday morning. They checked into a hotel, met Art for lunch, then drove back on Sunday and got home at midnight. They did this every six weeks for years. Something changed when Greg was at that first school. He could sense something special was happening. Art would make them feel special with time for lunch on Friday and hamburgers at Art's house on Saturday night.

ALW had a lot of adversity in the early days, but Greg had Bob Miller and his team to strengthen each other during the tough times.

Art would say, "We are probably not going make it, but if we do it's going to be big." Greg would think, "Whatever you're going to do, Art, even if it doesn't work, we're going with you."

Art came down to South Florida one time and Greg picked him up at the airport. Art asked, "How's it going?" Greg responded, "I just got a big chargeback. I just had an agent quit. I had somebody tell me this is a scam." Art said, "Is there any one single thing that could cause you to quit and not do this?" Greg replied that, no, there wasn't. Art said, "Get over it. This is a yes, no, yes, no, business that will allow you to have great success one day, but that is just how it works. Get used to it." Art didn't pull punches. Being successful isn't for sissies.

Art's commitment and conviction were evident when Bob Miller made a sale that was canceled by the client because his old agent came back and sold him term insurance that was $5 a month cheaper.

Bob called Art. Art said, "Set an appointment. I'm flying down to meet with him. "Art said to the client, "Here is what Bob Miller did for you, and for five dollars a month less you chose to not do it with him but with the guy who ripped you off." The client decided Art was right and he stayed with Bob. Art's commitment to fly down and support Bob set a great winning example. Greg said, "It proved Art's commitment to us. After that, we never questioned him again."

Art's effect was felt by people other than those in his company. Greg's son knows a couple who are in real estate and the wife is responsible for 275 real estate officers in the state of South Carolina. They somehow discovered Art's videos on YouTube. They told Greg that at least once a month she would show all their realtors the Art Williams "Do It" talk. Greg said, "Art doesn't realize the effect he has had on so many people that are not even in our company."

Greg only made 12 sales in three years, but Art kept a relationship going for those three years.

Art said the reason he did that was that Greg was the right kind of person, and he just didn't have the right kind of goals yet. As long as a person could hang in there, Art knew that eventually it would all come together for them. Art said, "I knew if I could keep you around long enough, you'd make a positive change."

Greg said Angela added a whole new dimension to ALW and brought the partners together. Everyone respected, liked, and listened to her.

What made Art so different? His beliefs and his winning ways. Greg learned from Art that relationships lock people in and that they can count on him.

Art created a phenomenon and encouraged his people to create their own phenomenon. Art's genius was his plan for us to build "a company within a company."

Greg said, "Art will never know how many people will be affected during his time here and how many generations in the future will be changed forever because of the Art Williams phenomenon."

Larry Weidel

Larry Weidel was a giant that Art counted on. In an interview with Art, he indicated that there were two people in the field he counted on to react and respond to his ideas. One was Randall Walker, and the other was Larry Weidel. Larry learned the business in the base shop of the legendary Bob Turley. Larry went to Greensboro, North Carolina to build his business and became incredibly successful. He and his RVP team set records that will stand for a long time. Larry had the ability to see through things and determine outcomes pretty quickly. He came from a construction background and that's probably where he developed that skill and talent.

Larry told me that in the history of the company he was the first person to make a sale with the new A.L. Williams. Larry said that Art was having problems getting materials and applications to write business. One day Art came to the office with a box full of much-needed life applications. Bob Turley had a contest because he wanted someone in his base shop to be the first one to write the very first life app and offered a $25 bonus as a reward. Larry jumped on it and has that claim to fame.

Larry tells the story of how Art could turn things from a negative to a positive instantly. A short time after the company was founded, everybody was angry because of legitimate problems that arise with every start-up. Art came to a meeting at Bob's office wearing a "Do It Big" shirt. Art started the meeting by saying, "Let me tell you something. We are not going to talk about problems. Today we're going to talk about doing something great." Larry said that Art knew if he allowed any grumbling it would explode into chaos. Larry said, "That's when I believe the company was born, and Art has never deviated from that same go-go-go philosophy. In the minds of the field, we always believed that somehow

Art would come up with a solution for every problem we had, and he did".

Larry mentioned that whenever he would intend to talk to Art about a problem at the end of a meeting, he realized when he walked out that he had forgotten to ask Art about the problem because Art was so good at promoting the future. Larry told the story of one RVP in Texas who phoned Art and was mad as a hornet. Art told him, "If you catch a plane and get here tomorrow, I'd be glad to talk to you about it." He arrived the next day and met with Art. On the flight back home, the RVP realized that he never asked Art about the problem, and he never even thought to bring it up.

Art had an RVP meeting every six weeks because, as he said, "If I don't get you together every six weeks y'all will be committing suicide out there." Larry described Art as a bouncing ball cheerleader in the early days.

One day when Art visited Larry at his office, Larry was having a problem with a client who wanted to drop the policy he just bought. Art said, "Let me have the phone." Larry was excited to see the master at work. "This was a plumber who didn't know anything about financial services, and he tore Art up. I saw Art fall flat on his face and I realized there were no magical comebacks. That did more for me than if Art had saved the sale."

Larry tells a story of how Boe Adams was at his home and avoided taking Art's phone calls. Finally, he answers the phone and Angela said, "You've got to get over here." Boe rushed over and had to dissuade Art from what he thought was a great idea. Just as McDonald's at one time listed the number of hamburgers sold on their signs, Art wanted to put a sign on a tall tower in North Atlanta that said, "X dollars of life insurance sold by ALW." Angela had spent the whole day Sunday trying to talk Art out of it. She didn't like the idea, Boe didn't like the idea, and guess who backed down? Art. Smart man.

Mike & Stephanie Tuttle

Mike Tuttle worked for a while with the Campus Crusade for Christ ministry. A fellow leader there was Bill Stewart who knew another fellow leader in California named Doug Hartman, who knew another fellow leader named Glen Plate. Because of these connections, when Mike Tuttle joined A.L. Williams, California exploded — all because the dots at Campus Crusade for Christ connected with ALW to form a mega-organization, starting with Mike Tuttle.

In 1971, after graduating from Mississippi State University, I started working with college students through the ministry of Campus Crusade for Christ. I was there for five years. In my last year with CCC, I came across the book <u>Mortality Merchants, The Legalized Racket of Life Insurance</u>. My degree in college was in accounting, so I liked numbers. After reading this book, I was enraged with the way the life insurance was ripping me off, as well as most Americans.

In August of 1978, Mike Utz, who was a general agent with First Life Assurance Company, called me and asked if I would be willing to fly to Atlanta and meet Art Williams. I'd known Mike for about a year and had been a part-time agent for him during that time. We were strictly doing term insurance sales. There was no building of teams, no building management, and so on. He told me that Art Williams was doing what we were doing but had a different approach to our business. It took a lot of faith for me to buy the airfare to go to Atlanta for a three-day meeting with some man by the name of Art Williams and a company that I had never even heard of, but I did. It was by far the best decision I ever made. I'd spent five great years in the ministry, then I had spent a miserable one and a half years working for an antique auction company. I was raised in a very poor rural community in Pine Ridge, Mississippi. I'd never even been around any businessmen, and I knew nothing about business.

Anyhow, I went to Atlanta, having no idea who I was meeting or what was going on, other than this guy had started a company. They were 18 months old, and they were mainly in Georgia and were just thinking about expanding to some other areas.

Now anyone who knows Art knows what I'm about to say is true. The minute you meet Art, you just know he's different. He's a leader among leaders. I have never met anybody else like him in my entire life. I often liken him to Jesus in the Bible. When Jesus went to his disciples and told them, "Drop your nets and follow me," they did it instantly with no questions asked. They didn't ask for his financial statements. They didn't ask for any BBB reports, reference letters, etc. He spoke with such authority. Just who Jesus was spoke volumes. He had such credibility that when he said, "Follow me," people dropped their nets and followed Him. Well, Art Williams had that kind of impact on me and countless numbers of other people. He said, "Mike, we're going to build a different kind of company. You've always been in a sales company. We're going to build a management company. In building a management company, you have unlimited security and unlimited income!"

That word, security, was a big, big factor in my life. At that time, 1978, as a 29-year-old person, I was only making $1,000 a month working for the auction company. But I also was making $3,000 to $5,000 a month working part-time with Mike Utz selling term insurance. Of course, all my friends were asking me if I was nuts. Since I was making so much more part-time than I was making full-time in the auction business, why I didn't quit the auction business and go full-time selling term insurance? My response was that I didn't like sales and I hated the insecurity of living on full-time commissions. I didn't want to be ten or more years down the road trying to think of who I can find to go make a sale to.

But now here I am in Atlanta hearing Art Williams saying that with him I could have a giant management company that would provide unlimited income for me and my family, along with unlimited security. Those were magical words to my ears. I had never been so excited about an opportunity in my life. Art hated the life insurance industry, just like I did. He said we were going to go on a crusade to revolutionize that industry. I caught his vision, and I was ready to sign up.

However, there was one hurdle I just didn't see a logical solution to. I was prepared to walk away from the greatest opportunity I thought I'd ever seen. Somehow Art found out about my hurdle. Back then, Art did a three-day school. I still to this day cannot believe Art did this, but at 7:00 a.m. that Sunday morning Art was knocking on my door. He was *there to discuss my hurdle and to see if the two of us could come up with a solution. He listened to me and told me that he completely understood my situation. He promised me that if I would commit to going to work with him, he would give me his word to solve that problem. Right then we shook hands, and I went to work full-time for A.L. Williams. To this day I get emotional when I think about that morning with Art. There I was, a nobody, a 29-year-old kid that Art had never even heard of. I had no credentials, other than I'd been in the ministry for five years with college kids. And yet Art had gotten up early that morning to come meet with me to see if he could help me clear my hurdle. I promise you that this is not how he normally operates. What possessed him to do that for me I will never know, but I will forever be indebted to him. He changed my life. I immediately went from working for the auction company for $12,000 a year to making $160,000 my first year with Art and $460,000 my second year with him. Now that is still a lot of money today, but it was a small fortune 40 years ago for a 29-year-old kid. I cannot tell you how many times I think back to where I would be today if Art had not reached out to me that morning and totally changed my life.*

One of my most fun memories of Art is the first time I met him, and he was talking to me about going to work for them. ALW was mainly in Georgia and Alabama. They were just beginning to expand to Florida and Texas. After listening to Art, I decided to sign up. I can still hear Art saying, "Now Mike, you're going to be our first new agent in Texas. You're going to be funding all your own expenses, you're on your own, so we're going to bring you in on a Division Leader contract. Mike, you can't tell anybody this, because we say that everybody has to come in at the bottom. So, on the reports what we'll do it will show you as a District Leader. But you will be paid on a Division Leader contract. Mike, you've got to promise me that you won't ever tell anybody this because it will create some real problems because we never do it."

Wow! I am thinking Art must see something really special in me to make such a special first-time-ever concession to me. Well, I took off, and I exploded. That December ALW had their first convention at Point Clear, Alabama. I will never forget how excited Stephanie and I were to be at such a special event. We had never experienced anything like this. We drove up, and it was so intimidating. All of a sudden here we are making lots of money and having great success. My business was exploding, and

I'd only been with the company four months. I'd joined in August of 1978, now this was December, and he was calling out the awards. He called me out as the No. 1 District for all of ALW. But I did not feel right about receiving the award, because I'm really a Division Leader, not a District Leader. It seemed like lying about your birthday in Little League baseball. But what could I do because I had promised Art I wouldn't tell anybody about our special arrangement? So, I went to Bill Orender, because I knew I could trust him. I said, "Bill, I've got to talk to you in confidence. I don't want to get anybody in trouble, but, Bill, I've got to turn that plaque back in. That award, I cannot accept it. It's not fair because in reality I am a Division Leader. Bill started laughing. Bill said, "Mike, Art does that for everybody. In fact, the guy you'd beat is on an RVP contract. This is one of the many ways that Art makes everybody feel special. He tells them all that he'll put that on the contract, and that that person is the most incredible guy ever, but they can't tell anybody." My response was, "Oh my gosh, well it worked." Art definitely had me thinking that he must see something in me because he is giving me a higher contract than all the other district leaders."

Another great early memory for me happened when I'd been with the company for just a month or so. Art asked me to come spend a day with him. I thought we would probably be looking at scripts, products, plans for recruiting. etc. Instead, he just brought me in his office and then when people would come in, Art would say, "Hey, I want you to meet Mike Tuttle. He's going to be a superstar. This guy's out in Texas. He's a pioneer." Needless to say, he made me feel very special, which is one of his greatest strengths.

After work we went to his house. He got a football and we started passing it around. He had been a coach. So, we're out there running routes. It's September and it's very hot. We're getting all sweaty in gym shorts, running around barefoot in his front yard when his wife Angela says, "It's time to eat." Well, I'm ready to go take a quick shower before we eat. But Art says, "Not at my house, you're going to eat just like you are." It was the first time I ever met in their big, beautiful home. I'm sitting there in gym shorts, T-shirt, barefooted, grass stains, and sweating like a pig. About this time his daughter April enters the dining room and Art says, "Mike, this is my daughter April, and she was just voted most beautiful girl in high school." April responds back,

"Daddy, I was not." "Well, in my eyes, you were, darling," says Art. "She also was voted most athletic." "Daddy, I was not!" "Well, in my eyes you are." I saw first-hand how much he loved his kids, and how he loved his wife. What he was doing was setting a picture of where I could be by being is this great business. Art was showing me that this is where I could be someday. I too could be financially independent and have a great relationship with my wife and kids. That was Art. There was never any high and mighty attitude from Art. He was just Art Williams. He related to the common man. And of course, he had me spend the night there. Many years later and many CEOs later, I have yet to be invited to come spend the night with any other CEO. But that was Art. He has to be one of the most real leaders in the world. With Art, what you saw is what you got.

I almost liken it to fishing. If you know anything about fishing, if a fish really ever swallows the hook, and gets it down in his gullet, he can't get away. You can tie your rod somewhere while you go into town and have supper. You can come back, and that fish will still be on your line. He can't get loose. But if you barely, barely get that hook in the side of his mouth, just the least tug, and that hook comes loose, and the fish gets away. I think Art knew that I was way out in Texas with very little support. He knew that there would be a lot of challenges starting up my business. I was a part of opening up a new state for him, so he wanted to get that hook way down in my gullet. What a great opportunity for me to really see who Art was and where he was going to take me. After that day, I was so in, so caught!

Back in the late '80s big-screen TVs had just come out and, if you remember back then, they extended about six feet out into your room. Art had recently bought one. I'd never even seen one in person. We'd gone over to Athens, Georgia, to see Steph's parents. Art only lived about 30 minutes from there. It was the second December that I was with Art. It was Christmas time and he invited Stephanie and me to come over for supper. I thought, "There's no way I'm going to bother Art during the holidays." Well, Art truly insisted on letting us know that he and Angela really wanted us to come join them for supper at their beautiful home. So, we went over there and had this great meal. While there he wanted us to watch the video of his son's last football game. His son had been a senior in football that year. They'd won the state championship with no timeouts left on the clock; they had to go for a two-pointer to win the game, so Art wanted us to watch it. Well, the problem is the TV is in their bedroom. So next thing I know, there's Art, Angela, Stephanie, and I laying on their bed watching this game on their giant screen TV. Talk about a proud papa! He had the pep rally videoed. So we had to watch the whole pep rally before the game. Then, we had the warmup before the game because little Art was captain of the team and was leading in the warmups. Then we finally got to the actual game when my in-laws called to tell us that our daughter, Stacey, had gotten sick and that we needed to come home. We had already been there several hours and hadn't even got into the heart of the game yet. I said, "Art, I'd stay all night to watch this, but I need to go," and we left. But I just thought again, that was Art. You know, he was just wanting to share his life with us. Art and Angela, they just endeared themselves to us.

One of the things I often tell people about Art was that he was always taking the time to handwrite personal letters, making us feel special and letting me know that we were going to be big in this business. I look at how many CEOs we've gone through since then, and I don't remember ever getting one more handwritten note from anybody. If you go across the country and visit the offices of any of our top leaders, I promise you that all of them, like me, will have framed handwritten letters from Art Williams hanging on their walls And even more amazing is that, even to this day, I still receive handwritten letters from Art.

Another thing that I have always been so impressed with is that he always delivered on everything he promised. I struggle with big talkers in business who always make these grand projections but never deliver. When I met Art, his company was only 18 months old. In the meeting he shared his 15-year game plan:

- *by 5th year to be writing $1 billion in insurance. People laughed. Impossible! But he did it in just 18 months!*
- *by 10th year to go nationwide. He did it in record time.*
- *by 15th year to go public. He did it in record time.*

What a "for real," honest leader Art was who always *delivered. No wonder we all followed Art and always bought into him.*

To this day, people who have not had the privilege of knowing Art often ask us what it was about Art and Angela that made us so committed to him. We knew how much both of them truly loved us. We knew that, regardless of what challenges in life we may be facing, they were always behind us. He always let us know that he loved us and was committed to us.

John & Gloria Roig

The Art Williams phenomenon was not just "buy term and invest the difference." It wasn't just transforming an industry. It was much more than that, because it transformed the lives of countless people who changed their life stories and generations of their family's life stories, as well." This is one story of the Art Williams phenomenon from an A.L. Williams giant.

I was recruited by Bob Miller in December 1977. Bob played basketball for Auburn University with Bobby Buisson and Randall Walker and was teaching and coaching. Bob joined A.L. Williams and was personally trained by Art Williams. Bob explained BTID and I bought into it.

Bob lived in South Florida and didn't have an office. He worked ALW out of his kid's bedroom. I joined just to make extra money. Several weeks after I joined the company, Bob drove six of us to Atlanta to attend something called a Fast Start School. We would leave at 4 p.m. on Thursday and drive 12 hours and arrive at 4 a.m. in the morning, go to a hotel room, get a quick nap, and then meet Art for lunch. Art ran the Fast Start Schools, and it was there that I got a glimpse of what this was all about.

I was shocked when Art talked about being a dreamer. I had taught school for 10 years and I couldn't see myself doing it for another 10 years, let alone 30 to 40 years. I went into teaching to change the world and change kids. But I found out that there was more to teaching than teaching. I started growing weary of it. It was at that first school that I got a glimpse of becoming a dreamer again. I identified with Art because he was a football coach and I, too, coached football.

When I first heard him talk about how I could be a dreamer again, it was like he was massaging my heart. I missed competing and I liked the fact that Art had an enemy that he was battling against, just like the opposing football team. It revived me and got me excited again about life.

I spent two years part-time and in January 1980 I decided I was going to dedicate the rest of my life to Art and his crusade. I recognized that I had the coach, I had the leader, I had the right concept and Art made me feel good about what I was doing. That gave me belief and confidence.

In the early days Art would constantly talk about how we probably wouldn't make it. He told us not to take out long-term leases for our offices because he didn't know if we would last long. Art would always end every talk with, "We probably won't make it but if we do make it it's going to be big and you're going to get wealthy." He sold us the dream. He told us that we would be the most respected people in our community. He sold us the dream that we could financially take care of our family and our extended families. The big dream I bought into was that one day I could be somebody. Who talks like that? We soon forgot that we might not make it because we got so excited about our futures. In December 1979 at the A.L. Williams convention in Sea Island, Georgia, Art's wife Angela spoke. She pulled the partners aside it became the very first partner's meeting ever. When my wife Gloria came out of that meeting, she was fully on board, thanks to Angela's meeting. I went full-time and six months later opened my own office in Miami. It was June 1980, and in November 1980 I became the 111th RVP in ALW history.

Because ALW had a system that offered financial independence, I soon had a dream and an obsession to become financially independent. I did not want to have to go through life struggling like I had for my entire life. I came here to be financially independent. I did everything I could to recruit people and recruit more people and more people because the more people I had to override the faster I would become financially independent. With a lot of people on a small override I could make a lot of money and save it toward financial independence and that's what I wanted.

I've followed that formula for the last 42 years, and I became financially independent. Financial independence to me means that I am debt-free and living the dream that Art sold me in 1978 at the first Fast Start School. I wanted to become financially bulletproof. I kept seeing Art's thumb on the palm of his hand saying to us, "I don't want anyone to have their thumb on me." Art used to say that being financially independent was 1,000 times better than we ever thought it could be, and it turned out to be that way for me. Imagine having a life with no bills coming in? No mortgage? No car payment? Every day seems like a weekend when you have 100% of your income coming from overriding brokers and their agents. Imagine the feeling of Friday night, after the work week, when you've got nothing to do for the weekend. That's how I felt every day. Art gave that dream to Gloria and me and we gave it to others.

Art's influence on me came when I wanted to become better in all areas of my life. He influenced me to become a better person, better Christian, better family man, better husband, better business leader and an influencer of others. He had a way of getting me to want to be better. I saw his relationship with Angela, and I desperately wanted that same relationship with my wife, Gloria. Every day I tell my Gloria how important she is to me and what she means to me. I got that from Art. Everything I did building my ALW business I did for the benefit and betterment of my family.

ALW provided the vehicle I needed to become financially independent. I was teaching and I saw my income potential for five and 10 years in the future and I knew I could never become financially independent on that schedule. We were just paying our bills and had a nice little life but not a great one. I desperately wanted more.

As a teacher we would save enough money to go to Disney World once a year. Because I joined Art and bought into his dream, we converted that once-a-year Disneyland trip to going on amazing trips like the Holy Land, the pyramids, Europe, and even walking the Great Wall of China.

I also loved the fact that I could build a legacy to leave to my children. ALW allowed me to build a company within Art's company. We used to have bumper stickers for our cars that said, "ALW changed my whole life." It had a double meaning because it could mean I changed my whole life policy or changed my whole life period. ALW changed both for me.

I saved up the money I'd been making on a part-time basis so I could be in position to go full-time. Starting part-time I built something while being coached by Art. I always had an admiration for people who went full-time and put it all on the line. We made money and bought the material things like our house, car, took vacations but it was mental things that really made all the difference. Just the thought of becoming somebody, like Art said, brought great satisfaction. The fact that I did something that other people couldn't do was extremely satisfying.

Art didn't just recruit people, he made them close personal friends. Nobody wants a boss, and Art was anything but a boss. He was my coach, mentor, friend, and cheerleader. You can't put a price tag on a relationship like I have with Art. It is worth more than any toy or material things I could purchase.

I wanted to be an example for my children, my grandchildren, my hierarchy, like Art was to so many of us. He had a level of integrity that you could take to the bank in all areas of his life.

My relationship with Art goes beyond mentorship. His example as a leader is so exceptional that I wanted to be like Art. I am proud to be a descendent of Art, his coaching, and his teaching. What kept me motivated? Art's example.

I love the fact that I've been coached by Art. That's what pushing up people means, and it means you win with your heart, not your head.

We were insanely addicted to ALW and his crusade.

I loved it when Art said, "Our company was built so that people who look like us and come from where we come from could become financially independent. Our company was built for people who were never given a chance any place else." That motivated me.

- *You can get what you want if you help enough other people get what they want.*
- *You can turn your life and your business around in 90 days by working hard.*
- *We build people, not sales.*

One of the first examples Art and Angela showed us was how to have a better marriage. Because we own our business, Gloria and I became closer. We worked together and did not live parallel separate lives with her having her job and me having mine, having nothing in common outside of our families. We talked about our business, our futures, our team. Angela would say, "When two ordinary people with a common dream come together, they can do extraordinary things." That's what happened to us in our life. While I was out on appointments Gloria worked in the office and we worked together, dreamed together. That brought our whole family together. We got close and our family got closer. Art was our example and we wanted to be examples to our children. Because of Art and this company, I had my dad live with us for 29 years and he didn't pay one bill. That's the value of being with his great company and seeing how other lives could be affected.

My family was originally from Cuba, before the revolution. Twenty-one years ago, I had a chance to go back to Cuba for 10 days and see cousins that I had not seen for 40 years. I was able to buy them refrigerators, stoves, and change a little part of their world. At that time anyone who could get out of Cuba had to win a lottery. If you won the lottery, you could leave Cuba, if you could find a sponsor that would pay for all the bills to leave. Since then, we've had six cousins leave who are now living American lives. This never would've happened if I had been a schoolteacher. This never would've happened if I had not been coached by Art. Art changed my whole life

I'm proud that I was an eyewitness to the great phenomena that Art Williams started. I saw it with my own eyes. I saw the growing pains and I saw the success of Art's dream. I lived the Art Williams phenomenon like so many others.

Andy Young

Andy joined A.L. Williams right out of college from Wake Forest University. He had played football there on scholarship.

Art's phenomenon reached young aspiring people like Andy who dreamed of living their best life possible and gave them a track to run on and the hope to realize their dreams. Art said that, even though Andy was young, he had "the eye of the tiger." He wanted to be somebody so bad "it was absolutely unbelievable." He was in the second wave of people in A.L. Williams and Art says he was one of the best.

Art got a vision after his family was impacted by having too little life insurance on his father's life because the old agent sold him the wrong kind of life insurance. He found the right answer to fix that same problem for millions of people and correct an industry doing it.

No matter what the industry put us through, we had an answer for them. Art's solution was, instead of being the one person who attacked the industry, he multiplied himself into tens of thousands to tell his and their stories. That turned out to be the catalyst to correct other industries as well. We started with the life insurance industry, but as a byproduct we discovered there were other enemies as well. Any institution that took advantage of middle-income families came into our crosshairs. Many credit unions, banks, savings and loans and stockbrokers all took advantage of the middle-income people we served. We soon realized that many financial companies were victimizing middle-income families. People trusted them, and their unfair treatment needed to be exposed. It became an all-encompassing crusade.

Art's genius was distribution. He needed thousands of people to come together to accomplish what he wanted to do in the insurance industry. As a football coach he always brought together 40 to 50 guys and made them into one voice. He built a nucleus of people from diverse backgrounds for a common cause. Because we were doing something that had never been attempted, we needed to be a tight-knit group. Art needed to make sure his team stayed on track. Art had to change personalities and do things that had never been seen before in the history of American business.

What did Art bring? He brought team-building and the ability to build your own team, to have your own company within his company.

There is a crusader inside of all of us. Art just planted his crusade in us, and we took it from there. To have a crusade you need an enemy. As Art would eventually say, 'The enemy gave up. We ran all their asses off.' We were educators and coaches, and our specialty was insurance, money, and the proper use of it.

Art's system made it possible to create our own dreams and make them come true. BTID was the football to us. Art was the coach. Blocking, tackling and the fundamentals were taught, and we became assistant coaches to Art. It's like we were players first, coaches second, and owners third. That was Art's business model.

There was a certain section of Washington, D.C. that had its own publication. In one of their issues, they put a picture of Art on the cover, and it said, "Is this any way to sell life insurance?" in bold headlines. There was an RVP who had an office on a street that wasn't very reputable in that area, and it was assumed that he wasn't representing a reputable company. That's the kind of challenges we faced. That kind of judgement came from the total trust people had in the insurance industry. Art's business model was set up to make us 'Little Arts' and those who became that had huge careers.

How did Art change me? By watching Art go through adversity, how he got tough when he needed to be, and witnessing how he never backed down no matter what the industry, old agents, or publications said or did. I saw how Art handled the troublemakers who occasionally crept into ALW, how he took action to remove them.

Art moved this company and his cause by recognition. Art loved us, but he could be tough.

Art gave us the perfect model of how to build a company and be a coach. As a coach, Art would call audibles and make adjustments that needed to be made. A typical football coach has 30 seconds to call a play. If the defense lined up differently for a given play, a coach would call an audible, which is a change of play. The life insurance industry would come at us one way then adapt; the term insurance carriers would cut our commissions; the BBB would come out with a scathing review; it didn't matter. Art always had an adjustment. It didn't always work, but Art said, "You have to keep calling the plays."

Art had the ability to challenge us and got us to keep fighting when the enemy attacked. One time our insurance carrier made us take an 18% pay cut if we wanted to stay in business, but we believed it was the right play that Art had to call. He made sure we all had the bigger picture in mind, and we all bought into that "bigger picture" game plan.

Art would always give us another mountain to climb. Whether it was a promotion to a new level, or something called the Inner Circle, Art always had something new and bigger for us to go for in order to move forward and achieve personally. Art always gave us another war to fight. He had a huge chip on his shoulder and made sure we all had one also. Art had the ability to challenge us to 'burn our boats' so we would give it our all.

Art loved saying, "I'm just a dumb 'ole South Georgia football coach." He was anything but dumb.

At ALW, Art created an atmosphere and an environment where the hungry people became like gym rats. We loved it. We couldn't get enough of working and winning, but it took a world-class coach to get us to do it. Alabama legendary football coach Bear Bryant had nothing on Art.

In Rudyard Kipling's poem, it says, 'If you can walk with Kings and not lose the common touch....' That was Art. He never forgot where he came from. Art became legendary on Wall Street, but he was a common man. He loved wearing jogging suits and intimidating people who used to intimidate him. Art was the everyman. That's who we were. ("If" by Rudyard Kipling)

We would give the same presentation to everyone, whether it was the president of a bank or a plumber next door. That's ALW to the core. Nobody got special treatment.

We were on a mission. I was always the kind of person who was going for something. I needed to hear, "Go for it" from a coach. I was always driven to go for things, to take my shot at becoming an RVP and beyond. I had a bumper sticker on my car that said, RVP or Bust. Art assembled a group of people who had a thread of success in their fabric of life.

Art lived for a fight. In August of 1981 in the Lexington North Carolina Dispatch, there was an article, "Pyramid insurance company operating in the area." That fueled us. Our attitude was, "What else do you have to throw at us? Because you're wrong."

These were the core traits of ALW:

- *Art kept a scorecard to show us how we were winning and what we were doing.*
- *Art loved to be around competitors.*
- *Life will give you what you are willing to fight for.*

Some of the quotes that served Andy come from the legendary "Do it" talk (many years later Nike would come out with an advertising campaign slogan using those exact words).

It takes a certain kind of mental toughness to be a success. Art had it and made sure we had it.

Some other core ideas:

- *Go five feet further than the finish line.*
- *Do what everyone else does, but a little bit more.*
- *The difference between winning and losing is "this much," (then hold up his thumb and forefinger with a space in between).*
- *There are no excuses in the big leagues.*
- *There are no junior RVPs.*

When Andy was having a tough time in the business, he asked his father if he could borrow some money. "My dad said, 'If you need money maybe you should go out and get a good job?' That angered me. I was humiliated. I had no resumé, so I had to come up with one and look for a job. I went to an interview and almost threw up. I said, 'I can't do this.' That incident inspired me so much that I went from District Leader to SVP in 12 months. Because of Art, we discovered that within us lies a dormant giant waiting to come out."

Art attracted the kind of people who were wired a certain way:

- *They were competitors.*
- *They wanted to build a company within a company.*
- *They had a chip on their shoulder.*
- *Their butts were always burning.*
- *They hated to be called average and ordinary. (Art would say 'Call me anything but average in ordinary.')*
- *They had the fiery drive to become financially independent.*
- *They loved that there was a track to run on and a game we could play and win.*
- *They all wanted to be the best person they could be and have the best life possible.*
- *They always relished having another mountain to climb.*
- *They were poor sports about losing.*
- *They loved a righteous fight and that we were the 'bad guys.'*

I never thought about becoming financially independent before I met Art. Financial independence to me is the ability to do nice things for people. I always felt like I was playing behind the eight ball until I became financially independent. I woke up every day scared. Financial independence meant I could do everything possible for my mom when she was ill. Being financially independent meant I could rent a house at the beach for five months for my family to live while my sister was going through the last stages of her cancer. Being financially independent meant I could hire a nurse and all of us could be with her, and we could let my sister go with all her family around her. Being financially independent meant being able to pick people up and move them in a different direction.

I get a kick out of seeing people succeed and taking their lives to new levels. I loved seeing people fly first class and stay in first-class hotels that had never done that before. I loved being in a position to write the checks when I saw a need. I loved building a business big enough to have my life matter, that made changes in other people's lives.

One of the best great things that Art taught me was, "When you die people won't remember what you said, but they will never forget how you made them feel."

Jimmy Meyer

Jimmy Meyer built one of the largest organizations in the company, based in New Jersey, before he expanded to Florida and beyond.

He was just a young 20-something when he joined ALW with stars in his eyes. He was working for a newspaper but wanted more. He wanted a phenomenal life and was ready for the phenomenon of Art Williams that would give that to him. He recalled Art's cornerstone words, "I want to be somebody so bad it borders on being an obsession." The first time Jimmy heard those words something moved inside of him. "When I heard those words, I knew he was talking about me," Jimmy said. Those Art Williams words became the soundtrack of Jimmy's life. Jimmy remembers as a youngster how he wanted to play basketball, because it was his outlet for being somebody. No job interviewer ever asked him about wanting to be somebody. Jimmy coined the

name "Maniacs" for his team's name because he saw a maniac as a person who wanted it more, who did more and worked harder.

It hit a nerve with me. When I first heard Art's words, it became a WOW moment in my life. I knew then that I wanted to be coached by a man like Art. With him as a coach I replaced basketball as a team and found my new team: A.L. Williams.

It was important to me that Art would downplay himself by saying, "I'm just a dumb old football coach." I identified with that because he was relatable to me. Art would say, "We are not looking for talent we're looking for desire." I may not have the talent but if desire would be what it took for Art's promises to come true, I had that desire one hundred times over.

When I joined ALW I worked like I never worked before in my life. Art was someone I wanted to emulate. I'd had success in basketball because I worked at it. I liked being an underdog because underdogs seemed to have big hearts for what they were doing and a great work ethic. ALW was an underdog company taking on the big-time insurance industry and that excited me. I bought into the idea that I could win by helping others win. This was explained in Art's book Pushing Up People. *I liked helping others succeed versus working hard to make my bosses look good at a job. I bought into having freedom by helping others get their freedom.*

I saw that Art truly cared. Every time I heard him speak, no matter how many people were in the room, I always felt like he was talking directly to me. I wanted to be coached by Art. I wanted to please Art. I attracted people by not having them follow me but follow where I was going and because Art had a plan for all of us.

I loved doing whatever it took to help my team win. Team is an acronym for Together Each Achieves More. I saw that on a basketball court and with Art as our coach I believed it would work here, and it did.

Any player wants to perform for his coach and make him proud. I was no different. I wanted to perform for Art and make him proud of me. Why? I admired what Art was doing, what he had done, and I wanted to copy that.

It's interesting how Art attracted top-tier followers. Bob Safford owned his own company prior to A.L. Williams. Bob Turley pitched in five World Series, won the Series MVP, the Cy Young Award and the

Hickok Belt for best athlete in 1958. If these two accomplished men followed Art, how could I not follow him?

I found a team at ALW that was in my wheelhouse. It's the relationship part of a team that I had missed since playing basketball and I believed that I had found it again. When a team comes together, it's powerful. Teams come together only through adversity and during hard times. Art made himself available during the tough times. He didn't flinch when adversity hit us, he attacked and that made us fearless. I felt a special kind of bond at ALW that I've never experienced at any other place. The bonding element to me was a sense of security when I had no security, because now I was part of something bigger than me. Bonding was also having a movement. It was "us against them" and I loved being part of the "us."

Art was a master at recognition. He had a unique ability to recognize you when he was recognizing other people and not you. Every time he recognized someone and started speaking highly of that person, I thought he was talking about me and when it wasn't it made me work harder.

I loved being part of our team. I loved being on a team and being a go-to person where people were looking at me and counting on me to lead. When you are the go-to person you can either forget where you came from or continue to help people get to where they want to go. I chose helping people like I saw Art help people like me. Former Dallas Cowboy head coach Tom Landry was famous for saying, "A coach is someone who tells you what you don't want to hear, who has you see what you don't want to see, so you can be who you have always known you could be." (Landry 2022) Art would tell it like it was and all it did was drive me to work harder and want to be bigger. I guess Art was a father figure to me, as all great coaches are to their players.

- *I was driven to make Art proud of me.*
- *I was driven to get Art to know who I was.*
- *I was driven to be that somebody that Art talked about.*

I figured if Art knows who I am, then I'm on the road to being a somebody that Art talks about.

Whenever I saw Art in the early days, I never assumed he knew who I was. I'd walk up to him and say, "I'm Jimmy Meyer from New Jersey under Joe Ensor and Bob Safford." I was hungry for him to recognize who I was and I let him know how bad I wanted to be part of his team.

"I never thought Art was too tough because I knew he loved us and wanted to make us better. Any championship coach is tough and will make an example of somebody on his team to motivate the rest. Art did what he had to do, and we rallied around him when he did it. There were some bad people in the company at that time and we knew Art was right in having to get rid of them.

Art wrote two books, Pushing Up People and All You Can Do Is All You Can Do. Art would say that the most powerful words in the universe are, "All you can do is all you can do but all you can do is enough." Just as he started to say those words, we all joined in and chanted the words with him. We were united with him and the crusade. We truly were,"One team, one dream," and I believed I was the go-to guy on that team.

I was obsessed to let him know I was doing all I could do. Great coaches get people to seize 'the moment'. I wanted it more than anybody else and I wanted it so bad, as Art said, "It bordered on being an obsession. My butt was always burning, and I wanted to deliver."

In 1984 Art was doing "BEAT PRU" meetings. They were meetings with no RVPs in attendance, only below RVP. His battle cry was, "It's now. We can beat them." I was just a lowly District when I heard those words, but I gave him the best six months of my life and went on to become a Regional Vice President because he called that play. Art knew he needed to get future RVPs in the game. Art had an up-and-coming leader with him at that meeting named Steve who was my age. I kept thinking, "Someday that's going to be me." I had an obsession to be somebody like I never had before. It was vitally important for me, and it drove me. Art had the ability to create an environment that made the ball busters like me go for it, build teams and have other people join us.

I never played football, never put a helmet or pads on, but when I heard Art say,"We are going to knock their asses off" in his knockout talk, I wanted to put on a uniform and hit somebody. Great coaches get people who don't know anything about the game wanting to play it and win at it.

Being in financial services and recruiting was something we never thought we could do and was not a game I was familiar with, but Art got me to want to play and win at it. I didn't join financial services, I joined Art's movement, Art's dream, a happening for the ages and a team. I wanted so badly to be part of it.

How did Art Williams change me? He did it by creating an environment for me to believe in myself because he believed in me and that caused me to try. He would say "Try. Just try." He allowed me to attract others that wanted to change like I wanted to change, and it made me want to be a better man, a better everything. He taught me how to fail forward and achieve financial success. Not just to make money, but to become financially independent like he was, so "no one's got their thumb on me." It gave me peace of mind to be financially bulletproof and I thank him every day for giving me that. He really did change my whole life.

Art taught me how to build a team. Art constantly preached teamwork. He told us that negatives go up and positives always go down. Art taught me how to build relationships and how to spend time with people.

He taught me how to have fun with my team. Back in 1984 we had field Olympic games in the grassy field behind the Boca Raton Club in Florida at a company incentive trip. Men and women of all ages, from all walks of life, were acting like kids with childlike enthusiasm, playing those games like they were teenagers and having the time of their lives on their individual hierarchy teams. It built incredible teamwork that served the A.L. Williams system and became the backbone that caused us to win.

Art was never too big to do the little things, and to let me know that I was connected with him and his team. We were going to Art's place in Georgia that he called Little River for a meeting with Art, but our plane got canceled and we got in late. When we arrived, Art stayed late and cooked us hamburgers. He did the little things to make us know we were a team, his team.

Art's personal relationship building is what he should be known for and not just being a great businessman. When Art saw something special in you he went out of his way to get to know you. He'd ask all about your life, your dreams. He wanted to know what made you tick. He wanted to connect with you on a deep and profound level and you felt it. Art never demanded loyalty and commitment; you willingly gave it.

John & Angela Lennon

John Lennon is a successful builder of his own A.L. Williams business. He started with A. L. Williams in 1980.

He was 35 years old and was selling tax-sheltered annuities to teachers when he first saw the opportunity. John is a graduate of North Carolina A&T University. He quickly understood BTID because he owned some whole life and some term insurance. But he couldn't understand how you could build something here. He struggled with the concept of building a company within a company which Art talked about constantly.

What attracted John was the crusade. He said, "I wanted to be part of a company to help people who have been sold the wrong kind of life insurance and I wanted to correct that injustice.

"When I first heard Art, I was moved by his conviction and his strong passion from his heart. Art projected a feeling and a vision that resonated inside of me to be part of the eradication of whole life insurance that was so destructive to families when the breadwinner died.

"It felt good to be part of something that gave people an opportunity to do something great with their lives, especially for people in the African American community. It gave them the opportunity to make part-time money and start a business venture that could help them create a great future for themselves and their families. When I realized how much ALW helped families and that I could get paid to do it, it blew me away."

John was moved by the impact and significance he could have by helping people change their lives through the company.

It was important for John to find something he could believe in and be involved in, something that was bigger than himself. He was haunted by the thought that he and so many others were living the mundane and average and ordinary lives that Art so rabidly talked about. John felt like one of those people who was locked out of a better life.

"In ALW I found a way to change my life and to change the lives of other people by finding a better way to use their money and obtain wealth."

John was 35 years old when he joined the company. He loved being coached by Art. Many other leaders that he encountered had lacked integrity.

"Art's integrity inspired me to rise above the position in life in which I found myself. The crusade motivated me to do more than I ever thought I could do. I fell in love with BTID and recruiting other people so they could fall in love with it like I did."

John loved the environment of the company. He was especially moved by the pivotal phrases that have become synonymous with the Art Williams Phenomenon.

"When Art said you could be somebody, I thought I was already somebody but found out there was so much more that Art meant.

"In my life I had never heard anyone talk like Art did. It strongly resonated with me. He talked about financial independence, becoming debt-free, and building a company within a company. I never thought about things like that before.

"As I listened to Art, I thought I could build something special, I could become financially independent, I could make a difference in my community, I could do special things with my family and, if I paid a big enough price, my life could turn out like Art told us it could."

Art always said, "Never forget what blew your butt out of the water." John paid a death claim for a man with children who had a $30,000 whole life policy he had converted to $100,000 of term and a year later died in an industrial accident. John saw the power, the emotion, and the effect that BTID made.

"Paying that death claim pushed me over from being in the business of selling insurance to being a crusader. It took me to a whole new level of confidence and belief. I didn't have the conviction that I should have had until I paid that death claim. It drastically disturbed me and caused me to continue to fight for the people in my community."

John saw that the ultimate fruit of the ALW recruiting opportunity was deeply rooted in paying death claims. He saw recruiting and building a company within a company as a total package to be able to create value, with a death claim check as the concluding piece.

"You can't imagine the feeling you get when you pay a death claim knowing all the seeds you planted and seeing the ultimate fruit harvested when a widow gets a check."

John was especially impressed with the fact that he could invite other people to work part-time, make money, be taught our system, and own a company like he owned one. He said, "I saw The Art Williams Phenomenon as giving human beings an opportunity and inviting them to participate in a life-changing crusade."

When Art talked about beating Pru, John said the crusade came alive to him and caused him to keep fighting and digging. With that one statement, John felt that Art created a prize, he created pride, he created a team effort that was going to win a championship. John wanted to be part of it. He wanted to be part of the celebration, part of the energy in it and he wanted to be part of the fight.

He loved that Art kept promoting that he wanted to build a company where the next generation's opportunity would be as good, if not better, than what the original people had. He wanted the future generations to make more money, have more success and build it bigger. John saw this happen over and over again, and it exhilarated him.

Angela, John's wife, became an integral and active part of everything that they accomplished. It seemed that Angela had found her niche. He had his niche of building and constructing a company, and she had her niche of connecting with people. Her strength was a strong part of what their team eventually accomplished.

John realized that everyone who joined ALW was not going to have a career, but they used what they learned here to have a great life.

John felt strongly about the Art Williams Phenomenon. "I had never been on a championship team. At ALW I felt like I was part of something that was changing America and changing the world. I wanted to play hard for Coach Art. He instilled in me and others what it took to succeed and have the life we could only dream about. I loved it when he said that I could be somebody. That resonated with me and still does to this day."

Today, John is financially independent, and he and Angela created a company from nothing that will leave a financial legacy to his family for decades to come.

"I feel fortunate and blessed to have been introduced to something as powerful as the Art Williams Phenomenon and to have met an individual like Art who shared his life with me and many others. The phenomenon caused me to be more decisive as to what I wanted to do with my life. It also gave me the ability to communicate and share that life with others. It seemed like every time Art talked, he knew exactly what I needed to hear at that moment."

Frances Avrett

Frances is one of the original two women who set the course for all the women to follow in ALW. Back when Frances got started, there were no women in financial services. Virginia Carter was the first woman in ALW, followed by Frances. Since then, there have been thousands who poured into our company because of their example.

Frances is from Sandersville, a small town in Central Georgia. She started with the company in 1981. Prior to that, she and her husband had a wholesale plant business that they owned. Her husband had been in ill health for many years, necessitating Frances' need of an opportunity.

Frances said about Art, "I was taken by his ability to share his vision for what we can do. I loved the fact that he said we can do something special with our lives. I loved the fact that he said we could do something special in the world. Art said he wanted to change the world and he knew how to do it. That attracted me. I identify with Art because he is from South Georgia, and we came from the very same kind of rural roots."

The person who recruited Frances was living in Colorado. Frances went to a Fast Start School in Atlanta by herself. Art was the main speaker and Frances thought, "He knows what he wants to do. I like his mission, and when he talks, I feel like he is talking to me, talking about my family, my issues, and my dreams. His mission captured me.

"I was in financial trouble at that time because of my husband's illness. But when I saw and heard Art I thought, 'I can do this.'"

Frances's husband's illness cost them everything. They owed over $400,000 when she entered the business. Frances was responsible for taking care of the children and looking after her husband. She had been praying for something that could fix her financial problems. When she saw ALW, she knew it was the answer to her prayers. Because of Frances' husband's health problems, he was only given three years to live, but because Frances prospered at ALW, she was able to provide better care and he ended up living for 13 years.

Frances had been looking for an answer and before the A.L. Williams opportunity came along, she had interviewed with Fireman's Fund Insurance Company. She told the manager that she needed to make $50,000 a year to be able to pay her bills. But the manager there was typical. He said, "You should be happy if you can make $35,000." It was both a sexist thing to say and also a mindset. Most managers don't want you making more money than they are making.

When her recruiter from ALW called she asked if she could make $50,000 a year at his company. His response was, "Is that all you want to make? I've got people like you making over $100,000 right now."

Frances made $67,000 her first year and over $100,000 her second year. What she prayed for came true.

When Frances joined ALW, 99% of the people coming into the company and the industry were men. She was a pioneer. Art never saw her as anything other than Frances, a special kind of person. He never viewed her as a woman trying to make it in financial services. He never saw anyone other than who they were. Frances didn't join ALW to be a crusader for women in financial services. She said, "I thought, 'What if I would get ill?' I didn't want my family's income to go away like it did when my husband got sick. I was looking for something where my income would continue no matter what. I desired a passive, recurring income stream and some kind of ownership because that's what I wanted when we were in the wholesale plant business. Everything I prayed for was found in the package the ALW system offered. I never saw myself doing this and I wouldn't have done it if my husband had not gotten sick. I didn't like talking to people. I would've been a great accountant. We had 1,000 acres in Central Georgia and had a great life until the illness devastated us financially. I found my way out with this company, and it worked. This company changed my whole life."

Frances witnessed Art's integrity, how he was committed and lived up to his end of the bargain. One time Frances achieved a goal and walked up on stage to receive a plaque from Art. While he was giving Frances the plaque he said,"I can tell you're happy about this plaque. But you are here to make money. I'm from Cairo, a small town like you are from. I'm anxious to see how you do working in small towns. It's important to me how much money people make and how much money you are going to make."

Frances discovered that Art had the ability to identify studs early. He would call me and say, "I will be running by your office in a little while. Meet me in the parking lot and talk to me for a minute." When we met, he would ask for my opinion. I liked knowing that he felt it was important to hear what I had to say. I trusted him. He respected my ability to build. I was a horticulturist in my former life and that required having a duplicatable and transferable system and that's how I ran my business.

I'm very proud of the fact that in some small towns old agents met together to figure out what they were going to do about me and how were they going to stop me. They never could. I had great organizations in Macon and Savannah, Georgia. I would do my meetings on Tuesday, and I noticed that the Life Underwriter's Association ran life insurance ads weekly. To my pleasant surprise, they ran those ads twice as many times on Tuesdays because I was doing my meetings on that day.

I couldn't understand life insurance agents who were smart and had plaques and certificates for achievement selling the kind of products they were selling. They were intelligent, they supposedly had character and supposedly had integrity. How did they not figure out this concept of BTID on their own?

Art made a lot of promises and every time he made a promise, it was kept. When the words came out of his mouth, "I promise you," you could take it to the bank.

Art was honest and transparent about the times we were in, and our chances of making it. He also told us how great it was going to be in spite of the difficult times if we did make it, and we did. Art and Angela are the most genuine down-to-earth humans you can find. They had all this massive success and yet were so grounded and giving. I've never seen so much grace in my life.

Art is often thought of as the crusader, but to me he was more known for his ability to connect with people as the cornerstone of why he was so successful and why his company worked. ALW was a people company, not an insurance company. ALW was a relationship company, not a sales company. ALW was a financial independence company, and not a 'just another way to make money' company.

Bob & Chris Tillery

Bob Tillery is originally from Columbus, Georgia. He took a job in Atlanta as the Associate Registrar for Georgia Tech. Bob was recruited by Rusty Crossland in 1976 and is one of the Original 85 people at ALW. In 1977 he went full-time and in 1978 moved to Greenville, South Carolina. Bob was promoted to RVP in 1980 and ultimately to National Sales Director.

A funny thing happened with a lot of my clients. They began asking how I got into the business and if I could teach them the business.

Since I wasn't in management at the time, another manager would train them and make overrides on their sales. One day an announcement appeared in the Greenville News that the Life Underwriters in the area were having a meeting to discuss how to run A.L Williams out of business.

I called the number listed and asked if I could attend. The lady with whom I spoke was excited to tell me that they had two outstanding agents who had met with the leader of the local A.L.William's office and that I should definitely attend. I arrived early and got the second seat from the head table.

The head table was on a riser, and our tables were lined up perpendicular to it. The president of the Association had been with a large whole life company for over 30 years, and he opened the session with the great news that after that meeting ALW would be no more. The agent sitting between me and the head table was about 6'5" and fairly large and obscured me from the vision of people at the head table. I had my trusty cassette recorder and began recording the session. The man across from me praised me for that, saying he wished he had brought his recorder.

The first speaker came to the podium and ranted and raved about the confrontations he had with the head ALW guy in Greenville and how he had sent me running and saved his business. After about 30 minutes of this, another guy spoke and pretty much said the same thing, but did add that we were stealing clients' cash values.

The first speaker never saw me, but when the giant man next to me leaned back, the second speaker saw me and turned white as a sheet. He could not continue and told the whole life guy who I was and sat down. The big company guy told the entire crowd of over 300 mad agents who I was, and they screamed at me and threatened to have me arrested. I heard an agent at a table behind me yell, "Let's hang him now!" The big guy next to me stood up and exclaimed, "My name is C. R.," and listed all his credentials.

He ranted about what he would do to me if I ever tried to steal one of his clients. When he finished, I told him that the only initials behind my name were STUD and asked him about a couple of dentists and doctors whose programs of his I had recently replaced.

I then held up my hand to ask to be heard. The big company guy wanted me beaten up and thrown out, but somebody a few tables over said that they should hear what I had to say. I told them that what we did was legal and right, and then made three challenges to them.

The first challenge was to pick their top six to eight people and sit them across a table from my top six to eight people and we would have an impartial person judge them on their knowledge of life insurance, investments, and how to build financial independence. In addition, they would be judged on background and standing in the community.

The second challenge was for them to produce one client in the history of the over 600 companies represented who had been able to retire in dignity on the cash values of his life insurance policy. With that challenge I told them I would close shop and move back to Georgia if they could produce one client. The big guy next to me swore he could produce hundreds, but that never happened.

The third challenge was to come to one of our training sessions that were held every Tuesday and Thursday night and Saturday mornings and see for themselves how well-trained our reps were.

The big guy next to me stood up and said he would be there and that we should be ready to have our theory debunked. He and another agent from another big company did show up one Thursday evening. We had 72 seats in our meeting room, and they were filled by new recruits and prospective recruits. I asked a couple of our new recruits if they would let the guests have their seats.

The four reps doing the presentation were all fairly new, and only one had been licensed for more than six months. In the middle of the cash value illustration, the big guy agent stood up and announced that he could use that example and make the whole life policy look better than buy term and invest the difference. The rep making the presentation was stunned and looked at me, and I told him to have the man come to the board and have at it.

The big guy began to make excuses. He didn't have his calculator; he didn't have his rate book. One of our reps went down the hall to our office and brought back a Flitcraft, and someone in the audience produced a calculator. The big guy said he would need some time, but could definitely destroy our presentation.

When I reiterated that we met Tuesday, Thursday, and Saturday, and for him to pick a day that was convenient for him, he said a few choice expletives and left.

A week later I was having lunch with a couple of clients when a guy in a three-piece suit approached our table and began screaming obscenities and knocked me out of my chair. The fight was on. When the sheriff's deputy asked me what happened, I simply told him to call my clients to get the whole story. He called them and then asked if I knew that the guy who hit me was their former agent.

We began building relationships with some key people in one of the state insurance departments, and any time I was in Columbia, I would invite an attorney or licensing department person to lunch. After giving them our basic presentation, each one would ask pretty much the same question, "Why have we not known about this before?" Today, our reps do not have to worry about enemy agent confrontations or insurance commissioners who don't understand our business.

I have even become friends with a couple of former whole life agents who left those companies and now have successful auto and home businesses. My local Kiwanis Club has six auto and home agents in it, and they are all decent people. One of them was at the Life Underwriters meeting and one of our training sessions. Shortly after that meeting, he left his job and became a property agent.

I am so proud of what Art Williams built and how he never wavered from his belief in doing what's right. All the attacks created something beautiful. Just like a pearl is the result of a grain of sand irritating an oyster, the industry created an unintended consequence that enabled game-changing value for all Americans.

The ALW Home Office

While the early home office leaders didn't carry a briefcase, they provided the kind of support that helped the crusaders in the field to keep moving forward and spread the "buy term and invest the difference" philosophy to the thousands of people who needed it.

Art recalled some of the people who made the home office run. "Treacy Beyer, Barbara King, Mary Durham, Kevin King – these four made a huge difference in A.L. Williams. There are many, many others."

Treacy Beyer, PennCorp Financial

Treacy Beyer, who was instrumental in the biggest growth period in ALW history, shared with me his unique perspective on the incredible trajectory of A.L. Williams. Treacy was with PennCorp Financial in Santa Monica, California. He started in 1972 and worked his way up the corporate ladder. When Art and Stanley Beyer of PennCorp aligned, Art negotiated the necessity of opening ALW's own home office in Atlanta. Naturally, problems occurred, and administration was a wreck. Penncorp called upon Treacy to fix the problems. Art would go on to say that they saw immediate changes with Tracy running administration. Treacy reflects here on meeting Art and Boe, and his time at A.L. Williams.

I remember in 1982 or 1983 when Art and Boe met with Stanley Beyer. I immediately thought that Art was an exceptionally brilliant businessman. He was smart enough to take advantage of the business opportunity of "buy term and invest the difference "as a solution to millions of people's insurance problems. Art recognized a moment and took it. It wasn't that he did what everyone else did, but he did it better; he revolutionized an industry.

Art was also an extraordinary human being. He was not without fault. But none of his faults were fatal as some successful businessmen have.

There was one breathtaking moment to me that I witnessed. There was an executive in A.L. Williams that had a difficult history and threatened to be a source of embarrassment to the company. Art had his nemeses in the insurance industry, as we know, who were renowned ALW haters and writers. They knew about this executive and were about to write about it. This executive was ready to leave the company. Art said, "No way you are leaving. I'm not leaving you and you're not leaving me." That was the most completely unselfish and extraordinary thing I've ever witnessed in business. That's what one friend did for another. I'm not sure I'll ever see anything like this in my life. It's one friend saying to another, "I owe you a lot, you're my friend, and nothing that you did before is an issue."

There was a whole industry of people trying to stop Art and ALW, including the regulators, the 400+ thousand insurance agents, the 2300 life insurance companies, and insurance publications, as well.

When Art and Boe showed up at PennCorp, it was impressive. We knew that ALW was a huge player in the industry. We thought it was brilliant the way Art and his team found a way to sell term insurance and, pay people to do it using part-time agents and a compensation system that would create growth. Stanley Beyer was keen on finding a big general agency to generate business, and he found it in ALW.

Stanley and Art hit it off immediately. Stanley became like an older brother to Art. Stanley had a heart for salespeople and field people because he had come from a sales background.

Stanley wanted to structure a deal where Art and the A.L. Williams people could participate in the success as Penncorp prospered from the A.L. Williams relationship. Stanley wanted to start a reinsurance company that would belong to ALW, where they would take 50% of the insurance business ALW created and reinsure it. A reinsurance company would take the term insurance ALW was selling and sell it off to a third-party insurance company that would back the policies. Stanley set a threshold of production at which time that would be enacted, and ALW reached it quickly. The reinsurance company that was formed was the thing that created the A.L. Williams Corporation (ALWC). It was a wonderful plan because that 50% was already a profitable business. It became a huge asset because A.L.Williams went public. Many, many people became wealthy as a result, not just ALW agents but many of their family members enjoyed the financial success.

The initial person sent to work with administration floundered. I was sent to Atlanta to take his place. I saw myself as Art and Boe's partner and not an overseer for PennCorp Financial. I liked and trusted Art and Boe, and so it was not hard for me.

Before I went to Atlanta, my wife and I went to an opportunity meeting in Los Angeles. Art didn't know we were there. We just sat in the group as normal agents. We were blown away. We saw this as an immediate once-in-a-lifetime opportunity. It was really one of the thrills of my life to be part of ALW. I ended up there for 13 years.

After Art left the company, it was not one of my favorite experiences. I was in a place I was unprepared for. I saw myself as an ambassador and not CEO to take Art's place.

Art had a way that was almost spiritual. He had a vision of what to do. I always felt a special affection for the A.L. Williams people, and I didn't want to leave them in a lurch, but I knew my strengths and leading the company was not one of them. Sandy Weill didn't have a clue of what he owned or how to manage it. He knew how to run multiple corporations, not just one. I didn't feel like I was making an impact, so I left the company.

My first ten years with the company were the most extraordinary ten business years of my life. Art and Boe's partnership was fascinating to me. They completely trusted one another. They gave to each other. They never asked each other for anything because they gave it first. When Boe gave half his income to the field to create the National Sales Director position, Boe felt that the company and Art needed it to grow. They were remarkably generous and trusting of each other, and each proved worthy of that trust.

Because Art was a football coach, he could be very insecure. He was frustrated a great deal of the time, always wondering what could go wrong next. Because there was so much on the line and so many lives at stake, Art needed to be constantly reassured. Boe was great at reassuring him. That's how Art coached football because winning had to happen.

Art scared Sandy because he couldn't control Art, and Art refused to be controlled. It was unsettling for Sandy.

Art, the person, was a natural gentleman. He was an honest and faithful friend. I don't say those things lightly. I would trust him in the most difficult of situations. He was completely trustworthy. His relationship with Angela was remarkable and extraordinary to see. His relationship with Boe was also extraordinary. Art could be vulnerable in private. He became very transparent with those of us he trusted. He was not oblivious to the dangers and pitfalls that lay ahead for the company. I don't know anyone else capable of being as great a friend as Art was.

Art had the concept of duty with the salesforce, what he owed them, and what they were entitled to ask of him. Someone asked me, "How did Art change you"? It was an extraordinary example to see someone that powerful and impactful up close. Art was careful to use his power and his charisma prudently and carefully, so he did not crush people or dash their belief in him.

I always felt Art could motivate even a waiter during lunch. Sandy Weill couldn't understand how Art could handle as many people hating him as he did. Art had a whole industry hating him. But Art knew who he was and what he stood for. It was such a big part of my life that I will never forget.

Barbara King

Barbara King's personal story resembles the one of so many legendary field leaders. She had absolutely no experience in the industry – and none in the critical role she would go on to play that would impact the company for generations.

"Barbara was working at General Motors, and her kids and my kids were close friends," Art explained. "She lived in our neighborhood. We just talked one day, and she decided to come aboard. She did not have a background in public relations, communications or the financial services business, but she brought so much to the table. She was typical of people we attracted who learned on the job and were dedicated to our cause."

Barbara was one of the pioneers in the home office and one of the company's most important executives. She founded all the departments that formed Art's massive marketing, communications and recognition machine that supported him as he led the company to become No. 1 in the industry and win seven consecutive national championships: Publications, which later expanded to include ALW-TV and much more, Public Relations, Meetings & Conventions and Awards & Recognition. She also started the company's women's organization and led the company to support many charitable causes, which live on today through the company's foundation. Barbara also built an unparalleled leadership tree that is still in place making a major impact on the company 40+ years later, long after she has been gone.

"Barbara commanded respect," Mike Burroughs said. "She was tough as nails, and she had to be with the role she played within the company and with the media. Barbara had a relentless work ethic and the highest standards of excellence, and she demanded the same from everybody on our team. I learned a lot from her that would serve me well throughout my business career."

Kevin King

Kevin King was ALW's first lawyer. Kevin was a historic fixture in our company's birth and beginnings. As one of the original ALW people, Ed Randle said about Kevin, "He was a good friend who meant a lot to us during some tough times."

Kevin had a unique background conducive to our business. In the early days we had to provide something called "comparison statements" to our clients with a copy attached to every life app. They required our agents to pick up life insurance policies and pull pertinent information from them, such as dividend projections, cash value amounts, premiums, etc. Some agents would hire people to do this because it was just tedious. At the University of Georgia, Kevin worked part-time doing that work. He was familiar with our BTID business and was already a crusader. Kevin became a major cog in fighting the insurance wars. Now we have a whole department of lawyers. Then it was only Kevin. He represented ALW to insurance commissioners and fought to get our name cleared with the BBB. Kevin had an attitude of lenience that allowed us to go into regulatory areas that could be grey. He was willing to fight the regulators that he felt would change if they knew our system.

"Kevin and I had a unique relationship, and it was a really good one, even though we were approaching everything from the exact opposite perspective most of the time," Mike Burroughs explained. "He was in charge of protecting the company, and I was in charge of working with Art to put together the most aggressive advertising campaigns and attacks on the whole life industry in the history of the financial services business. But it was an entirely different legal environment back then – far less strict than it is today – so Kevin always found a way to support Art. I would finish working on a new project in Art's office, and he would say to me, 'Mike, I want you to go down there and tell Kevin this is what Art's going to do – and you need to figure out how to defend it. And I want you to tell him exactly what I said.' I would always deliver the message, and Kevin was so good natured that he would often just sit there and laugh, while shaking his head. He respected my position, and I certainly respected his. We had a great working relationship that led to a strong friendship."

He was Boe's right-hand everything. When the company went public, it was Kevin who made it all happen. He loved Art. He loved our people. He was a respected and trusted executive during the most trying and daring times of our infancy. He brought an honesty and a special character that caused those in power who could make or break us, to hear us out and give us a fair chance to show how we benefited our clients. It would be safe to say there would probably be no ALW if not for the legal guidance and personal care of Kevin.

Mary Durham Cawley

Mary and her husband Ken Durham, who passed away in 1995, were at Waddell & Reed before Art started with the company. Ken started part-time and was a full-time band director for a local high school and eventually became the band director at Georgia Tech. Mary eventually came to work at A.L. Williams headquarters, was a cornerstone part of all its growth and was an important part of our company's history. Mary has a unique perspective because she worked directly under Boe Adams in almost every area of the company and then alongside Art for decades.

After Art left Waddell & Reed, Mary started working for Boe Adams. She remembers the first home office in a Northlake office park in Northeast Atlanta. This company had its first meeting to name the company in an office building that was under construction. With bare cement floors and sheet rock dust covering the furniture, the company's name was decided upon. It would become the foundation for the great phenomenon known as A.L. Williams.

Ken went to Art after he started A.L. Williams and indicated that the company needed to start its own securities company. Eventually, all the security sales would go through Ken. Art needed a facilitator for securities to start a broker/ dealer and Ken spent the remaining years of his life in the marketing end of the securities side of our great company. He led the company to initiate securities sales, stay compliant and become an active player in the "invest the difference" side of BTID. "He was very influential in creating our first brand of mutual funds exclusive to A.L. Williams, called the 'Common Sense' funds. Ken was also the brainchild *behind increasing a client's monthly investment by 10% per year. If a person invested $100 a month, the following year it would go to $110 and then to $120 and on and on and on. This brought an increasing yearly income to our agents.*

"We can't talk about Art without talking about Angela. Art always said that the spouses have the largest degree of influence on their husbands and thus the company. He would not be where he is today without Angela."

Art influenced Mary and others by his words and his life. Mary saw Art as a morally kind and compassionate person. That was important because those character strengths permeated down throughout the whole company. There were always struggles and adversity, but Art's commitment, integrity, and pure grit showed all of us how to handle them. Art couldn't show hurt to his people and he didn't.

Mary said, "Obviously, Art had his moments as we all do, but he never gave up, he always projected hope and he would just keep fighting.

"Eventually Art and Angela knew they had to get away. They sought the get-away dream on 'The Discovery,' the first yacht. Then he graduated to the next yacht, 'The Lady Angela.' This was shared as well with some very special builders of the dream. There was nothing that equaled being in the presence of Art and Angela.

"I saw his strength and his struggles when his mother died of cancer,' Mary said. "I also noticed that after her funeral he had a peace, and I witnessed how he handled all of it. That was especially memorable as one year later that was my example of how to handle the same situation. Art and Angela were always strength with compassion.

"The first meetings and trips were conceived and planned by Art and Angela. As the company grew, so did events. I was blessed by being in the right place to work with them and eventually headed up Meetings and Conventions. After an extremely brutal several weeks, Art called me into his office before a convention. I looked tired because I and many others had been working night and day. It was wonderful and none would have it any different. He got up from behind his desk and came over to me. He put his arm around me and said, 'Now don't you get tired on me' and gave me a huge hug. After that, I was ready for another 30,000 miles. All it took was hug and a good word from Art.

"Our Meetings and Conventions department got to be so big we had our own travel agents. That is an example of the great growth of ALW.

"On our very first trip as a company, we went to the Grand Hotel Resort in Point Clear, Alabama. The resort and convention center were so nice that I thought, "We don't go to places like this. This is a lot of money. It was surrounded by palm trees all over and this unreal gated driveway that was monumental. It was the very first trip Ken won as a division manager. At the time I never dreamed of working for the company. We drove by those big gates three times before turning in. From those gates forward, what a dream was about to become possible.

"The big meeting that created the most ALW memories was in Boca Raton, Florida in 1984. This was a cornerstone event that solidified our future as a company. Boca was a playground resort for the wealthy that took our breath away. It was a statement trip that said, "We are here to stay as a company."

"I organized trips to Hawaii, England, Scotland, but the very first trip in 1984 to Hawaii was to the main island of Oahu and then to Maui. That was a "wow" trip because none of us had ever been there before. Art promised, "I will take you to the greatest places in the world." The Hawaii trip gave all of us a vision for the better life the ALW opportunity promised.

"Art could be a jokester. He had this infectious laugh. At one of the conventions, Art gave out nightshirts to the wives of his top people that said, ' I Sleep with a Stud.' Angela was somewhat appalled, but Art had a cheeky smile, and everyone knew he was having fun. At that same time the partners organization had a dance team performing at the partner's breakout. Art had the same partners come on stage at the general session to do their dance routine for the entire company. It was spectacular. We all loved it.

"Art loved making the impossible happen and inspiring people to do what they didn't know they could do. That summed up Art.

"Through ALW, God even provided another wonderful husband, SNSD Bob Cawley. He and Ken were good friends.

"God puts people in your life and because they are there you become a changed person. Daily Bob and I thank God for his creation. We

thank God for family. We thank God for putting these special people in the path of our lives. Art and Angela were huge in my life.

"I was especially proud of the statement Art gave to his spiritual strength when he gave a worship service on Sunday on the last day of meetings. It was unheard of in corporate America. I believe that's the reason we got to where we got to. It was a part of Art and not something he dragged out just to impress people. His spiritual side was something he modeled.

"If you want to know about Art and Angela here's a quote from Alex Trebek that explains who they are: 'Don't tell me what you believe in. I will see how you behave, and I will make my own determination.' (Trebek, mydictionary.com)

"People who never heard of Art have changed lives because of the life he led."

Yvonne Tyson, ALW-TV

Yvonne had a major in radio and TV journalism and was skilled in still photography when she began working at ALW-TV. They had six staff people and six freelance people working in the studio. Yvonne ran the day-to-day operation at the studio for several years.

Yvonne said the biggest thing she learned from Art was to believe in herself and to just get the job done. All who worked at ALW-TV believed they were bigger and better because of their experience, and they gave all the credit to Art. The staff gave it their all.

Art and Angela had the ability to motivate people to work hard by building relationships with them.

Yvonne's observance of Art was that he could be the quietest person in the room unless he was talking about ALW or his family.

The Original 85

An Epoch is a period of time in history or in a person's life, typically one marked by notable events or particular characteristics.

- To change an industry qualifies as an Epochal achievement.

- To change the lives of hundreds of thousands of widows and their children qualifies as an Epochal event.
- To change financial lives and give people the opportunity to own their own companies, to open the door for them to become wealthy, qualifies as Epochal.
- To take 85 people and in a short seven years become a NYSE company qualifies as Epochal.
- To go to war with the largest industry in America and stand toe-to-toe with titans of wealth and survive, with your only weapons being the truth and those 13 magical words, "I want to be somebody so bad it borders on an obsession," qualifies as Epochal.
- To bring honor, respect, dignity and hope to millions qualifies as Epochal.
- These 85 people, led by Art, accomplished all these things.

Somehow even the word Epoch isn't a proper measure of what Art achieved, along with these "average and ordinary" folks who followed him without hesitation.

From a dream and a crusade to a movement that would transform an industry, eighty-five people led the way, endured the hardest times, suffered the harshest criticism, and went to bed every night thinking A.L. Williams wouldn't survive, but they persevered, attacked, and ultimately won.

To these people, all those who came later owe a debt of gratitude.

Angela Williams

You can't talk about A.L. Williams' people without talking about Angela, Art's partner. She was a key player in A.L. Williams, from working in Art's first ALW office to her formation of the Partners Program, a game-changer for many spouses in the company. I spoke with Angela about her own journey with Art and ALW.

It was never Art only. It was always Art and Angela. Art used to say the only partnership he wanted in life was with Angela. "I never want a business partnership," Art said, "because they rarely work."

Art and Angela married when they were 19 years old and had a family fairly quickly. She was not only Art's wife and the mother of his two children, but also his confidant, his sounding board, and his truth-teller. If Art was the heart of ALW, Angela was the soul.

Angela's contribution to the A.L. Williams system is monumental. Angela's opinions and insights can be seen all over the history of ALW. Her legendary Partners Program transformed ALW from an insurance distribution company to a group of family-owned businesses where husbands and wives worked together to accomplish their dreams.

From the very beginning, Angela stood with Art. Angela encouraged Art to go full-time at ITT. They talked about it and decided he could always go back to coaching if God closed the door. Angela's parents were very vocal against Art going full-time with ITT. In spite of their opposition, Art and Angela decided to move forward with his career change.

The Columbus superintendent of schools confronted Art about selling "buy term and invest the difference." The superintendent's information came from whole life agents and their denunciation of what Art was doing. Angela says, "Art wasn't going to put up with someone controlling his life like the superintendent tried to do." Art and Angela's commitment to BTID pushed him to go full-time.

Angela was thrilled when Art made $300 on his first sale. They both made a commitment that they would save every dollar Art made from his part-time business. In just two years, he had earned $42,000. That was in contrast to him bringing home $10,700 a year as a full-time football coach.

When they went full-time Art made Angela cut up her credit cards to keep expenses down. The $42,000 Art made over his first two years turned out to be the nest egg they needed in case the full-time business started off slow. When Art was promoted to run an office in Atlanta, Georgia, Angela was his secretary.

Angela's family background acclimated her to living a life with Art being away from home a lot of the time. Angela's father was a surgeon in Cairo, Georgia. Her father was on call, as most doctors were back then, so in many ways his life was never his own. Because she was raised as the daughter of a doctor, Angela was comfortable with Art working long hours and coming home late after appointments. Angela knew what her role was in helping Art, because she had seen her mother do it in her home. She paid the bills, did all the packing when they moved, got the car ready when they went on family trips. Angela witnessed how her mother was a loving and supportive spouse to her husband and she imitated those behaviors.

Like Art, Angela's father was passionate and loved his work as a general surgeon. Angela occasionally went with her father on house calls, so she was involved in his career just like she would become involved in Art's career and business.

Angela was Art's first secretary. There wasn't a lot of money for office expenses, but she wanted to make the office as professional-looking as possible.

The first ALW office was a little warehouse that had folding chairs and folding tables. Their first full-time person was Bobby Buisson. They gave Bobby a small desk right behind Angela's. Angela tells that sitting next to Bobby all day long was interesting. Bobby's vocabulary was very raw with curse words sprinkled throughout. Angela eventually started picking up some of the words that Bobby would use. Coming home one day she used the same words around Art, and he was astonished. It didn't take her long to adjust her language at the office and at home.

Angela never complained about Art working so many hours because she saw the value of his hard work, the difference he made for families, and his encouragement of part-time people trying to make a better life for themselves.

Angela also loved everything about the business. She realized it was a relationship business and she enjoyed that aspect. She loved interacting with the agents and their families.

When Art decided to start his own company, she was totally supportive. Angela endured along with Art as they moved from company to company looking for a permanent home that was big enough financially to accommodate ALW's growth.

Angela saw Art reward and punish himself. If he did what he was supposed to do he might watch a ball game on the weekend. If he didn't do what he should've done she saw him work all day on Saturday.

It was at a convention in Point Clear, Alabama when Art asked Angela to do a partners meeting. Art had asked Angela to speak to the partners on numerous occasions before, but she never knew what she would say. He told her, "They need to get their attitudes straight." It was obvious to Angela that Art didn't understand what the wives were going through. The Partners Program became a lifesaver to spouses in the business.

What gave Angela strength when there was so much adversity in the early days? She said, "I had a passion for reading and studying the Bible. I believed that God had total control and I trusted him to open a door when another door closed. I had total faith in God that all things would work out for good."

When Art left the company, both she and Art were devastated. She recalled, "I was sad that everything we had built and the relationships we made were gone.

Art went through a total depression after he left the company. Angela credits strong Christian friends like the Tuttles and Stewarts who connected with them and told them that they were being prayed for. Angela said, "Anything that happens, happens for our good and God's glory."

They had a home at Amelia Island, Florida and during Art's most desperate hours, Angela would get up in the middle of the night and pray that miracles would happen. She had a hallway desk in the middle of the house where she would read the Bible and pray regularly.

Whenever Art went in a direction that Angela might not have agreed with, she remembered the Bible verse, "Not being able to change his mind, Gods will be done."

When thinking about Art selling the company, her thoughts always would go to the reality that they couldn't keep going at the same fast pace they had for many years. Even after Art sold the company, he was traveling three times as much as he had before he sold. Angela believed that living that kind of life wasn't emotionally and physically healthy for either of them.

During his time with ALW, Art was treated like a rock star. Angela did not think it was healthy for him to be treated in such a way. She realized he was a great communicator; he had the ability to draw people to him, and he was a great motivator. He was admired by tens of thousands and, as with any star, he could burn out.

She passionately said, "No matter how good he was as the leader of ALW, he was a better football coach. He was magical with those young men."

Angela concluded, "The hard trials in life strengthen you and bring you closer to God. Because they do, they are important parts of the journey. When you search for answers, that's when you get close to God. You must be grateful for those times. All the things that happened during our A.L. Williams life brought us closer to God and created that special desire to be close to him."

Chapter 8:

A COMPANY OF DESTINY

"The reason I kept talking about a company of destiny was because so many things worked out that seemed impossible," Art says. "It seemed that someone was looking out for us. Every time I turned around everything in my path said, 'This is my destiny.'"

As the protagonist says in *Field of Dreams*, "There comes a time when all the cosmic tumblers have clicked into place and the universe opens itself up for a few seconds to show you what's possible." *(Field of Dreams, 1989)*

Art told us this powerful story just before Feb 10, 1977. "I can look back on my life and realize I never really gave it my all," Art said. "I never became the student I could have been. I never became the athlete I could have been. I never became what I was capable of being. I was afraid. I was afraid I couldn't live with myself if I gave it all I had and didn't make it. If I gave it all I had and fell short. So when I started the company it was that moment that Winston Churchill talked about in his quote, 'To every man there comes in his lifetime, that special moment when he is figuratively tapped on the shoulder and offered a chance to do a very special thing, unique to him and fitted to his talents, what a tragedy if that moment finds him unprepared or unqualified for that which would be his finest hour.'" *(Churchill, 1940)*

Feb 10, 1977 was Art's "finest hour," when all the stars were in alignment. When all the tumblers clicked perfectly. When Karma presented itself. When all the energies in the universe came together. When the universe conspired for him to claim his destiny. His opening. It was Art's and our "God moment."

Art has said, "When nothing seemed to be working and then we started to succeed I knew that the Lord's hand was on our company. I'm not smart enough, I'm not good enough to take any credit for what our company did. The Lord has blessed me beyond anything I had hoped for or imagined. I was blessed with the most wonderful wife a man could have. I fell in love with Angela in the second grade and she was the only girlfriend I ever had."

Art sensed the special moment as his calling. "Millions of people struggle all the days of their lives with no stronger urge than that of acquiring the necessities of life — food, shelter, and clothing. Now and then, someone will step out of the masses and demand of himself or herself, and of the world, more than a mere living. He is determined to leave a legacy — a solid faith in his mission — the rooted belief that this is the one thing to which he has been called." *(Kimbro, 2003)*

If Art had delayed, even a little bit, it would have passed him, and all of us, by. Art told us that if he had tried to do it years earlier or later it wouldn't have worked. Timing was his ally. When his moment came, he took it.

All the Stars Aligned

We were a company of destiny. We didn't realize it right away because it grows on you. Belief grows slowly, just like the crusade. Steve Jobs said, "You can't connect the dots looking forward, you can only connect them looking backwards. So, you have to trust that the dots will somehow connect in your future. You have to trust in something: your gut, destiny, life, karma, whatever. Because believing that the dots will connect down the road will give you the confidence to follow your heart, even when it leads you off the well-worn path. And that will make all the difference. *(Jobs, 2005)*

To anyone observing the whole life insurance empire, starting ALW was a risky, even reckless, gamble but Art pulled it off. Art was the defining element. Art knew ALW's hope for success was dependent on his decisions, keeping a positive attitude, and prayer. But Art was what's called a "force multiplier," which refers to a factor or a combination of factors that gave Art and his 85 the ability to accomplish greater feats than without it. All the right people came together at the right time to create a magical company. When all the cosmic tumblers clicked into place, all the people fell into place. Art, his cousin Ted Harrison, the men who introduced him to ITT, Joe Jack Merriman, Boe, Art DeMoss, Stanley Beyer, Gerald Tsai, and Sandy Weill were the people tumblers that unlocked the phenomena known as destiny.

In the fullness of time, all the stars aligned.

The People and Events That Connected the Dots

Art Williams

Art was the central person in the movement that changed an industry and thousands of lives. Art was always looking to make extra money because coaching couldn't support his family. He took all kinds of part-time jobs, refereed basketball games, sold Christmas trees, and made extra money, but didn't want limitations on his income. Because he had a family, he wanted a secure income (overrides).

He was a coach, so he knew how to work with people and get the best out of them. He wanted to have his own team, be the head coach (his own company). As a coach, he was most fired up when he had an opponent — "those people in the wrong-colored jerseys" (the insurance agents). As a coach, he saw coaching as a way to change the world (a crusade). His father died and left his mother to raise his two younger brothers with only a $10,000 life policy when she could have gotten $100,000 of term and he became angry (the whole life industry). Art was the centerpiece that started the dots connecting.

Ted Harrison

Ted was Art's cousin. At a family reunion, Ted introduced Art to term insurance. Art was flabbergasted at the difference it could have made for his mom. The crusade and its crusader were born. The seed of a movement was planted and could not be unplanted. If Ted had not been at the reunion, the crusade might never have begun. "I can't express the awe of the reality of what Ted Harrison told me," Art says. "I saw my mother struggle and it tore me apart. It left her financially devastated, and I couldn't believe it."

Forrest Smith - The ITT Connection

This was one of the most life-changing events in Art's life. Art met Forrest Smith at a PTA meeting. Art only went to two or three of these meetings in his seven years of coaching. In discussing what Smith did for a living, Art discovered the man worked for ITT Financial Services. Smith told him (can you hear the tumbler rotating?) he believed in BTID. Smith told Art that ITT didn't hire part-timers, but he called the VP of Sales, and a trial run began. Art became the first part-time insurance agent in history. What were the odds this VP would give Art a chance, when no insurance agency ever used part-timers?

Coach Tommy Taylor

Art's earliest hero was his football coach in Cairo, Georgia. Taylor convinced Art he was destined for greatness, that he was special and had an amazing future. Art said, "Everybody needs someone to believe in them. They need to believe that someone thinks they are special, thinks they are different, that they are going to be somebody. Everybody who achieves something has that kind of person in their life." In Art's life, that person was Tommy Taylor.

What if Coach Taylor hadn't instilled the desire to "be somebody so bad it hurts" into Art Williams? Later, when Art consulted his former coach and friend to advise him or whether to go into insurance full-time and give up coaching, Tommy Taylor said, "yes" and Art's future was sealed. What if he had said "no?"

Coach West Thomas

Art's other huge influence as a young man was West Thomas, a mentor who advised and guided Art, greatly contributing to the formation of the man who would become the

Art Williams we all knew. What if Art had not had these powerful influences in his life?

ITT

They gave Art his first job in life insurance and a way to discover that he could spread his crusade for term insurance as a salesperson. But he needed more freedom for himself and his growing team, and his dreams were far greater than any company could support. Before long, Art was looking for a better fit. Destiny intervened again.

John Kostemeier

The former head of ITT had moved on to another company, Waddell & Reed, and called Art to tell him about them. Waddell & Reed offered another level of overrides, and Art made the difficult decision to move there. What if Kostemeier hadn't bothered to call Art? What if Art had said no, and stayed at ITT? Just six months after Art left ITT to go with Waddell & Reed, ITT went out of business. Art himself said, "We truly were a company of destiny. They (ITT) had been doing financial services for 30 years, and it was over. If I had stayed at ITT, I wouldn't have continued in the industry. I would have quit and gone back to coaching." How did these situations occur just when they were needed? An accident? A miracle? Or just the "fullness of time?"

Bill Atkins

Art met Bill Atkins when he was at Waddell & Reed. He was the president of United Investors Life. At Waddell & Reed he had created the first permanent term insurance policy ever sold called annual renewable term (ART).

Art recalls the situation:

"The month prior to leaving Waddell & Reed I was looking for a company to go with. I had no success, and I was about ready to give up. We had the reputation and the statistics at Waddell & Reed to show other companies how well we were doing. I approached five to six different

companies and they all said no. We were an unknown entity, and we were revolutionary in the BTID philosophy. Out of desperation I remembered Bill Atkins and looked him up in the phonebook and called. Amazingly, he answered the phone. He intimated that he knew exactly the person that I needed to talk to. It was Joe Jack Merriman, who owned Financial Assurance Corporation (FAC). Bill told me he had lots of money and was at one time president of Waddell & Reed, so he was familiar with what they did there. They made a commitment to us, and it didn't bother them a bit that we were controversial." What if *Bill Atkin*s hadn't answered the phone?

Joe Jack Merriman

When Art contacted Joe Jack Merriman, the owner of Financial Assurance, he was willing to back the company in a variety of ways. This move turned out to be another tumbler turning.

Art recalls, "After four months we were doing two to three times more business than what I had talked to him about. We were driving Joe Jack crazy with how fast we were growing. I was at a Fast Start School in Atlanta when I got a phone call that told me to call him immediately. He said,'You've got to get another carrier.' To his credit, he gave us three to four months to find another carrier, which seemed impossible because I had already talked to all the others that I knew about. As fate would have it (the tumblers turned), Bob Turley had met Boe Adams and our recent association with him led us to National Home Life (NHL).

Art DeMoss

Art DeMoss' company, National Home Life, was a mail-order health insurance company that had been trying to expand into working with general agents, and the Vice President of sales was Bob Safford. When Art DeMoss died suddenly, his company's directors chose to go in a different direction, but this caused Bob Safford to join Art. Bob became a giant in ALW. The situation at National Home set the stage for another dot, Stanley Beyer. And

later, incidentally, Art's daughter April would marry Art DeMoss' son, Mark.

The FTC Report

The industry was bashing A.L. Williams, citing a lack of credibility. All the media outlets followed the industry's lead with newspaper and magazine articles that attempted to discredit the company. In late 1979 Michael Pertschuk, the head of the Federal Trade Commission, released the FTC report on the insurance industry. The report identified cash value insurance as "overpriced" and blasted insurance policy "cash values" as a low-return way to save money. The FTC Report was a seminal event in ALW history. It provided the perfect ammunition to counteract the claims of traditional agents. Why did the FTC decide to do this report at this time? Why would Pertschuk go out on a limb to criticize the largest industry in the country? Destiny.

Charles "Boe" Adams

The financial genius behind A.L. Williams was Art's partner and best friend. If you had to name one person without whom A.L. Williams wouldn't have been the same, it would no doubt be Boe Adams. Art nicknamed Boe, "the Mastermind," and trusted and depended on Boe more than anyone else. While Art managed the agency and led the ALW salesforce, motivating them on stage, in person, and through his writings, Boe preferred to manage the back-office operations from behind the scenes. Boe had been introduced to Art by Bob Turley.

Prior to Boe's business career, he had been a basketball coach. When Bob Turley introduced Art to Boe their coaching backgrounds helped bond them immediately.

Boe had run an insurance company in Denton, Texas, but it had failed. That failure led him to become a wholesaler for an insurance company calling on general agents in Atlanta (ALW was, basically, a general insurance agency). The relationships developed as a wholesaler would end up being key to the expansion of ALW. One of those relationships was with the owner of National Home

Life, Art DeMoss who had led Boe to Christ. Boe was responsible for connecting Art to Art DeMoss.

Boe was a charismatic figure who inspired awe and respect. Standing at 6'5", Boe made an impact when he walked into a room, and his incredible financial and business acumen impressed Wall Street giants like Sandy Weill. Along with his wife, Myrna, Boe became a fixture at the A.L. Williams meetings and trips, but he was most comfortable at his giant desk at the home office working on new products and new ways of acquiring all the financial and administrative support that Art's company needed. According to Art, "People have no idea how much money it takes to keep this thing running. That was Boe's real job. All the troubles we had in the early days had to do with finding the money to keep this thing going."

Boe & Myrna Adams

It's scary to think about A.L. Williams without Boe Adams. What if Bob Turley had never introduced Boe to Art Williams? What if Boe hadn't introduced Art to Art DeMoss, who ultimately led to Stanley Beyer?

Stanley Beyer

Stanley was a wonderful, caring man. His company owned an insurance company called Massachusetts Indemnity and Life Insurance or MILICO. It was the 600th largest life company in America and Stanley wanted to diversify from the health and accident business that primarily sold its products to rural farmers. Boe connected with Stanley, and they clicked immediately. Stanley appreciated the method Art used. He saw himself being a part of a ground-floor, life-changing, revolutionary company. He and Art hit it off and the field loved him.

Stanley was also honest. Eventually, he realized that his company wasn't financially strong enough to finance ALW's rapid growth. The upfront financial resources needed to pay commissions were compounding exponentially. He openly told Art and Boe that they had better seek deeper pockets. PennCorp Financial (MILICO's parent company) finalized a merger agreement with American Can Company in 1983. Art said about Stanley Beyer, "Stanley was a genius and a great encourager. He always made us feel good about what we were doing. In the toughest of times, Stanley never doubted. When the industry did something to us Stanley would say, 'They can't do that to you' and he encouraged us to take appropriate action to fight." Stanley Beyer was a critical "dot" that helped solidify ALW as a force in the industry.

American Can Company

American Can was one of the 30 companies that made up the Dow Jones Industrial Average. At the same time that A.L. Williams was rapidly outgrowing every company they worked with, American Can Company was making a move from heavy industry to financial services.

With American Can's storied history and ALW's gigantic sales force, this unlikely duo had the potential to dominate the financial services industry. American Can eventually did spin off its can division and became solely a financial services company. In 1987 American Can announced that it would change its 86-year-old name from American Can, in order to reflect that move. According to Art, "American Can loved us. They had been the largest can company in the world, but they understood us perfectly."

Sanford (Sandy) Weill

Sandy was known as "The Wizard of Wall Street." He built companies large through acquisitions. His company owned many household-name companies like Smith Barney and Travelers, and ALW would be an addition to a market that Smith Barney could not reach. In December 1988, Sanford Weill's Commercial Credit acquired the former A.L. Williams for $1.54 billion. (*Washington Post, 8/88*) On February 6, 1989, the new company began trading on the New York Stock Exchange.

Throughout the next ten years, A.L Williams, MILICO, and FANS all joined under the same umbrella. All the "people dots" connected. All the tumblers clicked, fulfilling the destiny of ALW. All the players had a need to grow and merge. ALW was like a chess piece whose future was determined before a move was ever made.

Napoleon Hill

Going to a Napoleon Hill seminar was a defining moment in Art's life. Art said, "He taught that every successful person did six things to succeed financially. My goal was to have $300,000 accumulated. I thought I could follow his plan and be set for life. That motivated me!" Art's realization that he could combine his crusade with financial security for himself and others was a "destiny" moment that shaped Art's future and resulted in the financial independence of millions of ALW leaders. What made Art suddenly decide to go to the seminar?

The Auburn Basketball Players

Tee Faircloth, Bobby Buisson, Bob Miller, and Randall Walker all played on the Auburn University basketball team together. Tee recruited Bobby; Bobby recruited Randall and Bob. The dots connected again. Those players would ultimately form some of the largest hierarchies in A.L. Williams and grow the company exponentially.

Scott Reynolds

One of the earliest believers in "buy term and invest the difference." Reynolds recognized the problems with whole life insurance early on and wrote a landmark book, *The Mortality Merchants* in 1968, subtitled, *The Legalized Racket of Life Insurance and What You Can Do About It.* Scott Reynolds became a friend of Art's. Scott knew another termite who agreed with Scott on BTID, and Scott introduced Art to Yankee's great Bob Turley, who gave the small A.L. Williams major credibility and who built an empire within ALW. The dots continued to connect.

Arthur Milton and Frank McIntosh

They were consumer advocates who clearly saw the crusade and were willing to help. At a time when A.L. Williams was brand new and desperate for some public credibility, these two giants put their reputations on the line to stand up for the crusade. Arthur Milton's *How Your Life Insurance Policies Rob You* was a breakthrough publication. Another publication, *What's Wrong with Your Life Insurance?*, was a key "kitchen table" weapon. Frank McIntosh spoke at many company meetings and appeared on ALW-TV. When the young company needed consumer support the most, Arthur Milton and Frank McIntosh answered the call.

Arthur Milton with Art and Angela

The State Insurance Commissioners

The competition was constantly complaining about A.L. Williams to state insurance commissioners. What if they had ordered a "cease and desist" without hearing Art out? Something always seemed to happen to show the commissioners that the claims about A.L. Williams were just "sour grapes." Once, appearing before Georgia commissioner Johnny Caldwell, they discovered that Caldwell's son played ball with Harold Tarrer. That personal connection made Caldwell take a closer look at the charges and realize they were untrue. When the company appeared before Commissioner Lyndon Olson in Texas, Olson was able to separate complaints from misdeeds and told the industry A.L. Williams was just competing, and there was nothing illegal about that. Every time, something happened to turn the tide in ALW's favor. Lucky breaks. Or destiny?

The California Expansion

Mike Tuttle had worked with Campus Crusade for Christ. When Mike joined ALW, he connected with fellow CCC leader, Bill Stewart in Lubbock, TX, who knew another leader named Doug Hartman in California who knew another leader named Glen Plate. California *exploded* all because the dots at Campus Crusade for Christ connected with ALW, starting with Mike Tuttle and eventual greats like Mike Sharpe. The California contingent in A.L. Williams ended up becoming one of the largest and most productive organizations in A.L. Williams.

And Last, But Not Least. The Insurance Industry

Seriously. If the industry hadn't focused on destroying A.L. Williams, we never would have risen to the heights we did. Their constant attempts to put us out of business kept us alert, determined, obsessed, and filled with a desire to win. If it had been easy, that would have been great, but we wouldn't have become the ALW we became – tough, resilient, unified, powerful. It was never easy but as Art said, it was "worth it." They never meant to, but they were one of the "dots" that connected to make us great.

The A.L. Williams' Coalescence

If just one thing hadn't worked out, ALW wouldn't have worked. Think about what had to be overcome:

- No applications
- Handwritten commission checks
- No credibility
- No name insurance company
- Insurance wars
- Bad press
- Old whole life agents
- Lost two of five policies
- Only Art's vision to keep things going in the right direction

Our weapons to battle against all the obstacles:

- Fast Start Schools

- A company built by and for rebels and crusaders
- Crusade of BTID and Financial Independence
- Art's ability to bond with his team
- Angela and the partners
- Competing against one another
- Excited to make money and build wealth
- Iconic and great people
- Teammates that depended upon each other
- Failure was not an option
- Release of pent-up demand to build RVPs (using the multiples) and make money, the dream to finally have financial freedom
- Playing scared drove us to do more
- Burning our boats

A Special Hour in History

God appoints men and women for a special hour in history. Art and his founding team were people appointed for that hour in the history of the insurance industry to right the wrongs and injustices that corrupted the goodness it was supposed to be doing. Yes, $10,000 of Insurance was "better than nothing," but the problem occurred when the choice of whole life insurance caused the agents not to provide $100,000 of insurance for the same dollars because the commissions for whole life were higher than term. The cost of traditional insurance was so steep that families couldn't get the coverage they needed to protect them against the untimely death of a breadwinner.

How could a football coach ever change an industry as old and established as the insurance industry, much less change the entire way it did business? No one told Art Williams he couldn't do it. His own mother's experience focused his attention, and he recognized his true destiny. "I didn't totally believe I had a destiny from day one. It came gradually," Art says. "After a while, I realized that all the things happening were not coincidental and were actual evidence that all the dots were connecting, and we had a definite destiny. Things kept falling into place over and over again."

No One Told Art

- No one told Art that he had to become financially independent, he CHOSE to.
- No one told Art that he had to save hundreds of thousands of families. He CHOSE to.
- No one told Art to create the largest financial services company on the planet, he CHOSE to.
- No one told Art to create more financially independent people in America, he CHOSE to.
- No one told Art to fight until the job got done, he CHOSE to.
- No one told Art to be somebody, he CHOSE to.
- No one told Art to use the power of the multiples. He CHOSE to because it was the only way.

And, if Art HADN'T made these choices, there would not be heroes like:

- Bobby and Red Buisson
- Rusty Crossland
- Bob Turley
- Virginia Carter
- Frank and Debbie Dineen
- Fred Marceaux
- Lafayette Walker
- Randall and Mary Walker
- Frances Avrett
- Jerry and Rhonda Beyer
- Ronnie Barnes
- Kip and Carole Ridley
- Larry Weidel
- Andy Young
- Jerry and Sherry Ward
- John and Gloria Roig
- Greg and Sharon Fitzpatrick
- Asaad & Lois Faraj
- Frank and Kim Joyce
- Jimmy Meyer
- Cheryl Bartlett
- Caroline and Ed Myers
- Larry Davidson
- Ivan & Sharon Earle
- Mike and Myrna Sharpe
- Cindy Kicklighter
- Bill and Leslie Whittle
- Bob Safford

Many more heroes and hundreds of thousands of lives changed…Billions of dollars in death claims to widows and families... over 125+ Million-dollar earners...$1+ Billion a year payroll to the sales force. And on and on and on and on.

And no one told *me,* no one told *you,* to follow in his exact footsteps and build a replica of what Art built. We all had to choose to. And so must *you*. If you haven't made that choice... ***What will it be?***

A.L. Williams' Impossible Dream

At most big schools in the early days, there would be a church minister type who wanted to let people know what a good singer he or she was. The song they always chose was "The Impossible Dream" from *Man Of La Mancha*. I remember at a big event in San Francisco where Carol and I were on stage with Art and Angela and Boe and Myrna. The leader got up and thanked us, then Boe leaned over to me and said, "Now comes the T-shirts," which the leader gave us. Then he leaned over and said, "Now comes the song where we sway." That song was "The Impossible Dream." Everyone in the audience and on stage would sway as the vocalist sang with immense emotion.

Boe was right, but there was a reason "The Impossible Dream" was always chosen. That song was the A.L. Williams theme song back in the day because it tells of deep devotion and an earnest quest that we related to:

To dream the impossible dream
To fight the unbeatable foe
To bear with unbearable sorrow
To run where the brave dare not go
To right the un-rightable wrong
To love pure and chaste from afar
To try when your arms are too weary
To reach the unreachable star
This is my quest
To follow that star
No matter how hopeless
No matter how far
To fight for the right

Without question or pause
To be willing to march into Hell
For a Heavenly cause
And I know if I'll only be true
To this glorious quest
That my heart will lie peaceful and calm
When I'm laid to my rest
And the world will be better for this
That one man, scorned and covered with scars
Still strove with his last ounce of courage
To reach the unreachable star.

(Man of La Mancha, 1965, composers Leigh and Darion)

It hit an emotional pitch that spoke about how we wanted our lives to turn out. Ninety-nine percent of those in attendance would ultimately quit, but for a few precious moments in the long years of life, their thoughts reached to new dimensions and fit with Art's belief that everybody wants to be somebody. And it is within them if they choose to be.

We "Bet the House" That It Would Work

We bet on something we all believed in. We knew it was a risk, but we wanted this dream, and we weren't letting it go. Art was the glue that kept us together and on track.

Art was a person that you felt like you'd known for 100 years when you first met him. He had a charisma that you couldn't duplicate. You never wanted to let him down. It wasn't hero worship or intimidation, it was kismet, fate, destiny. All the dots aligned with him and our futures.

We knew we could impact our worlds with our crusade. Art always stressed the crusade over making money. He built in us a throttle that was "pedal to the metal." We never knew how long it would last because of the power of the industry and whether a company would finance us.

Art made his stand, and we were in the trenches with him. The harder the enemy pushed, the nastier and testier he got, and the more we loved it.

It all connected, and our futures were better than we ever imagined.

Truly a Company of Destiny

Imagine *WHAT IF…*

What if Art hadn't gone to the family reunion?
What if Art hadn't gone to that one PTA meeting because he never went to them?
What if Art hadn't started part-time with ITT?
What if Boe hadn't decided to come with ALW?
What if Joe Jack Merriman and Stanley Beyer hadn't wanted to expand and grow?

The *"what if's"* had no space in the placement of the dots or tumblers. Art's and our destinies had to happen "as they should happen."

Art said, "There were many times in my life I thought what we were doing was hopeless. There were a lot of things I didn't know, but I was able to hire the people who did know. It seemed like whenever I needed someone, the right person at the right time came into my life."

How did we make it? All the tumblers fell into place at the right time.

Throughout the ALW story, **all the dots connected, and all the stars aligned.** Destiny was ours.

PHENOMENON SPOTLIGHT

Facts About Art

- Art attended Presbyterian College on a football scholarship.

- Art earned two degrees from universities:
    - A Physical Education Degree from Mississippi State University
    - A Master's Degree in Science from Auburn University

- Angela earned two degrees:
    - An Education Degree from Mississippi State University
    - A Master's Degree in English from Auburn University

- Art and Angela got married on December 10, 1960.

- Art and Angela have two children, seven grandchildren and sixteen great-grandchildren.

- Art was named Georgia Football Coach of the Year twice:
    - At Appling High School in 1965.
    - At Kendrick High School in 1968.

- Art coached nine players who went on to play Division I college football.

- Art played against legendary NFL player and coach Dan Reeves in high school and beat Reeves' team three straight years.

- Art's favorite places to travel to in Europe are Venice and Paris.

- Art "lettered" in three sports all four years of high school.
    - Baseball
    - Football
    - Basketball

- As a quarterback, Art called his own plays in football all four years.

- Art was 46 years old when he ran an incredible 5 minutes, 6 seconds in the mile.
- Art likes to swim for 1.5 hours each day.
- Art doesn't drink alcohol or smoke.
- Art and Angela own Old Edwards Inn and Spa in Highlands, North Carolina.
- Art is an avid golfer.
- Of the books he authored, *Common Sense* was his favorite.

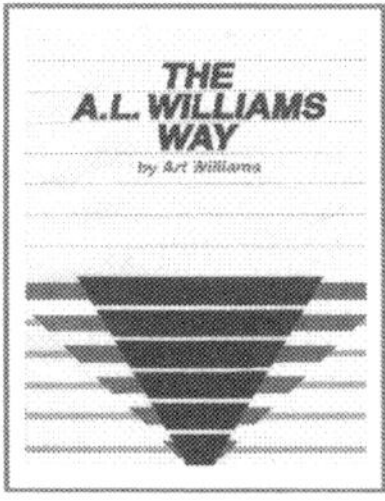

Chapter 9:
A LEGACY OF LEADERSHIP

What is a legacy? It is planting seeds in a garden you will never get to see bloom. Art dreamed big and thought long. While he wanted success for his family and for the families of the first 85 people, that wasn't what built his legacy. It was the things he did as a leader and a creator that built a business that would last long after he was gone. There are many good businessmen. There are few people who create something that has never existed before and change the business model of an industry forever. Those of us who were there in 1977 have seen amazing things happen in A.L. Williams, and we've seen another generation of "termites" rise up. But the opportunity and the crusade will go on for many more generations. Who can say how long?

God creates a twin soul for each person — that person's Godly soul and the soul of the purpose they were created for. It's a perfect match. They were made for each other. Without this connection, one's dreams would have no meaning. God has prepared a path for everyone to follow. And when a person's desire and purpose align, all the universe conspires to help them achieve it. It's something deep inside that has to be pursued. As Catherine Pulsifer said, "We all have a purpose in life, and when you find yours, you will recognize it."*(Pulsifer, 2022)* It's been said that the two most important days of your life are the day you are born and the day you find out why.

Art found his "why" when his father died and left his mother, Betty, with Art's two younger brothers and a measly $10,000 worth of cash value life insurance. When Art's cousin talked to him about term insurance, the twin souls came together. When ordinary meets extraordinary, "wow" happens. Art was ordinary and the revolutionary "buy term and invest the difference" concept created a "wow moment." His God-given purpose had appeared.

In the movie, *Ford vs. Ferrari,* Carrol Shelby says, "It's a truly lucky man who knows what he wants to do in this world, because that man will never work a day in his life. But there are a few, a precious few…and I don't know if they are lucky or not… who find something they *have* to do, something that obsesses them. Something that, if they can't do it, will drive them clean out of their minds." *(Ford vs. Ferrari, 2019)* Art was one of those men who was obsessed.

It's difficult to comprehend how unfathomably spectacular ALW was and is. With his relentless competitiveness and fierceness, Art earned everyone's adoration and will be celebrated forever. It has been a privilege to be coached by him.

Art opened his heart to us, and we opened our heart to him.

He taught us how and why to win. He got the most out of us and maximized everything we could give. As it says in the *Book of Job,* a leader "has the root of the matter in him." *(Job 19:28)* Art lived it and it shone in him. You can't fake the fire in him, that's a natural part of him.

Art had his "burning bush moment," and he couldn't retreat from it.

Creating Something from Nothing

Any idea that comes from our soul and mind and ultimately comes to fruition is creation.

We are literally being touched by the finger of God when we take an idea that God has given us and turn it into something fruitful that serves mankind.

Art's business creation was literally created from nothing. As of the end of 2021, Art's creation has produced:

- 5.7 million life insurance clients
- 2.7 million client investment accounts
- $903 billion of life insurance in force
- 130,000 licensed representatives
- 6,000 Regional Vice Presidents
- $1.1 billion paid in annual compensation to the sales force

- $97.3 billion in Assets Under Management
- $28.1 billion in death claims paid
- $2.245 billion in death claims paid in 2021
- Listed on the New York Stock Exchange
- Fortune 1000
- Forbes 2015 America's Most Trustworthy Financial Companies
- Forbes 2022 America's Best Insurance Companies
- Forbes 2021 The Best Employers for Women

All numbers as of Dec. 31, 2021

And, yes, that's all amazing. But Art was all about people, and it's the effect his greatness had on the lives of people – both those who joined him in the field and those who received the benefits of ALW's products and services — that is the true legacy of Art.

Perpetual Leadership

Mark Batterson said, "Legacy isn't measured by what we accomplish in our lifetimes. It's measured by our coaching tree, our mentoring chain. It's measured by the fruit we grow on other people's trees. It's measured by the investments we make in others that are still earning compound interest twenty years later. It's measured by every blessing we bestow." *(Batterson 2020)*

Many people are called leaders, but true world-changing leaders are a rarity. These are perpetual leaders whose ideas, philosophy, and charisma still develop new leaders today. This type of leadership is not easily copied and stand apart from the norm. Art led and inspired by giving us a sense of belonging. When we joined ALW, it was as if we arrived home. Our legacy began to form when we met Art. Why did we become crusaders? Art created an "us against them" mentality. Belonging meant everything to us.

Belonging is a feeling we get when we relate to those around us when they share our values and beliefs. We feel connected, and we feel safe. As humans, we crave the feeling, and we seek it out.

Art made us feel like we were on his team, he made us feel special, and that inspired us. He made us feel that we were part of something big, important, and necessary. We didn't need anyone applauding to know we were doing something important.

We had a strong bond with one another because of the "spirit of the culture," or *elan,* that our crusade created. As the saying goes, "People will live for a vision, but they will die for a cause." Our culture, our bonding, and our belonging created a unique universe that only we understood. If you weren't there you can't understand our dedication, our resolve, our passion, and our devotion to Art. We found a home where we spoke the same language. It's like moving to a foreign country and seeking others who spoke your native tongue. All our relatives thought we were crazy. All our friends thought we were nuts. It's like soldiers who were in foxholes with each other that had code words that only they understood. It's like the ex-military who go to the VFW hall or like the tv sitcom where, "everybody knows your name." Only A.L.Williams people "got us." In many ways, we felt complete when we belonged to this Special Forces group, this Green Beret, this Band of Brothers, all aligned for a common cause, a oneness, a reason for existing. This kind of unity was no accident. There was no "team" without a leader, and Art was a leader like no other I've seen in my lifetime.

A man is deemed great if he encounters and beats a great foe and survives great adversity. Art was magical to us. He demonstrated moral leadership. He set lofty goals for himself and us. We were like stallions that needed a spur occasionally. As a friend in ALW said to me, "I didn't know what courage was until courage was my only option." That describes our challenge. Art led us to go conquer the world."

Art's leadership and vision were an adhesive that kept us together. He was a bus driver, and we were passengers on his bus. He told us what to do and we all did it. Why? His way was better than any other ideas we may have had. He was a fighter. He was fierce. His vision was relentless.

We always cautioned people never to underestimate him. He was intense. Sometimes Art's steadfast intensity caused him to create an environment that would escape his core relationship building way of doing things. An example of this was at a senior leadership meeting in New Orleans before a convention. We all knew better than to talk while Art was speaking. He was in the focused zone of a general on a battlefield. We were used to those rare moments and felt the same way when we spoke to our hierarchies. During a meeting, one leader was asked a question by his spouse sitting next to him. He whispered back not to ask any questions. Art caught sight of him and devastatingly chastised him in front of all his peers. Of course, Art knew what he had done and profusely apologized after the meeting. People who are not directed by a crusade or haven't felt the pressure Art felt would think unfairly of Art. But it also shows that a person in a leadership role has to bear many responsibilities, and it is a very tough job.

Paternalistic Leadership

A paternalistic relationship resembles the parent/child relationship. A father figure is an example.

Art was not "our daddy," but he modeled a life that many of us had never seen from our own parents. As Art would say, "When you win, you win in all areas of your life, not just business. If you lose your family just to succeed here, then you aren't a winner."

Paternal advice is sought at various times through our lives. Many of the same principles that cause one to succeed in business are applicable to family, health, or spirituality. Things like focus, discipline, time, and goals aren't only found in business. Just as businesses have mottos, so do families. Just as businesses have mission statements, so do families. To win in all areas requires sorting priorities. Who doesn't want to succeed as a person, a parent, or spiritually? Who wants to be a "dud" as a father, a mother, physically? To be able to glean success thought patterns from a "father figure" is a rarity, because corporations only want you to succeed in one area, making them money. Art taught that success doesn't mean losing one to have the other. This paternalistic leadership kept us motivated, because it involved knowing we were more than just a number.

When you go to work for a corporation, they put a massive empty hypodermic needle into you and proceed to suck out everything good that you have to offer them. When you have nothing left, they dispose of you like an old used battery. When you joined ALW, because of what Art taught, a massive hypodermic needle that is full is put into you. It is full of all the good things, how to be a better father, better wife, better mother, better citizen, better leader, successful RVP and Godly person. Yes, Art could have used his influence to be like many hard-core CEOs, but, if you knew Art, you would never question his intentions. The proof? Angela was right by his side. They were the "father figure couple" anyone would like to be, or to have their child's business endeavors blessed by.

How to Fight - and Win

Winston Churchill was one of Art's heroes. Many of the things said about Winston Churchill could be said about Art. England was facing the daily reality of invasion by Germany during the early days of the war. As Eric Larson writes, "Here, as in other speeches, Churchill demonstrated a striking trait: his knack for making people feel loftier, stronger, and, above all, more courageous." (*Larson, 2020*) John Martin, one of his private secretaries, believed that he "gave forth a confidence and invincible will that called out everything that was brave and strong." Under his leadership, Martin wrote, Britons began to see themselves as "protagonists on a vaster scene and as champions of a high and invincible cause, for which the stars in their courses were fighting." (*Larson, 2020)*

We challenged the largest financial industry over the last 100 years. Art never wavered and called upon us to fight back, to pick up more policies, recruit more people, plant our flag and never back down. Art took something that wasn't supposed to work and made it work.

Mike Tuttle once discussed a book that became a movie called *12 Mighty Orphans* about orphans who wanted to compete in sports with bigger teams. They were ostracized and discriminated against because they were orphans. He saw the same thing in ALW. We were like the orphans.

"First off, nobody had ever promoted term insurance," said Mike. "No one ever went out and attacked cash value life insurance. No one ever hired part-timers in this industry. And just like they were trying to prevent this team (the orphans) from competing with bigger schools, the industry tried to do the same with us and totally shut us down and not let us be in business. Art built a company that was built for those people who had been locked out of corporate America. These orphans would have fit perfectly into our business. Art created warriors just like the football coach in the movie did. The head coach had such a life-changing impact on these young men's lives, just like Art had on our lives."

Art caused us to evaluate our life, effort, and results in all areas by reminding us:

"Life is just a flicker."

"One day they will be patting your face with a shovel."

"On your tombstone will be either dud or stud."

"You are supposed to be somebody."

"Life won't give you what you want, but only what you are willing to fight for."

"The only thing people remember is what's on the scoreboard. What's your scoreboard going to read when they click your light out?"

It was Art's way of encouraging us and motivating us to do the hard stuff. All these things told us, "Life is short. It will be over too soon. Do it *now*."

Art's main phrase was "You must see yourself involved in something bigger than your business." Who talks like that? What business leader sees themselves involved in changing the world?

When Steve Jobs was looking for a CEO for Apple, he was negotiating with PepsiCo CEO John Sculley. Sculley was a typical CEO looking at his stock options and bonuses. A frustrated Steve Jobs finally said, "John, do you want to sell sugar water for the rest of your life or come with me and change the world?"

Howard Shultz created Starbucks for a similar purpose. The title of his book was called, *Pour Your Heart into It*. His vision for Starbucks wasn't just to sell coffee, it was to, "bring people's front porch to America." The larger vision was reuniting people with a long-ago way of life, where people connected by sitting on their front porches and visiting with their neighbors as they walked by. Howard Schultz didn't see coffee, he saw creating a place where people could visit, conduct business, read a book — all while drinking their coffee. Coffee used to be called the "think drink" because great thoughts from great conversations would emerge.

Art saw what we were doing as going beyond insurance sales. We were righting wrongs, correcting injustices, and opening doors for people like us who came from where we came from to have an opportunity to make a difference.

The greatest fear in life is death. The second greatest fear is living an inconsequential life. Art knew how to create a vision in our minds that would cause us to go beyond our fears, beyond our comfort, beyond just eking out an existence. He believed that football prepared and taught kids about life, Art saw ALW as doing the same thing. We needed to belong to something bigger than us. As author Breńe Brown said, "We are biologically, cognitively, physically, and spiritually wired to love, to be loved, and to belong. When those needs are not met, we don't function as we were meant to. We break. We fall apart. We numb. We ache. We hurt others. We get sick. There are certainly other causes of illness, numbing, and hurt, but the absence of love and belonging will always lead to suffering." *(Brown, 2022)* Rallying around a cause made us feel like we were making a difference, that our lives mattered, that we weren't duds but studs, that our tombstones would read "winner."

Art gave us our mission with his "bigger than your business" vision. As the author writes in *The Alchemist,*" There is one great truth on this planet: whoever you are, or whatever it is that you do, when you really want something, it's because that desire originated in the soul of the universe. It's your mission on earth." *(Coelho, 2015)* Art left a deep footprint of entrepreneurial spirit in tens of thousands of "somebody" wannabes.

"Crusaders die-hard" was our battle cry. We felt like missionaries in a foreign land whose mission it was to leave this world a better place. With Art as our leader, we really believed we could do it.

He Taught Us How to Live

Art did more than teach us how to win in business. He taught us how to live our lives. When I worked in corporate America, the boss I had there was a good man, and he was very successful. The only thing he never taught me about was how to live. He never taught me how to have a better marriage. He never taught me how to be a better father. He never taught me how to live out my faith. Art Williams was a different kind of business leader. Like all great people who have a magnet on them to attract other people, Art taught the science of living.

He was a father figure to more people than I can count. It sounds strange that grown men and women are looking for a figure in their life that could be a role model, a person that they want to be like, a person that they can idolize. Most people look to sports figures, their teachers, parents, or movie stars. We looked to Art. He showed us that we could change our lives financially, build something to last for generations to come, and actually build a company of our own. He showed us that to do all that, you had to become a better person. We came to realize that the thinking that gets a person where they *are* is not the thinking that gets them where they *want to be.* Art talked about our thinking, our heart, wanting to be somebody, and believing that all those things add up and will build a successful business.

An example of Art's magnetism for attracting people from different backgrounds, even successful ones, is Bob Turley. Bob was a professional baseball pitcher for the New York Yankees for many years and won almost every award imaginable. After he left baseball, he ended up in the insurance business personally selling. He met Art and immediately saw what Art could do for him because of Art's coaching background and Bob's athletic background. Bob could work anywhere, and probably could have made more money initially, but he saw something in Art that he respected. Maybe it was his respect for coaches and managers that had influenced his career and life. He realized that you have to have a great coach and manager to get you to new levels and that you could not get there by yourself.

Another great example was Bob Safford. Bob was a millionaire at age 28 through owning a life insurance company. He sold his company and eventually went to work for National Home Life as Vice President of Marketing. He could've gone anywhere, he could've been hired anywhere, started his own company again and been very successful. But Bob knew he needed somebody in his corner like Art Williams to build something like he wanted to build. He saw Art not only as a leader, but as a positive asset that could help him get big. Bob created one of the largest organizations in all A.L. Williams' history and has been responsible for countless wealthy leaders who changed their lives because of Bob. He couldn't have done it on his own. He needed a partner, and that partner was Art Williams. Art would make you better, even Bob Turley and Bob Safford knew that. Their humility in wanting to have a gigantic team and needing to get better to do it caused their "followship" mentality and dedication to Art. Bob and Bob had the same unquenchable burning desire to compete, fight, leave this world a better place, and they partnered with Art who had the same kindred spirit.

Art taught us to create something that would last forever, that the purpose of life isn't to live forever, but to create something that does.

Art's everyday life was his message. How he lived is what he taught. What he taught we lived. He said, "You don't win some of the time, you win all of the time." It's very similar to the phrase, "How you do anything is how you do everything."

Art was more concerned about how our lives, our marriages, our families, our health turned out than how our businesses turned out. In reality he believed that if your family and marriage is great, those same elements that make them great will make you great in business, great financially, great as a leader.

John Barry, author of *The Great Influenza,* quoted author Albert Camus about the crisis of the 1918 swine flu pandemic in a quote that encapsulates Art during the "Insurance Wars." "A crisis helps men rise above themselves. It not only helps them rise above themselves, but crises make men discover themselves." *(Barry, 2004)* The wars brought out the best in Art. When Art left on July 1, 1990, our concern was the concern of those who knew General George Patton well: Could he survive without a war?

Men who blaze new trails, charter new roots, pioneer new methods, and make new discoveries are men who dare to do things that can't be done. They search, seek, and strive to accomplish things that even they didn't think could be done. While others falter, they go forward. Man needs to dare. He needs an incentive to undertake. That urge to begin turns most things into a blessing. He who dares to think stands secure in the majesty of his own might." *(Prevette, 2020)*

Art was an artist. Some artists work in paint — some in stone. Art Williams worked with people's hearts.

Freedom To Have an "Off the Menu" Life

Art Williams gave thousands of people the freedom to experience an "*off the menu life*." A menu life is where you are offered a limited life menu chosen for you by others who think they "know better." Many schools have agendas to push kids to orchestrated career paths that they predetermined to have merit. It's like an arranged marriage where you have no voice.

- No one asked me what it is that I really want.
- No one cared what my wishes were.
- No one challenged me to expect more.
- No one thought I should want or ask for more.
- No one saw me as anything but a clone of everyone else.
- No one was happy unless I cowered down and acquiesced to their thoughts of how my life should turn out.
- I was in their rut.
- I was on their Hamster Wheel.
- I was handed the basic ingredients and a recipe for a mediocre life.
- Who are they? Who are they to think they should run my life?

Art offered a customized life available to anyone who could break away from the mediocre, cookie-cutter thinking of frustrated, stuck people who think "you can't" because they settled. Our futures were their pasts, but for Art.

Art built this system for a different kind of person. People like us! He said, "People like us, who come from where we come from, nobody is going to find an oil well in our backyard."
Art's phrase, "I want to be somebody," was an essential mantra to those early A.L. Williams people. It ignited a fire in their bellies.

Art saw people, not as they were, but as they could be. And he showed them how to get there.

A "Hero Maker"

Art's life was lived as a hero maker. He built platforms and invited us to stand on them instead of building a pedestal for himself. *(Ferguson, 2019)* It can best be described in his philosophy that his fruit grew on other people's trees. The evidence was that, when Art retired, the business system he created didn't die. It exploded and created thousands of other "Arts," leaders that number over 5,000 today.

Author Dave Ferguson used the word Diatribo as a way to describe Jesus' method in apprenticing his 12 apostles. Diatribo means to rub off on. "Día" means against. "Tribe" to rub against or rub off on. *(Ferguson, 2019)*

Art took his crusade and turned it into a crusade movement. He took a drop of compassion for orphans and widows and turned it into a tidal wave of compassion. He turned a passion while in Columbus, Georgia into a North American movement, and phenomenon. He took a moment of caring and turned it into a movement of caring.

Art took that special moment of opportunity and turned it into a movement of epic proportions. Art's movement caused the tectonic plates of the insurance industry to be repositioned, and a new insurance industry world order was created.

His vision was not to build a castle for himself, but a kingdom where masses of average and ordinary people could thrive and succeed. Art served as a rocket booster in the career of others while catapulting forward himself. His wake propelled the lives of countless thousands who caught his wave. His forward thinking blessed those around him to strive for the best lives possible. It could be called the "Art effect."

Dave ended with the story of a successful church planter who challenged his son with the words, "Don't lose the vision." *(Ferguson, 2019)* We are challenged to do the same today. Many of us have dedicated the remaining years of our lives to keeping Art's system alive. Art's philosophy was that "Everyone deserves an ample financial life. Everyone deserves freedom of time, money, control, and financial happiness." His system provides the power and numbers of RVPs to make that happen.

God placed within us the influence and impetus to supply Art's vision with the masses of people that it takes. (*Ferguson, 2019)*

As MLK said "Life's most persistent and urgent question is, what are you doing for others?" *(King, 1957)*

The difference Art made was not in business and products, but in the essential difference he made in people's minds, hearts, spirits, and souls. He was the best servant-leader I've ever seen.

He was not only inspired but was inspiring. For many of us Art was the final piece of our personal puzzles.

As Richie Falcone said, "Art Williams gave average people a chance to be somebody. At least, that's what he did for me. I would do anything I had to do for Art to know who I was. I wanted him to know me. His concept, vision, and desire to win allowed me to become a multi-millionaire. I'm a better man because of Art Williams! I remember being in Boca as a District Leader thinking that I would be a speaker one day there. I was so excited, I didn't even know what I was saying. But Art got it."

Josh Huffman once said, "What an enduring privilege it was to be mentored by such an extraordinary person. He has made a permanent difference in my life, and I am certain, thousands upon thousands of others, as well. I truly believe Art Williams is the greatest leader in America. And not just in American business. The example that he and Angela set in their marriage, the way they live their life, and the way they treat others is a testament to their character and their authenticity. They truly love people and are masters at expressing it. Art broke all the corporate rules that say leaders should not get too close to their people. He and Angela had nothing to hide. The way they live their lives inspired others to be more, do more, and become more."

A Great Leader Takes the Bullets

Art always did it first. If there had not been that one person who was going to step out there and take the bullets, the life insurance industry would've continued for another generation. He was the man who stepped out of the foxhole to go and face the challenges. It's important for future generations to know the sacrifices people made in order to bring them the company and future they have today.

As Peter Drucker said, "Whenever you see a successful business, someone once made a courageous decision." They drew a line in the sand. Art was willing to do that, and all our histories have been changed. *(Drucker, 2022)*

When you look at his life and what he left us, you realize how much you can accomplish because he did it first.

Art Myers said, "Art was always the quintessential example of 'been there and done that.' You knew that he never asked you to do anything that he hadn't already done. He led by example."

I can't imagine how hard it was to have the weight of the world on your shoulders. One time Art spoke to us and said, "I was driving down the road the other day and saw a chain gang with a smoky-the-bear-hatted guard who was carrying a shotgun. I thought to myself, 'Now why don't I do that? Why can't I just stand and do nothing and watch over those prisoners?' Then I got realistic and realized I can do that maybe for two or three hours, but then I start climbing the walls. When you want to be somebody so bad it borders on being an obsession, doing nothing is not satisfactory. You've always got to be moving forward and you're never satisfied; that is the price of wanting to be somebody."

"Edward Jenner"

It was 1796 when Physician Edward Jenner made the first step in the long process whereby smallpox, the scourge of mankind, would be totally eradicated. He then presented the hypothesis that infection with cowpox protects against subsequent infection with smallpox. The Latin word for cow is vacca, and cowpox is vaccinia; Jenner decided to call this new procedure vaccination.

Dr. Jenner eradicated smallpox. He is the greatest lifesaving human in history because his discovery saved the most lives. If not for him 1/2 billion people would have died from smallpox disease, which had been the deadliest killer in world history.

Thomas Jefferson said of Jenner, "Humanity is so indebted to you sir, that mankind must never forget that you lived, that you cared, that you worked, that you served." *(Jefferson,1806)*

Can something similar be said of Art? Name another person in the financial industry who cared, lived, worked, and served more people financially than Art. Remember the Norman Dacey quote? "Where now, will the American people find a champion willing and able to harness the strength of this financial giant? Who will lay the present sorry mess open to the light of day? Where shall we find a man with the temerity to face these latter-day 'untouchables,' to stand in the path of this juggernaut and cry, 'Halt?'"

Although Art didn't invent BTID or the multiplication system that ALW used, this quote from science explains a great deal. "In science credit goes to the man who convinces the world, not the man to whom the idea first occurs." *(Darwin, 2016)* Art convinced the world. Art's conviction and tenacity transformed the insurance industry and brought widows, orphans, and retirees more financial peace of mind than any bank in America.

As a saying from the Talmud goes "Whoever saves one life saves the world entire."

Incomparable

When you think of incomparable you imagine unequal, matchless, one-of-a-kind. It's astonishing to think of someone against who no one can be measured in accomplishment.
Who comes to your mind when you think of someone you cannot compare to anyone? Perhaps cellist Yo-Yo Ma, composer John Williams, baseball legend Henry Aaron, or our very own Art Williams?

Art taught people that they could be valuable, that they could be important in this world. He taught that what we did here would last forever. He taught that we had a place here, that we were not just cosmic accidents. What Art created was incomparable, which makes him incomparable.

Johnny Mercer once referred to someone as being, "in a category called *beyond*." Art was in that category.

Helen Keller met Mark Twain and made a lifelong friend. She said about him, "There are writers who belong to the history of their nation's literature. Mark Twain is one of them. When we think of great Americans, we think of him and the age he lived in. To me he symbolizes the pioneer qualities, the large, free, unconventional, humorous point of view of men who sail the seas and blaze new trails through the wilderness." *(Flannery, 2016)*

Insert Art instead of Mark Twain. Art too belongs in the nation's history, not of literature but of business. Because of what he built and the countless lives he's affected, he too was a great American. Art symbolized pioneer qualities because he pioneered and revolutionized changes in the century-old insurance industry. Art blazed new trails through a wilderness and created paths for many to achieve great things with their lives and legacies for generations.

Art had what America wanted. He had courage, obstinacy, self-reliance, generosity of soul and spirit. As Flannery puts it, it's "the kind of spirit that makes firemen rush into a burning building - because it's the right thing to do." Art was bold, defiant, ambitious, and larger-than-life, just what we Americans like to see in our heroes. Art made the American dream a reality for himself and millions of others. As Jimmy Carter said about John Wayne, "He had personal conviction, courage and reflected the best of our national character." *(Carter, 1979)* Every red-blooded American is looking for someone to be like. Someone they hope to be.

Art's story is the story of America and the American spirit.

An Ultimate Team Builder

Sisyphus was a legendary king of Corinth, condemned eternally to roll a heavy rock up a hill in Hades only to have it roll down again as it nears the top. Art had a team we could join that gave us hope of being on a championship team and getting our lives "over the top" — never having to lose ground again.

Our vain attempts to believe that getting an extra degree, working a little harder, sucking up to the boss, playing their game, laughing at the bosses' jokes, and drinking the corporate Kool-Aid, would get us over the top had proven to be wrong.

It was pure naivety and an immature imagination. All we got was a sense of meaninglessness and frustration. Working at corporate America we became invisible and dispensable. We could be replaced.

We'd all had moments Art called "that Friday night feeling," that specialness that came when wearing a school uniform that said we belonged. Then we graduated only to become nobodies and irrelevant. We had succumbed to the tradeoff of security and a steady paycheck instead of a life of adventure. Getting that ball over the hill was still possible, wasn't it? Maybe if I just…

We had no control of our destiny, no hope of that ball finally rolling with us and not against us. Art gave us a team, a family, a feeling of importance and a life that mattered. No longer a Sisyphus but a *somebody*.

Being part of a championship team means suffering together. If you cut one of us, we all bled. We found a brotherhood and sisterhood that put us all through the same trials and "enemy confrontations." Just ask any of the originals what an enemy confrontation was. It was a glorious time of defeating and deflating an arrogant insurance agent at the kitchen table.

How badly people want to be part of a team can be seen in the extent people will go to be on one. They will even join a team that does bad things. Just look at gang members who will kill as part of their initiation. Look at the Mafia. But also look at the Marines, the Green Berets, Special Forces, the police, and fire departments — they are the epitome of good. We were fortunate to have a leader with character and a will — even a motto of "do what's right."

We planted our flag not only with Art but his crusade, which gave us a sense of purpose and meaning. We were his elite team. ALW became our brand like Nike, Adidas, or Under Armor. Our sponsorship was the compensation we were paid for delivering results for clients.

Art's team gave us hope, aims and rekindled buried dreams and a stubborn hope that the ALW way would get us finally and permanently over that hill.

The environment Art created was the best soil anyone could ever hope for to grow big dreams and make them come true. We were lucky to be the "seeds" in Art's soil.

All in the Family

Art's phenomenon is a reminder of how companies can turn themselves into families. Like a family will laugh together, reminisce together and, when one dies, grieve together, that's how we were. When veterans of ALW get together today, they rave about how this phenomenon changed our lives and we do it with passion and affection. Art taught us how to treat each other by remembering our names, asking about our dreams, and caring about how our lives were going to turn out. It all came down to Art, who had leadership abilities practically unheard of in most business circles, because his training field was the football field. Art would teach us that the *heart* of a leader is more important than our leadership *skills*.

When it came to relationship building, Art was beyond brilliant. He was a relationship savant. What other founder of a company would say his chief asset is his ability to build relationships with his people?

Art always believed that money was the byproduct of what you do. Because of his relationship passion, Art believed as Henry David Thoreau said, "The mass of men leads lives of quiet desperation." *(Thoreau, 2004)* He saw the strong desire in people to be coached, recognized and encouraged.

Because ALW was a totally different animal, it seemed like everything we did was being made up as we went along, and it was. Beating Pru was the company goal but, in reality, the only thing that was important was the ALW family, taking care of each other and building unity. Art's mantra was, "one team, one dream," and we accepted that vision and shared it with our teams.

Art said it best, "The thing that made A.L. Williams great was not that we had 225,000 players, but that we had hundreds of teams where everybody felt important and felt they were a part of something bigger than themselves. We were righting a wrong… while at the same time giving each family a chance to become financially independent and teach others to do the same. We built personal relationships with the people we recruited. We fought side by side with them, cried with them, hurt with them, and celebrated with them. The competition tried every trick to put us out of business, but the war made our people even more determined to fight. We were the little guys attacking a giant. And that gave us a huge goal. I would say, as I look back, it was an impossible goal."

Art always put in perspective our role in the making of history. Whether or not we "do it and do it and do it" will determine the outcome of the lives of widows and orphans, of people who are desperate for better lives. According to Art, "It did seem impossible, but ultimately the scoreboard showed that our little rag-tag army did the impossible. In 1977, the industry sold 90% cash value and 10% term. But, in just twelve short years, the industry sold only 10% cash value." What a legacy.

Art Inspired Us

Every time Art spoke, he inspired such confidence and enthusiasm. His talks were inspiring and quotable. It's an insult to call them speeches. His words transcended a speech and became placards for a movement. Words have power and his words transformed tens of thousands to want more, do more, and expect more. After every talk he gave, we were like a team of football players ready to run out of the locker room and conquer the world.

Think General MacArthur, Napoleon, Winston Churchill, General Patton — all great leaders who inspired men to give all they had for a cause that only they could see and understand.

Art Williams had a noble cause. All the others had war, freedom, and honor as their cause; Art had something that only he felt so deeply about. He inspired men and women with individual freedom from dreary, dead-end, purposeless lives. The vehicle? Life insurance. He found something deep down inside of a man's or woman's soul that could not be explained, understood, or satisfied. Who could hear, "I want to be somebody so bad it borders on being an obsession" and not feel a sort of spiritual wanderlust?

There is an Academy Award-winning movie from 1945 called *The Best Years of Our Lives*. It's a picture about men who fought in WWII that came back to their families, never to be the same again. Their "best years" were fighting for something they believed in. ALW was the best years of our lives. We fought our own kind of war that came about during our "Moment of Greatness." As the words to the Whitney Houston song, *One Moment in Time* describe: *(Bettis, 1988)*

> I want one moment in time
> When I'm more than I thought I could be
> When all of my dreams are a heartbeat away
> And the answers are all up to me
> Give me one moment in time
> When I'm racing with destiny
> Then in that one moment of time
> I will feel…
> I will feel eternity.
> I've lived to be
> The very best
> I want it all

No time for less
I've laid the plans
Now lay the chance
Here in my hands
I want one moment in time

What red-blooded person doesn't get inspired by these words? The pulsation of blood going through our veins calls us to create a life that most men can only dream about.

Who could hear William Wallace in *Braveheart* inspiring his men on the battlefield with, "Fight and you may die? Run, and you'll live, at least a while. And dying in your beds, many years from now, would you be willing to trade all the days, from this day to that, for one chance, just one chance, to come back here and tell our enemies that they may take our lives, but they'll never take our freedom!"

"In the year of our Lord thirteen fourteen, patriots of Scotland, starving and outnumbered, charged the fields of Bannockburn. They fought like warrior poets. They fought like Scotsmen. And won their freedom." *(Braveheart,1995)*

We Paid a Price

How can anyone ever know the price these pioneers paid to get the company off the ground, fight a formidable enemy, fight regulators, fight to find a product company that would finance and believe in us, fight to get people licensed, fight losing people because of chargebacks from old agents coming back, fight to get policies issued, fight one of the largest, most robust industries in the country?

How will they ever know how many times we had to rebuild our base shops, recruit another 100 people just to make $10,000 a month, how many nights and weekends we had to work, the endless hours it took to build our own company and forge a destiny for ourselves and finally, after years and years and years, to have it pay off? There's no telling how many people lost their health because of the fight, how many people with the hearts of champions couldn't sustain the fight because they had families that needed them. We didn't know how tough it would be. We didn't know the sacrifices we would have to make. The risks we took were huge.

Most people would have been terrified to leave the comfort of a solid, lucrative position to launch into completely unfamiliar territory. Especially people who had no business experience, no MBA, no financial expertise. Where did Art get the courage to launch a company from thin air? Where did someone just a few years out of coaching football get the belief that he could actually succeed in an industry that had been around for decades?

Art dared greatly. All great men have one quality in common, the daring ability to start something, regardless of the cost. Historically, none of these people have been rich or privileged.

Eli Whitney, the man who invented the cotton gin, was a schoolteacher in Connecticut. John Rockefeller was a clerk in the produce house. Andrew Carnegie was a bobbin boy. Thomas Edison was a newsboy. Henry Ford was an electrical mechanic. Benjamin Franklin was a printer's apprentice. Bell, the inventor of the telephone, was a teacher of sound. Eastman, the Eastman Kodak king, was a bank clerk. Art Williams was a small-town football coach.

"Men who blaze new trails, charter new roads, pioneer new methods, and make new discoveries are men who dare to do things that can't be done. They search, seek, and strive to accomplish things that even they didn't think could be done. While others falter, they go forward. He who dares to think stands secure in the majesty of his own might. *(Prevette, 2020)*

"Where there is no struggle, there is no progress. Those who profess to favor freedom and yet deprecate agitation, are men who want crops without plowing up the ground, they want rain without thunder and lightning. They want the ocean without the awful roar of its many waters." *(Douglass, 2016)*

Art said, "If I had known financial independence was so great, I would've paid a bigger price." To succeed, Art not only had to determine what he was going to do, but also how much he would give up doing it.

Every leader will find him or herself at a crossroads like the one Art experienced. Why? "Courageous leaders determined to make a big, worthy impact are often single-minded. Many live and breathe the cause they've embraced. Indeed, such investment is usually essential to fulfilling their purpose." (*Koehn, 2018*). This means that leaders like Art need people around them who can facilitate their single-mindedness. The result is the huge price of loneliness. The term, "It's lonely at the top" comes to mind. You can be in a large group, but ultimately you are alone. You pay a big price, and your family pays a big price when you are in a people business and you are obsessed.

Few can understand Art and the price he was willing to pay in leaving friends behind and marching toward his goal. If you are not outgrowing your friends, you stagnate. It's not that leaders lose friends, but that the old set that accompanied them must move over and make room for the next set of friends that will carry them farther. It's unusual to have the same set of friends all of your life. You can mark your life by friends who took you to new levels, and then the next set of friends, then the next friends, and on and on. People are put into your life to be friends, to bring some value to you, to escort you to a new level, then hand you off.

Genius

"Genius is not enough; it takes courage to change people's hearts." *(Green Book, 2018)*

Art is that same kind of rare breed, the likes of whom we likely won't see again. A genius is a "person exerting a powerful influence over others for good."

Genius can be a convenient catchphrase for someone who does something extraordinary but requires a heightened level of courage. Art "gave up" two careers to strike out to the unknown. He left coaching where he was respected, revered, and earned a livable salary to get into an uninspiring life insurance sales business. (Comedian Woody Allen described Hell as being with an insurance agent who wouldn't leave for three hours). He left Waddell & Reed where he was earning $100,000 a year. But he had that "itch" to do something special with his life.

Art didn't back off on his dream and our dreams. "Endurance is a much better test of character than genius." says Dennis Kimbro. *(Kimbro, 2003)*

Like Art, Charles Schwab understood. "I wanted to know how to be successful. That was important to me. I wanted to make money and have resources to have choices in my life. I thought financial services was the way to do that. I felt that it was my purpose in life to start this company, to be the heart and soul of free enterprise. With great humility and with a team around you, you can do so much more for so many more people."

A genius? Art would say no, but when the dust settles, Art may stand as the most important and influential person in the financial industry of the late 20th century.

What is a Legacy?

We all want to leave something behind to mark our time on earth: our children, our work, the impressions we made on those who knew us. Our Creator hides a high ideal in every human soul — the desire to continue to live in the hearts of mankind long after our time has passed. People with legacies are rich in values that endure, in qualities that can never be lost. In spite of any obstacles, they manage to leave a legacy and lift humanity from groveling pursuits to the achievement of great and noble deeds. Every individual needs inspiration. *(Kimbro, 2003)*

What's a legacy? It is a gift, especially of money or other personal property. What was Art's legacy? He created a system of distribution. Most think it was of the concept of "buy term and invest the rest." But it wasn't. Every meeting we had in the early days Art would get up and say, "We probably won't make it, but if we do it's going to be big." This lasted for several years. During one meeting where he said the same thing, some courageous RVP boldly asked, "Art, if we don't make it, what are we going to do?"

Art spoke his legacy, his gift to all of us and to future generations. The gift? "We are not an insurance company or a financial services company, we are a *distribution* company. We know how to create distribution systems. If they put us out of business we will get a hotel room, get a whiteboard, draw circles, then find a product to distribute through those circles. The product is important because we are crusade driven, but without distribution, the crusade fails."

The legacy of Art was the system of RVPs creating RVPs who create RVPs. The core of Art's legacy was the power of the multiples. Art repeatedly talked about the concepts that amazed him, the Rule of 72 and the magic of compound recruiting.

That's how Art went from 85 people in 1977 to 225,000 licensed people in 1990. It's similar to the "Give a man a fish and he eats once. Teach a man to fish and he will eat forever."

Most people would love for Art to bequeath them a portion of his wealth. But they would eat once. His legacy was his innovative financial services distribution system. His system created untold wealth. It was the hidden secret to generational wealth. The fascinating reality is that no other company has copied Art's system. They are blinded by the myths and prejudices of old-line companies that couldn't lower themselves to do that. The value was seen by Sandy Weill when, in 1989, he purchased ALW from Art for a sum that made Art one of the wealthiest people in America. He spun off our system in 2010 and it became one of the most gigantic and successful IPOs in America. In 2021, the NYSE company that was once A.L. Williams is approaching $1 billion in compensation to the field, $1.3 billion in annual death claim payments and $1 billion in profits. He bequeathed the system to generations beyond his.

As was said earlier, "We all want to leave something behind to mark our time on earth." Art bestowed a legacy, a precious gift that allows each of us to do the same.

A Compelling Duty

Art's words will be quoted by future generations, whether they know they're quoting Art or not. His words have become part of our culture. I believe his words will continue to have the power to inspire and encourage others.

One author said of Rogers and Hammerstein, and it is true of Art, that they left a legacy of hope that affected generations.

As is said by Dr. Howard Thurman: "There should be something in a person's life greater than his vocation, grander than material possessions or wealth, higher than genius, more enduring than fame. Here lies your greatest challenge, as well as your most compelling duty. Whoever uplifts civilization is rich though he dies penniless, and future generations will erect his monument. No matter who you are, no matter the odds, regardless of what lies in your path, you must leave your mark—you must tell future generations that you were here!"*(Kimbro, 2013)*

It is said "An inheritance is what you leave for someone. A legacy is what you leave **in** someone." Legacy is the influence your dream has on others, even after you die. *(Lounsbrough, 2022)*

They say there are no irreplaceable people. Whoever said that never met Art. There will never be another like him.

The "Trickle Down" Effect

Endless waves of blessings come from well-lived lives. I heard a great statement recently: that you will never know how you did as a parent until you see how your grandkids turn out. Our company is abounding with families whose parents came here part-time, built their businesses here, became successful here, raised and taught their children the beliefs they adopted here, and saw those children become pillars in their communities. I'm not saying that the truths for a better life in Art and Angela's messages to us made all the difference, but that they contributed to better marriages, better schools, better kids, and more honorable and generous lives. In talking with numerous RVPs that planted their family flags here, we hear that the biggest change in their lives is the kind of kids they've raised. They are proud of their biggest success, the quality of their children and now, grandchildren.

The "trickle-down" effect can be seen in RVP Ace Acevedo's family. He said, "My son has goals to play division one soccer, MLS, and the World Cup, then SNSD. My daughter is involved in Rhythmic Gymnastics and training for the 2024 Olympics in Paris." The amazing children that have come from ALW's RVPs are extraordinary, because of Art's teaching, and he and Angela's modeling behavior.

There are also stories of immense generosity. Mike and Stephanie Tuttle enjoy going to Cabo San Lucas in Mexico. On one particular trip, Mike took a cab and asked the driver (in broken Spanish) about his family. The man said he had six children, four of them were quadruplets.

After talking for a bit, Mike asked if he could visit the man and his family at their home. The man said yes. Later, when Mike came to visit, he saw that two quadruplets were boys and two were girls. Both boys could not walk because their eyes were crossed from birth, and they had not developed proper equilibrium. Mike was able to get a translator who helped express Mike's desire to find an eye surgeon to correct the boys' vision. He hoped that this could lead to them being able to walk normally. After a successful surgery and recovery period, the boys were able to walk! What an incredible gift to the boys and the family.

Andy Young had a great perspective on the "trickle-down" effect. He said, "I didn't come here to feed the hungry. I didn't come here to take care of the homeless. I didn't come here to contribute to the building of orphanages. I came here to make money, change my life, and build a successful business. Because I did all that, I am now able to feed the hungry, take care of the homeless, and contribute to the building of orphanages."

John and Gloria Roig have made a difference as well. John was originally from Cuba and when it opened, he rushed back to have his effect. "I rebuilt my aunt's kitchen with all new appliances," he said. "About 20 cousins each received a new refrigerator and stove. I paid for my cousin's wedding, which we attended. I took a busload (50) of family members to the world-famous Tropicana nightclub in Havana. In the last 20 years, Gloria and I have been able to sponsor six families (cousins) out of Cuba and resettle them in Miami. One cousin is a District Leader with the company today, along with his son. Another cousin owns the franchise which delivers furniture for Miami's largest furniture company. Children raised here number a few PhDs, pharmacists, teachers, and business owners. All are living the American dream because of A.L. Williams. Thank God for Art and Angela Williams!"

There are many stories like this throughout the company that Art and Angela built. There are orphanages that have been built, gymnasiums that have been built, and tens of thousands of kids who have had their private school tuitions paid. There have been moms and dads being retired early by their children and paid a salary to do whatever they wanted to do; there were new cars bought for dads, new houses bought for moms. The stories are endless because of the "trickle-down" effect of Art and Angela's decision to build a company and to take thousands with them to financial independence.

The "trickle-down" effect of normal people in Art's extraordinary business system empowered many of Art's leaders to change their lives. Without Art's system, these miracles could never have happened.

Timeless

As of this year, Art has been gone from us going on 31 years. It's fascinating that those of us who were witnesses to his leadership are now quoting words that will be quoted forever, words that describe the man, but also the "timeless" wisdom and life philosophies that transformed a generation and the next generation. Art taught us a new way to fly.

Art, like many great leaders, had the devotion of us who became spellbound by the hope he shared. Grown men and women loved his forceful way of stating what we had not heard from anyone but coaches. *(Goodwin, 2013)*

The cause of his timelessness? "The Founding Fathers of the United States were larger-than-life figures. They lived and breathed their "just cause." This is often the case with inspirational leaders in business as well. *(Sinek, 2017)*

Art's just cause was the legacy of freedom he fought so hard for and built for us.

Chapter 10:

PANTHEON OF DREAMERS

Art Williams created one of the greatest American success stories in history. In his wake he created more than a company, more than a business. He created a phenomenon.

A phenomenon is an astonishing occurrence, a prodigious event, a marvel. We all have a destiny and Art's phenomenon opened the threshold that exposed our destiny to each of us. His phenomenon helped us take hold of this destiny.

Art's company was named A.L. Williams, the name signifying not so much a specific company as a new kind of existence, a life of expanse and possibility for generations to come.

He shifted the shape, nature, and methodology of the modern insurance industry. In the big world of business and in the annals of business history in the United States, Art and A.L. Williams have become a towering presence.

How did this phenomenon occur? It stemmed from Art, his humble beginnings, and the death of his father at age 48 which left his mother financially devastated. Art took the life and lessons of Cairo, Georgia and used them to change the world. Art may have left Cairo and the people of Cairo, but they never left him.

The phenomenon began when Art chose to be a football coach and to coach lives, not just football. He became the coach we chose to invest our years with.

For us, ALW was a lighthouse in the darkness for people who had unfulfilled dreams. ALW was a harbor for eager and hopeful hearts who desired to be a part of something special.

Art was the one person who stood by us because he was one of us. He created the best possible environment to help us reach our potential.

He believed in us, and we believed in him. He was in our corner and would fight for us. He would throw himself on barbed wire for us. His will to win became contagious and became the impetus for our will to win.

We were proud insurance industry outsiders, and we all had an outsider's soul. He wanted to champion our cause, and A.L. Williams won the insurance championship because of it.

He loved looking out for us and filling a "father figure" role every young person needs. The cornerstone of his character was that he cared about how people's lives turned out. His unrelenting enthusiasm for relationship-building stemmed from this passion.

Eventually, he sold his company, and Camelot was no longer.

Did we expect Art to stay with us forever? He said he was going to be here until he died, until one day he wasn't. But his absence set off a business leadership explosion that created tens of thousands of Arts.

I'm sure there is a part of Art that doesn't want to be forgotten. His phenomenon solidifies his place in history and his relevance will be felt for generations to come.

Art Williams the man could not have been invented. Even Arthur Milton, who could only opine as to what man would take on the whole life insurance industry, could not have invented Art Williams.

Imagine… three or four lifelong insurance executives getting together and concluding that "buy term and invest the rest" is better than whole life. They want to start a movement to change the insurance industry, to get people properly protected, invested properly, and to eradicate whole life insurance in America.

And one man asks, "Who are we going to find to lead the growth of this idea?" One man says, "Let's look for a football coach. Make him from the South with a deep accent. He could hire other football coaches, pharmacists, firemen, nurses, and policemen — those are the best kind of people who would do this well. We definitely don't want him to hire anyone with an insurance background. We will let him hire people on a part-time basis. And one day he should let every one of them own their own company."

As I said, the insurance industry could not have invented him. Art was different, an odd duck to the industry. And that's the very thing we needed to change a stuffy, arrogant, elitist, spineless insurance industry.

This quote explains how Art was the one it took to lead us. Heraclitus, a philosopher born in the Persian Empire back in the fifth century B.C., had it right when he wrote about men on the battlefield.

> "Out of every 100 men," he wrote, "ten shouldn't even be there, eighty are just targets, nine are the real fighters, and we are lucky to have them, for they make the battle. Ah, but the one, one is a warrior."

Art was that one warrior who made the difference.

It's the end of an era, and those who have been fortunate to be a part of it are grateful for that era. How often can anyone say they were a part of a company that made history?

Why Do We Remember?

Why is it important to remember Art, what he did, and the people he did it with?

Acknowledging our history and celebrating it is critical to having a great company in the future. It's particularly important to acknowledge where we came from. Celebrating the lives and the stories of the great people who fought alongside one another is a huge part of it.

These people have become some of the best parts of our lives. They spoke at legendary Fast Start Schools; we heard them on conference calls; we were in meetings with them; we fought wars with them, took pay cuts with them and became financially independent with them. They are a part of us because they gave so much of themselves to us.

The fabric of our company was woven with these historic men and women who, through their courage, crusading spirit, and belief in Art, changed the insurance industry and brought security to families.

There was no greater loyalty than we had for Art. We were a band of troopers and survivors, people who kept going for their sheer love of Art, the fight, the crusade, the desire to make our marks on this generation.

There was a single-mindedness and a warmth within Art that created a unique magnetism. We all looked for people to emulate, whether Mickey Mantle or Ernie Banks, my favorites. It was how we grew — trying to play, think, aspire, and succeed like our chosen heroes.

These mighty 85 pledged their futures and their dreams to a cause bigger than themselves.

Historians who look back at the rise of ALW must put Art in the pantheon of legendary entrepreneurs. A pantheon is a group of illustrious or notable persons. Yes, Art had a dream and this pantheon was achieved.

Art's story is the story of America and the American spirit.

Will There Ever Be Another?

Will there ever be another ALW? The concept of BTID is not owned by us. Our recruiting and RVP system can be copied. There have been copycats that have tried without any success.

Gary Kornegay is a California giant in our company. He says it perfectly. "Will there ever be another ALW? Only if the leader of a company who had a father that died at age 48 with only a $10,000 insurance policy, leaving a broke widow with two young boys still at home, who is a football coach who is angry at the insurance industry because that policy should have been $100,000. ALW started as a crusade and built crusaders, while other companies start as money-making ventures. ALW was built *by* crusaders *for* crusaders. That passion cannot be duplicated."

ALW is a phenomenon that was created to accomplish a mission that necessitated a generational leader like Art Williams to emerge and influence a small band of followers who changed the world.

When Art Williams' chance came, he was ready. And his mission, and his destiny turned out to be ours as well.

About the Author

Bill Orender was living in Atlanta and joined Art Williams at Waddell & Reed in June of 1974 on a part-time basis while working for a steel company. Bill went full-time within six months and was one of the Original 85 people that launched A.L. Williams. In fact, it was in the home of Bill and his wife Carol where A.L. Williams company was named.

Bill and Carol, who have been married 54 years, built the "Company within a Company" that Art and Angela had envisioned. Bill made A.L. Williams history by becoming the first RVP to move out of the state of Georgia and move west of the Mississippi. Bill was only the ninth RVP promoted in a company that now has more than 6,000 RVPs. He and Carol were the pioneers of A.L. Williams' hugely successful westward expansion, which triggered explosive growth that helped take the company to the next level.

Bill and Carol were inducted into the company's Wall of Fame and are also members of the company's highest honor, the Circle of Champions. Still an active leader in the field, Bill now has a team of more than 4,000 licensed reps, including 200 RVPs in 32 states. Approximately two death claims are paid every single day within Bill's organization, and he and his team have more than $4.5 billion in assets under management.

Bill has made many other contributions to A.L. Williams over the years. Bill wrote two books that helped reps tell the company story for decades: The Deception of the Corporate Dream and The Last Love Letter. Bill also wrote Locker Room Notes, which was adapted from notes he had taken, covering a period of over 10 years, while Art was speaking at A.L. Williams meetings.

Bill, who was born and raised in Chicago, and Carol now reside in Graford, TX. They have four children and nine grandchildren. He graduated from Eastern Illinois University with a BS in Business.

About the Co-Author

Dona Bunch (known as Dona Janeway in the early ALW days) spent 25 years at A.L. Williams and its subsequent companies, from early 1981 to mid-2006. Dona was the first writer hired for the young company just after its move to its original offices in the Northlake Parkway area of Atlanta. There was also one artist, named Nancy Trude, and together the two made up the A.L. Williams Publications Department, which eventually grew to contain 20 plus writers, artists, and production personnel. She was the Executive Vice President of Communications for many years and member of the Company Planning Group.

Dona worked with Art Williams as a writer and editor on *Common Sense, Pushing Up People, The A.L. Williams Way,* and *All You Can Do Is All You Can Do.* Today, she lives in Knoxville, Tennessee.

Bibliography

Americanhistory.com. (1806). Thomas Jefferson Letter to Edward Jenner. Americanhistory.com.

Angelou, M. (n.d.). *Top 25 quotes by Maya Angelou (of 1010): A-Z quotes*. A. Retrieved April 6, 2022, from https://www.azquotes.com/author/440-Maya_Angelou

Atkinson, A. (n.d.). *Get guided help with your narcissistic abuse recovery*. The IT Factor: What it Looks Like and 12 ways to get it. Retrieved April 6, 2022, from https://queenbeeing.com/the-it-factor-what-it-looks-like-and-12-ways-to-get-it/

Bailey, B. (2021). The Science of the power of Unity. *The Science of the Power of Unity*.

Barry, J. M. (2004). *The Great Influenza*. Penguin.

Batterson, M. (2020). *Double blessing: Don't settle for less than you're called to bless*. Multnomah, an imprint of Random House.

Bob Dylan: Thoughts on johnny cash. M.Soul. (n.d.). Retrieved April 6, 2022, from https://www.m-soul.com/bob-dylan-thoughts-on-johnny-cash/

Breaking news, U.S. and World News. HuffPost. (n.d.). Retrieved April 9, 2022, from https://www.huffpost.com/

Bristol, C. M. (2016). *Magic of believing: The science of setting your goal and then reaching it*. Lulu com.

Brown, B. (2022). *Meet your next favorite bookB*. Goodreads. Retrieved April 9, 2022, from https://www.goodreads.com/

Caprino, K. (2019, September). What it takes to be a rare breed. *Forbes*.

Carter, J. (1979, April 9). *Speech on the death of John Wayne*. Welcome to The American Presidency Project | The American Presidency Project. Retrieved April 9, 2022, from https://www.presidency.ucsb.edu/

Churchill, W. (n.d.). *A quote by Winston S. Churchill*. Goodreads. Retrieved April 6, 2022, from https://www.goodreads.com/quotes/67420-to-each-there-comes-in-their-lifetime-a-special-moment

Coelho, Paulo (2015). *Alchemist*.

Commercial credit buys Primerica. (1988, August). *Washington Post*.

Dacey, N. F. (1968). *What's wrong with your life insurance*. Macmillan Publishing Company.

Disraeli. (2011). *I have a dream: Inspiring words and thoughts from history's Greatest Leaders* (Vol. Disraeli). Quercus.

Dreamworks L.L.C and Universal Studios. (2000). *Gladiator*.

facebook.com/DrNerdLove. (2013, January 14). *What is the 'it' factor?* Paging Dr. NerdLove. Retrieved April 6, 2022, from https://www.doctornerdlove.com/it-factor/

Farrelly, P., Burke, J., Wessler, C. B., Currie, B., & Vallelonga, N. (2018). *Green book*. United States; Universal Pictures.

Ferguson, D., & Bird, W. (2018). *Hero maker: Five essential practices for leaders to multiply leaders*. Zondervan.

Frankl, V. E. (2006). *Man's search for meaning: An introdcution to logotherapy*. Beacon Press.

Gladwell, M. (2021). *The Bomber Mafia: A dream, a temptation, and the longest night of the Second World War*. Little Brown & Co.

Glannery, C. (2020, March). Mark Twain and Helen Keller [audio blog].

Goggins, D. (2020). *Can't hurt me: Master your mind and defy the odds*. Lioncrest.

Goodreads. (n.d.). *Peter Drucker quotes (author of the effective executive)*. Goodreads. Retrieved April 9, 2022, from https://www.goodreads.com/author/quotes/15162571.Peter_Drucker

Goodwin, D. K. (2013). *Team of rivals: The political genius of Abraham Lincoln*. Thorndike Press, a part of Gale, Cengage Learning.

Gordon, J., & West, D. (2019). *The Coffee Bean: A simple lesson to create positive change*. John Wiley & Sons, Inc.

Hebel, B. W., & Hebel, T. (2011). *Forgiving forward: Unleashing the forgiveness revolution*. Regenerating Life Press.

Houston, R. (2017, November 16). *Becoming a better you (grace)*. LinkedIn. Retrieved April 6, 2022, from https://www.linkedin.com/pulse/becoming-better-you-grace-robert-houston

James, P. (2021). *Alchemist*. Orion.

Kennedy, R. (2013, August 27). *"few will have the greatness to bend history itself, but each of us can work to change a small portion of events. it is from numberless diverse acts of courage and belief that human history is shaped....".* Nelson Mandela: My Inspiration (and "Inspirator"). Retrieved April 6, 2022, from https://mandelamadiba.wordpress.com/2013/08/27/few-will-have/

Kersey, C., & -. (2021, October 6). *"believe in yourself and there will come a day....* Good News Network. Retrieved April 5, 2022, from https://www.goodnewsnetwork.org/cynthia-kersey-quote-about-believing-in-yourself/

Kimbro, D. (2003). *What makes the Great Great: Strategies for extraordinary achievement*. Broadway Books.

King, Jr., D. M. L. (1957). *Dr. Martin Luther King, Jr.* Speech, Mongtomery, Alabama .

Koehn, N. F. (2018). *Forged in crisis: The Power of Courageous Leadership in turbulent times*. Scribner.

Landry, T. (n.d.). Inspiring quotes. Retrieved April 12, 2022, from https://www.inspiringquotes.us/

Lapin, D. (2014). *Business secrets from the Bible: Spiritual success strategies for financial abundance*. Wiley.

Larsson, E. (2020). *The splendid and the vile: A saga of Churchill, family and defiance during the Blitz*. William Collins.

Lounsbrough, C. (n.d.). *Quote of the day*. BukRate. Retrieved April 9, 2022, from https://bukrate.com/

Marceau, S., McGoohan, P., & McCormack, C. (2000). *Braveheart*. Twentieth Century Fox.

McKay, F. (2021). *39 Fascinating Life Insurance Statistics*. Spendmenot. Retrieved from Spendmenot.com

"nuts!" - mcauliffe's 1944 Christmas letter. War on the Rocks. (2021, December 23). Retrieved April 4, 2022, from https://warontherocks.com/2021/12/nuts-mcauliffes-1944-christmas-letter-2/

The P.T. Barnum of the Life Insurance Industry. (n.d.). *Barrons*.

Pauley, J. (n.d.). CBS Sunday Morning.

Philosiblog. (2012, March 8). *Great spirits have always faced violent opposition from mediocre minds*. philosiblog. Retrieved April 5, 2022, from https://philosiblog.com/2011/03/30/great-spirits-have/

Prevette, E. (2020). *How to turn your ability into cash*. Duke Classics.

Primerica. (1988, August). *Washington Post*.

Pulsifier, C. (n.d.). *77 Quotes to Help You Find Your Life's Purpose*. graciousquotes.com.

Reynolds, G. S. (1971). *The mortality merchants*. PaperJacks.

Roosevelt, T., & Gable, J. A. (2003). *The man in the arena: Selected speeches, letters & essays*. Theodore Roosevelt Association.

Schwab, C. (n.d.). essay.

Sinek, S. (2017). *Find your why*. Portfolio/Penguin, an imprint of Penguin Random House, LLC.

Stanley, A. (2020, March 17). *Top 73 blessing quotes*. Christian Quotes. Retrieved April 5, 2022, from https://www.quoteschristian.com/blessings.html

Stanley, A. (n.d.). *Next generation leader quotes by Andy Stanley*. Goodreads. Retrieved April 4, 2022, from https://www.goodreads.com/work/quotes/1247764-next-generation-leader-5-essentials-for-those-who-will-shape-the-future

Sun-tzu, & Minford, J. (2002). *The art of war*. Penguin Books.

T. Ellery Hodges quotes. Quotefancy. (n.d.). Retrieved April 6, 2022, from https://quotefancy.com/t-ellery-hodges-quotes

Their finest hour. International Churchill Society. (2021, May 11). Retrieved April 5, 2022, from https://winstonchurchill.org/resources/speeches/1940-the-finest-hour/their-finest-hour/

Thomas, B. (1998). *Building a company: Roy O. Disney and the creation of an entertainment empire*. Hyperion.

Thoreau, H. D. (2004). *Walden, or, life in the woods; and, "on the duty of civil disobedience"*. Signet Classics.

Trebek, A. (n.d.). *Alex Trebek quotes*. Quotes By Alex Trebek. Retrieved April 12, 2022, from https://quotes.yourdictionary.com/author/alex-trebek/

Twentieth Century Fox . (2019). *Ford vs. Ferrari.*

Twentieth Century Fox Film Corp. (1969). *Butch Cassidy and the Sundance Kid.* United States.

VanCaspel, V. (1975). *Money dynamics: How to build financial independence.* Reston Pub. Co.

Vincent, T. (n.d.). *The law is a jealous mistress*. State Bar of Michigan. Retrieved April 6, 2022, from https://www.michbar.org/

Wallace, D. F. (2007). *Consider the lobster and other essays*. Back Bay Books/Little, Brown and Co.

War and politics. Society of Gilbert Keith Chesterton. (n.d.). Retrieved April 4, 2022, from https://www.chesterton.org/quotations/war-and-politics/

Ward, Lock & Co. (n.d.). *The poetical works of Henry W. Longfellow.*

White, J. (2022). God Uses Ordinary People to do Extraordinary Things. *The Southeastern Sun.*

Wicked, a Broadway musical. (n.d.). Song "For Good". Stephen Schwartz, 2003

Wikimedia Foundation. (2022, April 5). *Primerica*. Wikipedia. Retrieved April 7, 2022, from https://en.wikipedia.org/wiki/Primerica

Wikimedia Foundation. (2022, April 6). *Winston Churchill*. Wikipedia. Retrieved April 6, 2022, from https://en.wikipedia.org/wiki/Winston_Churchill

Wikimedia Foundation. (2022, March 28). *Isoroku Yamamoto*. Wikipedia. Retrieved April 5, 2022, from https://en.wikipedia.org/wiki/Isoroku_Yamamoto

Wikimedia Foundation. (2022, March 28). *Leymah Gbowee*. Wikipedia. Retrieved April 5, 2022, from https://en.wikipedia.org/wiki/Leymah_Gbowee

Williams, A. (2013) *COACH: The A.L. Williams Story,* CreateSpace Publishing

Worsley, F. A. (2003). *Endurance: An epic of polar adventure.*

Made in the USA
Columbia, SC
13 March 2025

55100591R00191